D1566508

The Civil War Diary
of a
COMMON SOLDIER

Pvt. William Wiley

THE CIVIL WAR DIARY
of a
COMMON SOLDIER

William Wiley of the 77th Illinois Infantry

Edited by TERRENCE J. WINSCHEL

Transcribed by MIKE EDWARDS

LOUISIANA STATE UNIVERSITY PRESS

Baton Rouge

Manufactured in the United States of America
First printing
10   09   08   07   06   05   04   03   02   01
5   4   3   2   1

Designer: Barbara Neely Bourgoyne
Typeface: Minion
Typesetter: Coghill Composition, Inc.
Printer and binder: Thomson-Shore, Inc.

Library of Congress Cataloging-in-Publication Data

Wiley, William, 1838–1902.
    The Civil War diary of a common soldier : William Wiley of the
77th Illinois Infantry / edited by Terrence J. Winschel ; transcribed by Mike Edwards.
        p.   cm.
Includes index.
    ISBN 0-8071-2593-8 (alk. paper)
    1. Wiley, William, 1838–1902—Diaries.   2. United States. Army. Illinois Infantry Regiment, 77th
(1862–1865)   3. Illinois—History—Civil War, 1861–1865—Personal narratives.   4. United
States—History—Civil War, 1861–1865—Personal narratives.   5. Illinois—History—Civil War,
1861–1865—Regimental histories.   6. United States—History—Civil War, 1861–1865—Regimental
histories.   7. Soldiers—Illinois—Peoria—Diaries.   I. Winschel, Terrence J. II. Title.
    E505.5 77th.W55   2001
    973.7′473′092—dc21

00-012718

Frontispiece photograph courtesy Mike Edwards

To Bobby and Bonnie Evans, my in-laws, whom I dearly love, and Rita Faye Riddle Evans (1934–1991), whose beauty was taken from us all too early.

—TERRENCE J. WINSCHEL

To my late parents, my wife Vicky, my oldest son Jason, and especially to my youngest son Joshua, who has faithfully followed me in the fields and woods searching for relics left behind by the men who fought the "War between the States."

—MIKE EDWARDS

CONTENTS

INTRODUCTION

We are coming Father Abra'am, three hundred thousand more,
From Mississippi's winding stream and from New England shore;
We leave our plows and workshops, our wives and children dear,
With thoughts too full for utterance, with but a silent tear;
We dare not look behind us, but steadfastly before,
We are coming Father Abra'am, three hundred thousand more!

With the strains of "We Are Coming Father Abra'am"[1] echoing throughout the land, thousands of men responded to the call made by President Abraham Lincoln in the summer of 1862 for three hundred thousand men to fill the ranks of Union armies thinned on the bloody fields of battle in a war that already had lasted longer than most people had anticipated. Among those who flocked to the colors in response to the president's call was William Wiley, a twenty-four-year-old farmer from Peoria, Illinois.[2]

Born in 1838, the new recruit stood slightly over five feet five inches tall, had sandy hair, blue eyes, a fair complexion, and weighed 130 pounds. A long flowing mustache graced his face but could not conceal the visible effects of long hours of exposure to wind and sun. His hands

1. Luther O. Emerson, *We Are Coming Father Abra'am* (Boston: Oliver Ditson, 1862).
2. The "Muster and Descriptive Roll of Company F, 77th Illinois Volunteers" gives England as Wiley's place of birth. Yet his discharge, dated July 10, 1865, states that he "was born in Miami in the State of Ohio." Office of the Adjutant General, Springfield, Ill.

were rough and calloused from work in the fields; his body was strong and robust.

As a farmer who relied on unfettered navigation of the Mississippi River to send his harvest to market, Wiley and men like him throughout the Midwest were directly affected by the secession of the southern states and the subsequent closure of the great river to northern commerce. Wiley's personal economic interests, coupled with patriotic fervor, compelled him to join the Union army. An ardent Scottish Presbyterian, his faith was the foundation on which his life was based. In an hour of national crisis, Wiley prayed earnestly for divine guidance, for strength, and for courage. He went off to war determined to do his duty, as he saw it, in the eyes of God.[3]

Wiley enlisted on August 5, 1862, and was mustered into Federal service on September 18 as a member of Company F, 77th Illinois Volunteer Infantry Regiment. Commanded by Captain William W. Crandall of Elmwood, the company consisted of men from Knoxville, Metamora, Yates City, Belle Plain, Low Point, Minonk, Rosefield, Whitfield, Washburn, Fairview, Lacon, Kickapoo, and Elba—all small towns scattered about west-central Illinois, most within a forty-mile radius of Peoria. Situated due north of the state capital of Springfield, Peoria was the social and commercial center of a vast farming region that thrived along the banks of the Illinois River and its tributaries. Small farmers such as Wiley constituted the bulk of Company F, which also boasted a few merchants, lawyers, and other professional men.[4]

Although he shared much in common with the men who formed Company F, Wiley knew few of them personally and on October 1 secured a transfer to Company C, which was composed mostly of men from Peoria and the adjoining counties of Woodford and Marshall. The company was commanded by Captain Joseph M. McCulloch of Cazenovia, and included William's older brother John P. Wiley, who had signed the rolls nine days after his younger sibling. There was a strong bond

3. E. J. Blair, Physician's Affidavit, received in the Pension Office on October 29, 1898, contained in Pension Records of William Wiley, Soldier's Certificate No. 984626. Pension Records, National Archives. Hereafter cited as Wiley Pension Records.

4. Ibid.; *Report of the Adjutant General of the State of Illinois*, 9 vols. (Springfield, 1900–02), 4:668–9. Hereafter cited as *AG*.

between William and John, stronger than between most brothers, and at various points in their military service that fraternal bond helped ensure William's survival.[5]

For William and John Wiley, as with most soldiers North and South, the odyssey on which they were about to embark would be the most frightening, yet rewarding, experience of their lives—an experience in which manhood would be forged in the crucible of war and their mettle tempered on the field of battle. Recognizing that the Civil War was a pivotal moment in his life, William Wiley decided to maintain a record of his service. The diary you are about to read is that record. It begins in August 1862, when Wiley enlisted in Peoria for three years or the duration of the war, and concludes in July 1865, when he was mustered out of service.

Although Wiley faithfully performed his duty as a soldier, his story was all too common; it failed to measure up to the level of historical importance necessary to attract attention in the years following the War of the Rebellion. Upon his death on November 12, 1902, Wiley joined that vast army of nameless faces whose record of service faded from memory.

Yet Wiley's diary would eventually come to light. A hundred years after the election of Abraham Lincoln as the sixteenth president of the United States, a man named Bill Brady (a former employee of Perkin Elmer, now retired) bought an estate in Newtown, Connecticut. The estate was formerly owned by S. Wirt Wiley, a longtime resident of the town, who had moved to Florida, where he died. While cleaning out the attic of his new home, Brady found the diary of Wirt's father, William. Curious to learn of the man who had kept this journal, Brady dusted off the leather cover and slowly deciphered the pages of the faded scrawl. It was as if William Wiley had returned in person to tell his story. Years later, Brady's nephew, Gene Johnston, a quality-assurance director in North Carolina, borrowed the diary to share with one of his employees, Mike Edwards, an avid Civil War buff. Edwards, who now works for the State Fire Marshal Office and the North Carolina Fire and Rescue Commission, first became interested in the Civil War when his Cub Scout pack went on a field trip to Bentonville. Since then he has read extensively on the war and has become a member of the Sons of Confed-

5. AG, 4:660, 662.

erate Veterans. He boasts of having two great-great-grandfathers and eight great-great-uncles who fought for the South.

When Edwards read Wiley's vivid account of the war, he was immediately enthralled. The words he read were those of a haunting voice yearning to be heard after more than a century of silence. Recognizing the historical importance of these faded pages and wanting to share these words with others, he made several attempts to purchase the diary. Brady was reluctant to sell until assured by Edwards that he would attempt to publish it. True to his pledge, after laboring to transcribe the diary for several months, Edwards sent copies to various publishers for their review. Fortunately, David Madden at the United States Civil War Center on the campus of Louisiana State University in Baton Rouge recommended that Edwards submit his work to LSU Press. In accepting the transcript for publication, the Press judged that, as the diary deals largely with campaigns in the Lower Mississippi River Valley, the editing and annotation should be done by someone whose studies have centered on those operations. At that point, it became my good fortune to be selected to edit and annotate the text.[6]

It quickly became evident upon reading the manuscript that Wiley's account was not a diary in the usual sense of the term. Rather, it was a postwar memoir based in part on entries contained in two small pocket diaries purchased by Wiley in Baton Rouge during the war and maintained by him in the spring and summer of 1864, and in part on a loose packet of diary-style entries later found in his personal papers. Further investigation revealed numerous similarities between Wiley's entries and the narrative of operations contained in former lieutenant William H. Bentley's *History of the 77th Illinois Volunteer Infantry, Sept. 2, 1862,—July 10, 1865*, which appeared in 1883. The similarities of wording are sometimes so remarkable that it strongly suggests that Wiley frequently referenced Bentley's history to refresh his memory and flesh out his own narrative.

The first dated entry in Wiley's account—August 5, 1862—reveals that his text is more of a journal or memoir than a diary. In that entry, Wiley frequently jumps ahead of himself to tell the fate of a wounded comrade or a member of the regiment who was taken a prisoner of war. Such foreknowledge is impossible in a true diary. A more glaring matter is the fact that Wiley writes in the first person of events in which he did not participate. One example is his account of the Vicksburg campaign. In January 1863, following the Battle of Chickasaw Bayou, he was taken gravely ill with malaria. So severe was the illness that he remained in the hospital while his regiment received its baptism of fire at Arkansas Post. Although Wiley briefly returned to duty, a relapse sent him back to the hospital, where he remained for several months while his comrades crossed the Mississippi River, battled their way deep into the Magnolia State, drove the Confederates into the Vicksburg defenses, and stormed the city's fortifications, only to be driven back with heavy losses. Wiley did not return to his regiment until June, as Union forces were waging siege operations to compel the surrender of the "Gibraltar of the Confederacy." Yet he writes of the long marches as if he had been in the column, describing the weather and condition of the roads, and he vividly details many furious engagements, especially the May 22 assault in which the 77th Illinois suffered its heaviest loss of the war.

When viewed as a postwar memoir instead of a period diary, Wiley's narrative assumes greater interest, for his pages weave an account of army life that was probably more common than not. Rather than focusing on the noble and heroic aspects of war, as many postwar memoirs do, this narrative reveals how simple most soldiers were. Wiley writes at length about his experiences with sickness, both on land and at sea, and about the monotony of daily life. Army leaders are seldom mentioned, which stands as evidence of how little private soldiers knew of them and the larger drama of which they were a part. Instead, Wiley writes of day-to-day duties and about his small circle of friends in the regiment, demonstrating that he was much a loner. The anecdotal materials contained in these pages make a refreshing read.

This diary of a common soldier nicely complements the growing body of scholarship on those who served in the ranks during the Civil War. Notable contributions to this field include James McPherson's *For Cause and Comrades*, Reid Mitchell's *Civil War Soldiers*, James I. Robertson's *Soldiers Blue and Gray*, and Gerald Linderman's *Embattled Courage*. Like these works, the diary of William Wiley provides us with a deeper understanding of and appreciation for the experiences of the common soldier North and South.

Wiley has been described as an "ingenious misspeller," and his words are transcribed as he himself wrote them more than 130 years ago. In cases that might cause confusion for the reader, misspellings are corrected in brackets. A biographical appendix to the text provides supplementary information on many of the people Wiley names in his diary; those names are marked with an asterisk.

THE CIVIL WAR DIARY
of a
COMMON SOLDIER

～ 1 ～

WE ARE COMING FATHER ABRA'AM

August 1862

In the Spring of 1861 when the great political agitatation on the question of human slavery in our nation culminated in civil war between the northern and southern states of our union. The slave olagarchy of the southern states having failed in all their efforts for the extension of their slave territory and having lost their former political control of the government and not being minded to submit to the humiliation of sharing that control with the mud sills[1] of the north. And perhaps fearing for the safety of their institution of slavery in the states where it existed owning to the growing antislavery sentiment among our people. And in order to assure the safety and purpeturity of their per [peculiar] institution. The slave holding states had determined to suceed from the federal union and form a confederacy of their own based on the foundation rock of slavery and the long pending conflit was brought to crises by the confederates firing on Fort Sumter.[2] Somehow from the day war was declared I felt that I was to have a hand in the conflict, but not being disposed to rush into it heedlessly and in deferance to the feelings of my parents who felt very keenly the dire necessity that might cause myself and my brothrs

---

1. *Mud sills* is a derogatory term referring to people who lived in log cabins. They were considered the lowest stratum of society in the northern states.

2. Situated in the harbor off Charleston, S.C., Fort Sumter was one of the few Federal military installations not seized upon the secession of southern states. Confederate and state troops fired upon the fort on April 12, 1861, in what has become known as the opening shots of the Civil War.

to have to take up arms in defense of our country. I put off enlisting until I felt it to be my imperative duty. And in the summer of 1862 when President Lincoln made a call for 600,000 more men I felt that the time had come and that I must make one of that number and verified my convictions by my actions.[3]

August 5th 1862

Mr. Samuel M. Hart[4] and I went to Peoria Ill. and inlisted in the US service under Mr. W. A. Woodruff[5] who was recuiting for the US Army in Peoria at that time and were sworn into the US service by John A. McCoy (Justice of the piece). During the following week several other young men from our neighborhood had went to Peoria and enlisted. Those enlisting in the same company with myself[6] were J. P. Wiley,[7] G. A. Hart,[8] William Pinkerton,[9] J. H. Pinkerton,[10] J. R. McCracken,[11] Albert Shepherd,[12] J. H. Vanars-

3. Wiley doubles the number of volunteers that Lincoln had called for.

4. Samuel M. Hart from Woodruff County enlisted in Company C on August 5, 1862, and was mustered out with the regiment on July 10, 1865. William H. Bentley, *History of the 77th Illinois Volunteer Infantry, Sept. 2, 1862–July 10, 1865* (Peoria: Edward Hine, 1883), 49 (hereafter cited as *RH*); *AG*, 4:661.

5. William A. Woodruff of Peoria was actively involved in raising and recruiting the men who eventually became Company C of the 77th. In recognition of his service, Woodruff was elected first lieutenant of the company and mustered into service at that rank on September 2, 1862. He was soon appointed as acting adjutant for the regiment, and served in that capacity until poor health compelled his resignation on March 17, 1863. *RH*, 46; *AG*, 4:660.

6. By placing himself among members of Company C, Wiley implies that he had joined that company at the beginning of his service. *RH*, 52; *AG*, 4:669.

7. John P. Wiley from Limestone entered service on August 14, 1862, and was promoted to first sergeant. He gained the trust and admiration of the men in the company. Mustered out with the regiment on July 10, 1865, he was commissioned captain on July 24, 1865, but not mustered. *RH*, 51; *AG*, 4:662.

8. George A. Hart from Woodford County enlisted on August 14, 1862, and was elected sergeant. He was the first man in the company to die, succumbing to typhoid fever on October 2, 1862. *RH*, 46; *AG*, 4:661.

9. William Pinkerton from Logan joined his brother John in Federal service on August 14, 1862. He was mustered out on July 10, 1865. *RH*, 50; *AG*, 4:661.

10. John A. Pinkerton from Logan enlisted on August 7, 1862, and was mustered out on July 10, 1865. *RH*, 50; *AG*, 4:661.

11. James R. McCraken from Logan enlisted on August 14, 1862, and was mustered out with the regiment on July 10, 1865. *RH*, 50; *AG*, 4:661.

12. Albert Shepherd from Logan was appointed corporal in Company C after he enlisted on August 9, 1862, serving at that rank until he was mustered out on July 10, 1865. *RH*, 47; *AG*, 4:661.

dall,[13] T. S. Patton,[14] W. M. Wright,[15] Dennis Duff,[16] John Dunbar,[17] P. H. McCartney,[18] S. A. Lesly,[19] W. S. Stevenson[20] and M. J. Wald.[21] Seventeen of us who went out in the same company and all returned but J. H. Vanarsdal, who died of measles at Memphis Tennisee. Mr. Woodruff was then recruiting in connection with Mr. Fanistock of Lancaster Ill., they intending to unite their forces and form a company but Mr. Fanistock getting recruits enough to form a company as his own. Mr. Woodruff united with Mr. J. M. McCullock* [McCulloch] of Lowpoint who was recruiting in Woodford county and they formed a company.

August 14th

Our company met in Peoria and after shaking hands and some speach making we took dinner at the Central Hotel and in the afternoon we formed in line and marched out to the fairgrounds where we camped for the night.[22] This being our first experience in camping out and the

13. James W. Vanarsdall from Linn enlisted on August 11, 1862. He died of measles at an army hospital in Memphis on February 23, 1863. *RH*, 51; *AG*, 4:662.

14. Thomas S. Patton from Logan enlisted on August 9, 1862. He was one of several men appointed corporal upon formation of the 77th Illinois, and served in that capacity until he was mustered out on July 10, 1865. *RH*, 47; *AG*, 4:661.

15. William M. Wright from Peoria enlisted on August 9, 1862. Reenlisting as a veteran, he was mustered out on July 10, 1865. *RH*, 51; *AG*, 4:662.

16. Dennis Duff from Logan enlisted on August 9, 1862, and was mustered out on July 10, 1865. *RH*, 48; *AG*, 4:661.

17. John C. Dunbar from Logan enlisted on August 11, 1862. Badly wounded in the attack against Railroad Redoubt at Vicksburg, he was discharged for disability on January 16, 1864. *RH*, 48; *AG*, 4:661.

18. Philip H. McCartney from Logan enlisted on August 9, 1862 and was discharged for disability on April 3, 1863. *RH*, 50; *AG*, 4:661.

19. Samuel A. Lessly from Woodford County joined the regiment on August 14, 1862, and was discharged for disability on October 20, 1863. *RH*, 49; *AG*, 4:661.

20. The roster for Company C in *RH* lists both a William Stevenson from Linn and a William Stephenson from Cazenovia. *AG* lists both men as "Stephenson." In both lists no middle name or initial is provided. Due to Wiley's often inaccurate spelling of people's names, it is impossible to know which of the two men he meant. William Stevenson from Linn enlisted on August 13, 1862, while William Stephenson from Cazenovia entered service on August 22, 1862. Both men served with the regiment throughout its term of service and were mustered out on July 10, 1865. *RH*, 51; *AG*, 4:662.

21. Merrick J. Wald from Woodford County enlisted on August 11, 1862, and was mustered out on July 10, 1865. *RH*, 51; *AG*, 4:662.

22. The Central Hotel was situated at 107 South Water Street, and owned by John E. Phillips. The fairgrounds were located along present-day North Reservoir Boulevard, north of Peoria,

change from a feather bed to the soft side of a board. Being a little sudden our slumbers were not very sound or refreshing but knowing that these were some of the things that a soldier had to get used to we made the best of it. We thought that was a terrible long night but the morning came at last and we proceeded to cook our first breakfast and talk over our experience of the night. And many was the night in the years that followed that we would have thought that nights accomodations a glorious luxury.

August 15th
We elected our company commisioned officers. For Captain, J. M. Mc-Cullock, First Lieutenant, W. A. Woodrough, Second Lieutenant, P. H. Jenkens.[23] Our company being assigned to the 77 Regiment Ill. Vol. Inf. we marched down to the campground assigned to that regiment on the [Illinois] river bottom north of the city near the Peoria pottery where we were furnished tents and set up our camp in regimental order where we spent our next night with mother earth for a mattress.[24]

August 16th
We were allowed our first furlow to return home and settle up our business preparitory to assuming the life of a soldier.[25]

August 23th
We laid aside civil life and returned to camp and took up the life of soldiers which was all life bustle and excitement at that time new compa-

---

and were the site of Camp Mather, which had been renamed Camp Lyons on August 17, 1861, in honor of Nathaniel Lyons, who had been killed while in command of Union troops at the Battle of Wilson's Creek on August 10. The men of the 77th Illinois lived at Camp Lyons for the next two months as they learned the rudiments of soldiering. Telephone interview with Elaine Sokolowski, reference librarian, Peoria Public Library, August 19, 1998; Cloyd Bryner, *Bugle Echoes: The Story of Illinois 47th Infantry* (Springfield: Phillips Bros., 1905), 27.

23. Philip Jenkins from Cazenovia was mustered in as second lieutenant September 2, 1862. Promoted to first lieutenant on March 17, 1863, Jenkins resigned his commission on February 12, 1864. *RH*, 46; *AG*, 4:660.

24. This is evidence that Wiley edited and added to his diary in the postwar period. The Peoria Pottery was located at 1500 North Adams Street and operated by C. W. Fenton and D. W. Clark. Founded in 1859, it was known as The American Pottery Company from 1859 until 1873, when its name was changed to Peoria Pottery. Telephone interview with Elaine Sokolowski, reference librarian, Peoria Public Library, August 19, 1998.

25. Such a courtesy was standard practice throughout the North and South in this spring of mobilization to enable the volunteers to settle as best they could their personal affairs and see to the comfort of their families prior to departure for active duty.

nies and regimenets were coming in every day. That evening we drew some blankets and after beding ourselves freely with straw we retired for the night.

August 24th

We arose with the reveilee and made some coffee and prepared for the duties of the day. We chose our noncommissioned officers as follows first sergent C. T. [F.] McCullock* [McCulloch], 2nd G. A. Hart, 3rd John [Jehu] Buckingham,[26] 4th J. S. Hornbaker,[27] 5th Anderson Wright,[28] First corporal J. A. Hutchinson,[29] 2nd A. G. Thorn,[30] 3rd John Sewel,[31] 4th A. S. Shepherd, 5th J. C. Herron,[32] 6th J. P. Black,[33] 7th T. S. Patton, 8th J. H. Drenon,[34] Musician E. Buckingham,[35] wagoner M. Carles.[36] The

26. Jehu (possibly Jahew) Buckingham from Cazenovia enlisted on August 13, 1862. Promoted to sergeant major, he was later reduced at his own request and mustered out on July 10, 1865. *RH*, 46; *AG*, 4:661.

27. John S. Hornbaker from Peoria enlisted on August 9, 1862. He was Company C's flag bearer until badly wounded during the Vicksburg campaign. He was discharged for wounds on August 28, 1863. *RH*, 46; *AG*, 4:661.

28. Anderson Wright from Cazenovia enlisted on August 13, 1862. He was promoted to first sergeant and on April 8, 1864, was elevated to first lieutenant. Due to the orders consolidating the 77th and 130th Illinois regiments, Wright was mustered out on January 15, 1865. *RH*, 46; *AG*, 4:660–61.

29. Joseph A. Hutchinson from Cazenovia enlisted on August 13, 1862. Mustered out as a sergeant on July 10, 1865, he was commissioned a first lieutenant two weeks later but was not mustered. *RH*, 47; *AG*, 4:661.

30. Alfred G. Thorn (also listed as Thom) from Linn was mustered in as corporal on September 2, 1862, serving in that capacity until he was mustered out on June 17, 1865. *RH*, 47; *AG*, 4:661.

31. John Sewell from Peoria served as a corporal in Company C throughout the term of his enlistment. On July 24, 1865, two weeks after being mustered out, he was commissioned a second lieutenant but was not mustered. *RH*, 47; *AG*, 4:661.

32. John C. Heron from Metamora enlisted on August 13, 1862, and was discharged for disability on June 16, 1864. *RH*, 47; *AG*, 4:661.

33. James P. Black from Richland enlisted on August 13, 1862. Reduced in rank during the course of his service, he was mustered out as a private on July 10, 1865. *RH*, 47; *AG*, 4:661.

34. James H. Drennan from Cazenovia enlisted on August 13, 1862. Promoted to sergeant, he was mortally wounded at Vicksburg on May 22, 1863, and died four days later. *RH*, 47; *AG*, 4:661.

35. Enoch Buckingham from Cazenovia enlisted on August 13, 1862. A talented musician, he helped transform the band (which is frequently mentioned in the pages of Wiley's diary) into the pride of the regiment. He was mustered out with the unit on July 10, 1865. *RH*, 47; *AG*, 4:661.

36. Moses Carles from Peoria enlisted on August 14, 1862. After reenlisting as a veteran, he was mustered out on July 10, 1865. *RH*, 47; *AG*, 4:661.

most of our time was now spent in drilling. We were put through the drill pretty thoroughly as we were needed at the front and they wanted to get us ready for active duty as soon as possible. We had company drill twice each day and regimental drill once each day. We also had considerable guard duty to do as we had a camp guard around our camp to keep the boys from straying off and getting into mischief. We also had some other guard duty to do at Regimental headquarters guarding supplies. After we had been put through the drill for some days we began holding dress parade in the evenings and after we had drawn our new muskets and uniforms we thought we could make quite a fine display.[37] In the mean time our regiment was thoroughly organized and officer[ed] Charles Ballance* of Peoria was commissioned our first colonel, L. R. Webb* of Peoria as Lieutenant [lieutenant colonel], M. V. Hotchkiss[38] as major, Adjutant, John Hough,* quartermaster, David McKinney,* Surgeon, Charles Winnie,[39] assistant surgeon[s], J. M. Cowan[40] and John Stover [Stoner],[41] Chaplain, W. G. Pierce,[42] Seargent Major, John Buckingham, quartermaster Seargent, J. H. Stevenson [Stevison],[43] Commis-

37. The 77th Illinois was initially furnished with flintlocks, probably manufactured at the armory in Springfield, Mass. Prior to leaving for the field of active operations, the regiment was issued British Enfield rifle-muskets. The .577 caliber Enfield, which weighed a little over nine pounds, had an accurate range of 800 yards. Mark Mayo Boatner, *The Civil War Dictionary* (New York: David McKay, 1959), 266.

38. Memoir V. Hotchkiss of Peoria entered service on September 3, 1862. As major of the 77th, he was despised and hated by the men, who considered him harsh and incompetent. After proving their estimation of him correct, he was given the opportunity to resign, which he did on February 2, 1864. *RH*, 31; *AG*, 4:654.

39. H. S. Balcom was mustered in as surgeon of the 77th Illinois on September 3, 1862. He was not commissioned, however, and it is assumed he left the service. Charles Winnie from Somonauk, who had been mustered in as assistant surgeon of the 55th Illinois Infantry on November 25, 1861, was promoted to surgeon of the 77th Illinois. Mustered in on December 20, 1862, he tended to the medical needs of the regiment until the unit was mustered out on July 10, 1865. *RH*, 32; *AG*, 4:654.

40. Jesse M. Cowan from Magnolia was mustered in as first assistant surgeon on September 30, 1862. He served in that capacity until the regiment was consolidated with the 130th Illinois on January 21, 1865, at which time he was mustered out. *RH*, 33; *AG*, 4:654.

41. John Stoner from Minonk was mustered in as second assistant surgeon on September 30, 1862, and was mustered out on July 10, 1865. *RH*, 33; *AG*, 4:654.

42. William G. Pierce from Elmwood was mustered in as chaplain on September 12, 1862. He ministered to the regiment until January 7, 1864, when he resigned from service. *RH*, 33; *AG*, 4:654.

43. Joseph H. Stevison from Magnolia enlisted on August 5, 1862, and was mustered in as quartermaster sergeant on September 12. He was promoted to second lieutenant of Company

sionary Seargent, W. H. Wakefield,[44] Hospital Steward, A. B. Wells [Niles],[45] Principle musition, D. B. Allen.[46] Colonel Ballance was quite an old man his bodily strength, military tact or military education was not as great as his patriotism. He made such a fible appearance and made such a poor out in trying to drill the Regt. that the other officers feeling that he was not capable of filling the postion properly prevailed on him to resign his postion in favor of Captain D. P. Grier* of the 8th Missouri who had gone out from our county and been assigned with his company to the 8th Missouri Reg. Who was accordingly commissioned as Colonel of the 77th Regt. September 12th. Our encampment at Peoria was interfered with various incidents and experiences both amusing and otherwise. Our first experience at cooking the army bean [being] sow meat[47] was rather droll and we soon began to think that it would be a good thing to take mother along to do our cooking and make our bed if the regulations would only permit of it. But that was one of the many good things the stern rules of war would not permit of. But our kind friends helped us out very much with their baskets of good things which they brought into us once or twice each week and Colonel Ballance's barbacue which he made for the regiment on one occassion. When he had a couple of fine Elk (which he had received from the west some years before). Slaughtered and cooked for the regiment in regular barbicue stile by digging a trench in the ground and builing a fire in it then hanging the quarters of elk over the coals. But his cooks not being very well schooled in the barbicue business they did not get a very good scald on it and the elk being very tough and hardly half cooked it was not very palatable. We thought it would be better diet for coyotes than for new soldiers. But if we had had some of the colonel's elk at sometimes in after years we

B on January 16, 1863. Two months later he was promoted to captain and served in that capacity until he was mustered out on June 13, 1865. *RH*, 33; *AG*, 4:655, 658.

44. Nathaniel H. [or R.] Wakefield from Peoria entered service on August 9, 1862, and was mustered in as commissary sergeant on September 12. On December 21, 1862, he was reduced in rank to private and transferred to Company C, where he served until June 6, 1863, when he deserted. *RH*, 34; *AG*, 4:655, 662.

45. Ambrose B. Niles from Eugene enlisted on August 5, 1862, and served as hospital steward until mustered out for disability on June 20, 1864. *RH*, 34; *AG*, 4:655.

46. Daniel B. Allen from Elmwood enlisted on August 12, 1862, and was discharged for disability on March 15, 1863. John W. Carroll of Peoria and Lemon Wiley (possibly a cousin of William Wiley) were the other principal musicians. *RH*, 34; *AG*, 4:655.

47. Sow meat, or fatback as it was often called, refers to bacon. Along with hardtack and coffee, bacon was the staple of the army diet.

might have got with it better shape. But we had too much respect for the good intentions of the old colonel to say anything out loud but let on as if we enjoyed the colonel's elk first rate. Soon after going into camp they put up barracks for us out of lumber something after the stile of the sheep and hog sheds on the fairgrounds simply roaghs of boards sloping each way with sides about two feet high a man could stand strait in the center. In these we slept with our heads to the center and our feet out. We had one long shed for each company with company officer's quarters in one end next to regimental headquarters.

Our encampment at Peoria was a very pleasant one and we might mention as some of the incidents of our camp in Peoria. The tendancy with the boys especially after we had drawn our uniforms to get a pass and go down town and have our pictures taken with acoutraments and musket in hand in the atitude of attention and a revolver and a big knife our belts. As we often remarked afterwards we looked lots braver then than we did when we got down where Johnnie was. Another incident was the raiding of the Sulters tent which was on our regimental grounds.[48] He had got to making bad whiskey, his princple stock in trade to the demoralization of some of the weaker comrades and getting then in trouble so the boys by the encourgement of some of the officers concluded to abate the micense [nuisance] by making an assault on his works they upset his tent, confiscated his goods and demoralized his business in general.[49] Also the milking of the city cows which would come about the camp once in awhile while some of the boys would get around them and

48. Sutlers accompanied the armies of the North and South wherever they marched, offering for sale a variety of food, drink, and supplies. Boatner, *Civil War Dictionary*, 822.

49. Bentley describes the incident more colorfully: "There was an establishment in camp purporting to be a sutler's shop, but which was, in reality, a *whiskey shop*. This was an eye-sore to the members of the regiment, and they resolved that the nuisance should be abated. Many of them were religious, and many of those who made no pretensions to a religious character, were temperate in their habits, and they were not willing that the Seventy-Seventh should become addicted to the vice of intemperance at the outset. They notified the 'sutler' that he must remove his stock in trade within a specified time, or suffer the consequences. With this order he promised compliance, but failed to make his promise good. As mild measures had failed, other means were resorted to. On the night of September 1st, the forces were formed in line of battle, completely investing the enemy's works. After brief skirmishing an assault was ordered. The assailants moved forward in handsome style with unbroken lines, and after a faint resistance, the works were carried by storm. This was our first engagement and our first victory. It was complete, bloodless and decisive. It was a harbinger of good things to come, of greater victories to follow." *RH*, 21–2.

coral them while some of the boys would milk them and then divide up and have some cream for their coffee until the citizen caught on to the trick and herded their cows away from camp. The mustering of the Regiment into the United States service on Sept 2nd. Also the presentation of 10 libraries of religious books one for each company by the ladies of Peoria. On the 3rd of Sept the regiment was drawn up on the parade ground when Colonel Ballance took formal leave of the Regt. The old fellow shed tears and said if he only had 20 years of his life back how gladly he would have led us to the front. But he felt that he was leaving us in good hands that he knew Colonel Grier was better capable of leading us than he could be at his age. Then he formally turned the command over to Colonel Grier. On the 20th of Sept the 77 Regt. was marched down to the city when a beautiful flag was presented to the Regt by the ladies of Peoria. The presentaion speech was made by Washing[ton] Cockle* of Peoria and replied to by Col Grier after which we were treated to a rousing speech by E. C. Ingersole* [Ingersoll] which was perhaps more patriotical than orthodox. He told the boys that they need not fear to go into battle that any one who was killed in such a holy cause was sure to go strait to Heaven. Also our first experience of standing guard with the old worn out flintlock muskets and the pitiful and often repeated call of corporal both day and night as some poor inexperienced guard would get into trouble. Religious services was held in camp almost every evening by Wm Rennolds* [Reynolds] and others. One of our reg was drowned while bathing in the river and was burried with the honors of war in Springfield Cemetery.[50] Also Seargent G. A. Hart of company C was taken sick with tyfoid feavor while in camp and died at his home and burried with the honors of war by a part of company C at Smithville.[51] There was in camp at Peoria at that time the 85th–86th–102nd–103rd–108th–112th Ill. infantry.

On the 27th of Sept seven regiments passed in review before Col [John] Brier* [Bryner] who was commanding the post which made quite

---

50. Wiley may be mistaken. Regimental records list only one man as having drowned during the war, and that was Pvt. Daniel Chambers of Company D. Chambers, from Roberts, present-day Ford County, enlisted on August 9, 1862, and drowned at Young's Point, La., on January 31, 1863. *RH*, 54; *AG*, 4:663.

51. Here again is evidence that Wiley edited his diary in the postwar era. G. A. Hart died at his home in Peoria several weeks after Wiley's entry of August 24 noting his death. Smithville is located in Peoria County, approximately six miles southwest of Peoria.

a display and drew quite a crowd. But these scenes like everything earthly was destined to have an end and marching orders came. And on Oct 4th we were ordered to pack our tarps and be ready to march at a moments notice with two days cooked rations in our haversacks. And all absent ones were ordered to report immediately to their company and all absent sick not able to march to furnish a phsisians certifiate to that affect and report to their company as soon as able to travel. This being our first marching orders we thought it sounded considerably like business.

2

REAL SOLDIERING

After just a few short weeks of training at Camp Lyons, William Wiley and the men of the 77th shouldered their muskets and left Peoria behind. The comforts of home and family became only a memory as they boarded the train for the journey into an uncertain future. The men shared dreams of glory and heroism on distant fields; yet few then realized what fate held in store for them. Ahead lay the monotony of a soldier's life: grueling marches under the hot sun or in pouring rain, bivouacs in the snow or in disease-ridden climates, extended periods on reduced rations, sickness, more sickness, and death for many. The experience of real soldiering would change each man forever.

Oct 4th
At 2pm we slung knapsacks fell into line bid farewell to old camp Lions and our many friends and marched down through the city to the depot amid the waving of hankerchiefs hats and flags all along our line of march. And many blessings was involked upon us as we march away. On arriving at the depot we found that the accomodations furnished for us in the way of transporation was not excately what we had expected from the hands of a generous goverment but perhaps the best they could furnished for us under the circumstances as a great many regiments was being hurried to the front and transporation was pretty well employed. Our cars were not the modern pallace cars but simply box cars with seats improvised for the occasion around the sides and through the center with rough two inch lumber. But we were just begining to learn that

anything was enough for a soldier so we piled into our cars remembering that this was no picnic and soon bid farewell to the city of Peoria and went bumping on our way watching the spires of the city receed from view wondering if we would ever see them again. We put in a very uncomfortable night as there was no chance for any sleep. Some got so tired and sleepy that they laid down on the floor of the car in the dirt and tried to get some sleep and morning found us very sore and tired.

Oct 5th
We arrived at Logans Port Ind. early in the day and turned south towards Indianoplois and went bumping along on our weary way during the day our boards seeming to grow rougher and harder all the time and the distance between the board and the bone seemed to grow less and less all the time. This was the Sabbath day in Gods country but we were begining to learn that there is no Sabbath in the army. We arrived at Indianopolis at 5pm where we stopped for some two or three hours and went out in town and got some supper. And soon resumed our journey towards Cincinnati Ohio we had to stop frequently and fill up the tender with wood which was piled up along the track our train ran on. Until about two o'clock that night when we stopped at a small station in southern Indiana and remained until morning. The citizens of that part of Ind were generally bitter copperheads[1] and they [the military authorities] were afraid they might try to wreck our train so we waited until daylight and proceeded on our way arriving at Cincinati at about noon pretty badly worn out not having slept any for two nights and our sitters were getting pretty tender. We bid adieu to our old box cars fell in line and marched out through the city crossed the Ohio River on a ponton bridge and out through Covington Ky and went into camp just beyond the town where there was several other regiments encamped.[2] The 108 Ill. which

1. Copperheads were northern Democrats who opposed the war policy of the Lincoln administration and favored a negotiated peace. These "Peace Democrats," as they were also called, formed many organizations, such as the Knights of the Golden Circle, Order of American Knights, and Sons of Liberty. Best known of their leaders was U.S. Representative Clement L. Vallandigham of Ohio, who was banished to the Confederacy. Boatner, *Civil War Dictionary*, 175.

2. The pontoon bridge referred to by Wiley was stretched across the Ohio River east (downstream) from the then unfinished Roebling suspension bridge. The pontoon bridge constructed by the Federals during the Civil War robbed John A. Roebling of the distinction of building the first bridge across the Ohio River at Cincinnati. Geoffrey R. Walden, "Panic on the Ohio: Confederates March on Cincinnati," *Blue & Gray Magazine* 3 (May 1986): 10–1.

had been encamped with us at Peoria rejoined us here.[3] We here first met the 19th Kentucky Regt which was our right hand regt ever after.[4] That night not having any tents we slept on the bare ground wraped in our blankets with the Heavens for a covering and the big full moon looking us in the eyes. Sometime during the night we heard yelling off to one side of the camp and looking up we seen a horse running through the camp jumping over the sleeping men but no one was hurt.

Oct 7th

We drew some large bell tents[5] 12 or 15 to the company and set up our camp in order our mess No.3 occupied one tent.[6] There was some 14 or 15 of us and we filled our tent pretty full but as we wanted to keep together and would rather put up with a little inconvenience than to be seperated. We had plently of room to sleep and as we had plenty of straw to lay on and plenty of blankets to cover us. We fared pretty well but missed the baskets of good things which our good friends supplied us so abundantly while we were encamped at Peoria and had to content ourselves with Uncle Sam's rations or if we got any extra we had to buy them from the town or the sulter. Our first day in camp here was pretty well occupied in fixing up our camp setting up our tents and writing letters. We remained in camp at Covington until the 17th of Oct. During our encampment at Covington our adutant John Hough was detached from the regiment as assistant adutant general on the staff of our division commander Gen A. J. Smith* and our first Lieutant W. A. Woodruff was

3. Like the 77th, the 108th Illinois had been organized at Peoria and mustered into Federal service on August 28, 1862. Led by Col. John Warner of Peoria, the 108th Illinois shared much the same destiny as the 77th through the Vicksburg campaign. Frederick H. Dyer, *A Compendium of the War of the Rebellion*, 3 vols. (New York: Thomas Yoseloff, 1959), 3:1092. Hereafter cited as *Compendium*.

4. The 19th Kentucky was organized at Camp Harwood in Harrodsburg, Ky., and mustered into Federal service on January 2, 1862. William J. Landram, colonel of the 19th, became commander of the brigade to which the 77th Illinois was attached. The association of these two regiments continued through June 1864. Ibid., 3:1079, 1205–6.

5. Also known as the Sibley tent, because it was designed by Henry Hopkins Sibley, a hapless Confederate general. Referred to as a bell tent due to its distinctive shape, the Sibley tent could easily accommodate twelve soldiers and their accoutrements. Boatner, *Civil War Dictionary*, 760.

6. The soldiers, each of whom took his turn at cooking, messed (or ate) in squads. This practice continued throughout the war despite the fact that in March 1863 Congress required that cooks be hired to prepare the food by companies. Ibid., 545.

assigned as acting Adjutant of the regiment. Before accepting the position Lieutant Woodruff came to Co C and told the boys that the Colonel wanted him to act as Adutant of the regiment that of course it would be a better position for him and lighter duty as he would have a horse to ride on the march but if we prefer that he should not leave the company he would not accept the position. But we told him to accept the position by all means that althro we regreted to loose him from the company it would be better for him and that he needed all the advantage he could get as his health was very poor (having been discharged from a former service on account of lung troubles). While at Covington J. P. Wiley was appointed 2nd Seargent of Co C in place of G. A. Hart deceased. The 77–97–108–112 Ills.[7] Regiments were formed into a temporary brigade under the command of Colonel John Coburn* of the 33 Ind. We had one team and wagon assigned to each company. Three for the Regt headquarters and one for the hospital. And our teamsters had a serious time getting their teams broke in as they consisted of wild and vicious mules bought up all over the country and every one that had a mean vicious mule or horse sold them to the goverment. These mules were corralled on the Ohio side of the river and our teamsters in the first place had to go over to the corall catch their mules harness and hitch them to the army wagons get them down through the city and across the Ohio River on the pontoon bridge and out to camp the best way they could. The greater part of the mules were young and had never been handled. A detailed of soldiers would be sent over with the teamsters to help them. They would try to get one mule that had been broke for each team for a saddle mule and the ballance they would just take whatever they could get a hold of. The greater part of them would just have to be lassoed and choked down until they would get the harness on them. Then they would let them up and get them hitched to the wagons the best way they could. The teams consisted of from four to six mules. When they would get them hitched to the wagons the teamsters would mount his saddle mule and get two or three soldiers on each side to scare them along thus they

7. The 97th Illinois was organized at Camp Butler and mustered into Federal service on September 16, 1862. The 112th Illinois was another regiment organized at Peoria and mustered in on September 20, 1862. These four regiments formed the Second Brigade, First Division, Army of Kentucky. Dyer, *Compendium*, 3:1088, 1093.

would go down through Cincinnati to the pontoon bridge which consisted of boats made like very large skiffs anchored in the river about
twelve feet apart with timbers laid from one boat to the other and two
inch plank spiked onto the timbers. The bridge was twelve or fourteen
feet wide with no side railing whatever. The bridge would sway up and
down and sideways when the weight would come on it and was not the
best kind to drive a big team of wild mules over. But by proding, whiping
and scaring they would get them foured onto the bridge and the noise
and swaying of the bridge would scare them and away they would go
across the bridge each mule a pushing with all his might for fear of being
pushed off the bridge which was at least 80 rods long and then by the
same scaring process they would force them out through the town of
Covington to camp. They would continue to drive them around until
they were tired out before they would unhitch them but the harness was
never taken off until they were thoroughly broke. Two assistant teamsters would be detailed for each team and the breaking process would be
kept up until they were well broke. Then they would have to be shod so
they could stand the rackett over the racks and pikes of Kentucky. This
was a accomplished by getting them in the stocks and straping them
down so they could do nothing but bray and then the shoes would be
fitted and drove. While we remained at Covington we were put through
the drill of the soldier each day exept Sabath. We had company drill in
the forenoon and regimental drill in the afternoon and dress parade in
the evening. Our company drill was principally in the skirmish drill.
Covington is surrounded by a range of hills almost mountains and over
these hills we were put through the skirmish drill almost every day. I
suppose they thought it was good way to strengthen our wind and
muskle at any rate they ran us over these hills until we thought the wind
was about all out of us but as we found out afterwards this drill was very
necessary as we were put on the skirmish line in the face of the enemy
very frequently during our term of service.

October 16th
We got orders to be ready to march on the next day with 40 rounds of
catridges in our catridge boxes and 2 days rations in our haversacks.
This we thought began to look business like espically the 40 rounds of
catridges as this was our first introduction to the inevitable 40 rounds

that being the number our catridge boxes would hold.[8] We felt that we were now going to the front and we were anxious to be off. We though that we had been playing soldier long enough we were getting pretty well drilled and felt that we were ready for more serious business.

October 17th

At 12 o'clock we broke camp at Covington Ky and commence our forward march. That afternoon we marched 9 miles out on the Covington pike and by night our 60 lbs of bagage to the man weighed 160. That night we encamped in the Boon county fairgrounds (not much of a looking fairgrounds by the way). That night we carryed off an old chaps straw-stack to bed ourselves with despite the serious objections of the owner but we consoled him the best we could told him that we simply wanted to borrow it for the night and that he could have it again in the morning and that he ought to be willing to make a little sacrifice for the cause as we were making so many. But we had some straw all the same.

October 18th

We arose at the reveiler. The orderly seargent called the roll and we were found still all present so we got some breakfast struck tents fell into line and resumed our march at an early hour. That day we marched about 12 miles. Early in the day we left the pike and marched over some very rough hilly road. The hills were so steep and rocky that our raw mules could not pull the wagons up so a detail of soldiers would have to be sent to push the wagons and mules up the hills. We though this was a little rough but we looked at it as being a military necessity and tooks turns at playing mule. During the day we also found persimons growing on the hillsides and got pretty badly puckered. That night we camped on a farm belonging to a Dr. who we were told was no neutral but a full-fledged reb and away with the rebel army. So the boys concluded during the night that it was a part of their duty at least to confiscate his property such of it at least as suited there purpose best. So that morning such things as hogs sheep chickens honey had become rather scare about that ranch.

8. Forty rounds was the standard issue of paper cartridges and was carried by each man in his cartridge box. If battle was expected, the men were often issued an extra twenty rounds that were placed in their pockets.

October 19th Sabath

We were aroused at an early hour by the sound of the fife and drum playing the reveilee and the order to fall in for roll call after which we breakfast on chicken and resumed our march. This was the Sabath but not a day of rest to us as we marched some 15 miles over a very rough hilly road through a very poor rocky sparcely settled country making mules of ourselves as on the day before pushing the wagons up the hills. That night we camped on the Licking River. That night some negroes came in and reported to the officers that there was an old reb living out a few miles from camp that had a lot of horses belonging to men that were away in the rebel army. So lieutenant Jenkins of Co C was sent out with a squad of soldiers to capture the horses and bring them into camp which they did.

October 20th

Resumed our march at an early hour. Marched to Falmouth Ky.

October 21th

Remained in camp at Falmouth. That night it was reported that there was a number of rebs at a house out aways from camp and lieutenant Jenkins of Co C was sent out with a squad of men to try to capture them. They went out and surrounded the house but the rebs were gone. Some of the rest of us detailed ourselves to go out and capture some rebel sheep but the sheep were too fleet footed and we had to leave them out there in the brush. Captain [Robert] Erwin of Co I got on a big drunk that night and abused his men shamfully and had them out in line at all hours of the night.[9]

October 22th

We left Falmouth Ky at an early hour having orders to report at Cinthiana [Cynthiana] Ky that evening a distance of 25 miles. But the roads being rough and hilly we failed to reach Cinthiana. Night coming on and being very dark we went into camp in a field some three miles from Cinthiana. The boys skirmished around in the dark to find some water

9. Robert Irwin of Magnolia was mustered in as captain of Company B, not Company I as Wiley states, on September 2, 1862. Irwin inspired confidence in his men and was well respected throughout the regiment. He was killed in action at Arkansas Post on January 11, 1863. *RH*, 41; *AG*, 4:658.

to make coffee. They found a pond out in the feild a little ways where they got water to make coffee that night and the next morning before daylight and after daylight they went to the pond to fill their canteens before starting on the march again when they discovered a big rotten hog or two floating around in the water which made their coffee set a little unsteady in their stomachs. But we did not alow such small matters to disturbe us but we filled our canteens later on.

October 23th
We marched to Cinthiana and through the town and went into camp on the other side of the town near Licking River. Here we remained until the 26th. It was reported at this time that Morgans* geurilla forces[10] were in that part of the state and we were expecting a visit from them which made us feel a little uneasy as we did not feel that our small brigade was able to cope with them. So we were kept on the alert day and night.

October 26th Sabath
There had about six inches of snow now fell during the night. We were aroused at an early hour shook the snow from our tents and started on another Sabath days march of 20 miles in the snow to Paris Ky where we went into camp on a hillside just outside of the town. After scaping the snow away we set up our tents and carried off a neighbours strawstack to bed ourselves with. We remained in camp at Paris one day.

October 28th
We marched about 15 miles and went into camp within three miles of Lexington Ky. This night we borrowed a citizens haystack to sleep on and some of the boys went foraging that night and brought in some sheep and had some mutton for breakfast. The owner came to our colonel the next day and complained that his men had taken some very fine sheep form him one in particualr which had cost him a big sum and wanted the colonel to make his men pay him for them. But the colonel told him he was not in the sheep business just then.

---

10. Confederate guerrilla Colonel John Hunt Morgan commanded a brigade of cavalry that gained fame raiding in Tennessee and Kentucky. Wiley writes from faulty hindsight, as the period of Morgan's raids did not begin until late 1862. Ezra J. Warner, *Generals in Gray* (Baton Rouge: Louisiana State University Press, 1959), 220–1.

October 29th

We marched on through Lexington and about 3 miles beyond to the north and went into camp in the timber.

October 30th

We marched some 15 or 16 miles towards Nicholasville Ky on a acaddamised road which was very hard on our sore feet.[11] We camped that night in the timber at the side of the pike within 4 miles of Nicholasville.

October 31th

We marched to Nicholasville Ky and went into camp.

November 1st

We were ordered to march to camp Dick Robinson.[12] Marched some 7 or 8 miles and were then ordered back to Nichoalsville and await orders. On arriving at Nichoalville we were ordered to march to Richmond Ky a distance of 25 miles. We marched some 4 or 5 miles that evening and went into camp near an old grist mill where we got a lot of meal and had mush for supper. Some of us went and bought some milk at a house a little ways from camp and our mess known as mess 3 had good old mush and milk for supper, to which feast we invited our company officers and carried a portion to our sick in the regimental hospitile.

November 2nd Sabath

We marched to Richmond Ky and went into camp in a small grove just outside of the town where we remained until the 11th of November. We had a very pleasant time the weather being very pleasant athro our duty was pretty heavy our regiment being the only troops there and between pickett camp and patrol guard and other duties we were kept pretty busy. There had been a battle at that place a short time before and there was quite a number of the wounded both union and rebel left in the hospitle there and details were made from the regiment each day to help take

11. A macadamized road is one that is paved with layers of small stones.

12. Camp Dick Robinson was the first Union camp established in Kentucky and was located south of Bryantsville.

care of the sick and wounded.[13] The union wounded were in one building and the rebs in another. The rebel drs and their assistants were left there to take care of their wounded. The people of the town were very generous and brought in many good things to the sick and wounded of both sides. Captain J. M. McCulloch of our company was appointed provost martial of the town and kept things in good shape. During our stay some of our dashing young officers got quite sweet on some of the young ladies of the town and they on them and they were invited out quite frequently to take tea with the ladies and had a good time generaly. One evening they went downtown to seronade the young ladies selecting a fine mansion where some fine young ladies lived. They squared themselves and poured forth their sweetest strains for quite a while being cheered on by waving hankerchiefs fans. After they had pretty well exhausted themselves a duskey face appeared at the door and said wees very bliged gemens for de music but I is very sorry to tell you dat de white folkes is all gone from home. About that hour of the night our young brave retreated silently and in good order but as it happened some of our patroll guards were close enough to see and hear and it was some days before our young gallant heard the last of that. So time passed on until on November 11th.

November 11th
We left Richmond and marched back towards Nicholasville. But after falling into line the regiment was marched down into town and was drawn up in front of an old dr's house who had two or three particualy fine daugthers in whom our galant colonel and other young officers had been very much interested and we were requested by the officers to sing some of our patrictic songs but the boys seemed to be badly out of tune that morning and did not sing worth a cent. So the colonel faced us to the right and marched us away. The band struck up old gray horse get out of the wildness and the boys set up the yell like a set of comanchees. We marched 12 or 15 miles that day and camped on the Ky river.

13. The Battle of Richmond had been fought on August 29–30, 1862, between Confederate forces under Kirby Smith and Union troops led by William "Bull" Nelson. In this spirited action, the Federals were driven from the field with a loss of 206 killed, 844 wounded, and more than 4,300 missing out of 6,500 men engaged. Smith's Confederates lost a total of 451 men killed, wounded, and missing. Boatner, *Civil War Dictionary*, 697–8.

November 12th

We marched to Nicholasville and went into camp. The boys had gathered up some chickens by the way and we had chicken for supper and were very much rejoinced to get mail and letters from home.

November 13th

Marched about 16 or 18 miles and went into camp about 2 miles beyond Marsails [Versailles] Ky. That evening a young refugee from east Tenisee by the name of Dudley Lindville came to us and enlisted in our company.[14]

November 14th

We marched to Frankfort Ky the capitol of the state where we arrived about noon. As we entered the town some old chaps raised quite an excitement in the regiment by taking some darkies away from the rear guard who had escaped and come to us as we marched through the state and were acting as cooks hostlers. They were some distance behind the regiment with the rear guard which always marched some distance in the rear of the army to guard against a suprise from the rear and to bring up all straglers. The rear guard was commanded by a young seargent and the old fellows took him by suprise and dashed in and grabed their boys as they called them and the seargent let them take them without making much resistance. When the word came to the regiment it raised quite an excitement. Our abolition blood got up and the colonel wanted to march back and retake them but the brigade commander wouldn't allow him to.[15]

November 15th

We marched towards Louisvlle. Colonel Grier placed Lieutenant Jenkins of our company in command of the rear guard and told him to take 20 good men and take all the darkies back with him and if any one attempted to interfere with them to make it hot for them but they concluded not to tackled them. As we marched down through the town

14. Dudley Linnville may have been born and raised in Tennessee but is listed in *AG* (4:662) as being from Versailles, Kentucky. He enlisted on November 18, 1862.

15. The brigade commander referred to here by Wiley was Stephen G. Burbridge, to whose unit the 77th was attached in November 1862. Dyer, *Compendium*, 3:1079.

Adutant Woodrough rode back along the line and told the boys to sing John Brown for them and we give it to them with a vim and then switched off onto (We will hang Jeff Davis on a sour apple tree) and a few such more. The old chaps looked like they would like to kill us but didn't. We marched some 16 or 18 miles towards Louisville Ky and went into camp. That night the boys gathered in some honey to sweeten their hardtack with.

November 16th
We marched some 18 miles to Louisville Ky and went into camp south of the town near the Ohio River. The negro catchers were there waiting for us and as we marched through the town we had the darkies skattered along beside the regiment and a lot of the massas were secerted in the stores along the street and when they seen their boys they charged out and made a grab for them. The darkies ran in among the soldiers and begged at them not to let massa have them. The boys interfered and the old fellows got away up on their shiverly [chivalry] and pulled their revolvers and swore dire vengence on the d——d yankee abolition niger thieves. The company officers drew their swords and the men fixed byonetts and it began to look like as if we were about to have our first battle. When Lieutenant Colonel [Lysander] Webb came dashing back on his big bay horse right through and over the old fellows with a revolver in each hand and ordered the old chap to hunt their holes and do it d——d quick and they concluded to retreat without their boys as their fugitive slave laws did not seem to work that day. That night for fear the general officers might order the darkies turned over to their masters some of the boys got some skiffs and rowed the darkies over the Ohio River into Indiana and gave some money and grub and told them where and how to go. Some sent them to their homes in Illinois to work for their people on their farms. A great many of them reached their destination and made faithful hands.[16] We remained at Louisville until the 20th. We had a very disagreeable time while there as it rained nearly all the time.

16. As William Bentley observed: "To such an extent was this slave enticing propensity indulged, that Gen. Burbridge, a Kentuckian, was reported to have said that the Seventy-Seventh was an abolition regiment, and would steal all the niggers in Kentucky if they had a chance to do so. . . . At all events we had quite a regiment of darkies following in our wake, like a troop of boys following an organ grinder, with a monkey on his 'masheen.'" *RH*, 103–4.

November 20th
We marched down to Portland below the rapids on the Ohio River where our regiment after loading our traps on the boats embarked on the transports Starlight and Ben South for Memphis Tenn. Company C was on the Starlight.

November 21th
We started down the Ohio river the guerillas and bushwackers being very troublesome along the river. We traveled by daylight and tied up and throwed out pickets at night. Their skeem was to shoot the pilots and let the boats run ashore and try to capture them. To prevent that they had to have all the pilots houses lined with heavy boiler iron, a half circle of it on each side of the pilot house. On our way down the Ohio River we stopped at Evansville Ind. and left some our sick. T. S. Patton and S. A. Leslie of company C was left at the hospitle. At that place T. S. Patton returned to the regiment in March. S. A. Leslie never returned to the reg but was discharged from service at Memphis Tenn the next spring and returned home.

November 25th
We arrived at Cario Ill. at the mouth of the Ohio River where we stopped for a short time. It made us feel like we were almost home again to see the black mud of the sucker state once more, which some of us were destined not to see again for almost three long years and many never saw it again.[17] We soon pulled out form Cairo and floated down the Mississippi River for the next three days tieing up at night. As on the Ohio River we had a very pleasant trip and a very agreeable change form tramping the pikes of old Kentucky. We had several boat races and as the river was very low we stuck fast on sandbars on several occassions and had quite a time getten off, but always got off and on.

November 28th[18]
We arrived at Memphis Tenn where we disenmarked and marched out through the city and went into camp about one mile east where we re-

17. Illinois is often referred to as the Sucker State. The origin of this nickname is uncertain, but appears to be attributable to the lack of water on the prairie. Those traveling across the prairie would "suck" fresh water that collected in small crawfish holes. Oral interview with Laurie Trimble, reference librarian, Peoria Public Library, August 19, 1998.

18. Bentley gives the date of arrival in Memphis as November 27. *RH*, 105.

mained until the 20th of December. While in Memphis we had a very pleasant time. We were getting too far south to see much old weather. It seemed very pleasant to us coming from the colder climate of the north. We had little snow once or twice but it did not remain long. We got some brick from an old brick kiln and built walls around under our tents to raise them higher and built a fire place in one end where we kept some fire on the coller days. While there the measels broke out in the camp and nearly all who had not had them were taken down and but very few ever got over them. They would get over the first attack but when they became convalescent they were sent to the convalescent camp at old fort Pickering where they had to lay on the damp ground and nearly everyone took a relap and died.[19] Andrew Dorson, Edward Hall, Reuben Parnham, James Vararsdall, Edward Wallace and James Yeldon of Company C died from the effects of measles at Memphis.[20] General Sherman* was organizing an army at that time to cooperate with General Grant* in an assault on the rebel works at Vicksburgh Miss and shortly before leaving Memphis the whole army passed in review before General W. T. Sherman and staff.[21] The army was drawn up in line just south of the city near Fort Pickering and made a very fine apperance. It was the largest demonstration of the kind that we had as yet taken part in.

19. Located on the Mississippi River on the south edge of Memphis, Fort Pickering guarded the southern approaches to the Queen City and provided the Federals with a fortified position on the river's east bank. In the course of the Civil War, the 77th lost 110 men to disease, many of whom died in Memphis of measles between November 1862 and February 1863. Ibid., 361.

20. Andrew Dorson from Cazenovia enlisted on August 13, 1862, and died December 25, 1862; Edward Hall of Logan enlisted on August 11, 1862, and died December 23, 1862; Reuben Parnham from Woodford County enlisted on August 11, 1862, and died April 21, 1863; Edward Wallace from Logan enlisted on September 2, 1862, and died January 26, 1863; James Yeldon from Cazenovia enlisted on August 18, 1863, and died February 26, 1863. Ibid., 48–52.

21. For a judicial account of Sherman's life, see John F. Marszalek, *Sherman: A Soldier's Passion for Order* (New York: The Free Press, 1993). Dr. Marszalek's work was nominated for the Pulitzer Prize in biography.

Few works on the Civil War are more a delight to read than the *Personal Memoirs of U. S. Grant*. Originally published by the Century Company in 1885, the two-volume work became an instant classic. Frequently reprinted, it is readily available.

3

Seeing the Elephant

The test of a soldier's mettle comes in combat. For Wiley and his comrades, that test would come in the winter of 1862–63 on a muddy field
of battle in Mississippi, just north of Vicksburg—the "Gibraltar of the
Confederacy."

To seize the river stronghold, Major General Ulysses S. Grant split his
force in two. One wing, consisting of 40,000 troops under Grant's personal command, marched south along the line of the Mississippi Central
Railroad from Grand Junction, Tennessee, into north Mississippi. The
objective was to draw Confederate troops responsible for the defense of
the Vicksburg-Jackson area into the northern portion of the state and
keep them pinned along the Yalobusha River near Grenada. The other
wing, consisting of 32,000 soldiers under Major General William T. Sherman, was to make an amphibious thrust down the Mississippi River from
Memphis and capture Vicksburg. Wiley and the men of the 77th Illinois
were attached to Sherman's Expeditionary Force.

Pushing deep into Mississippi over muddy roads, Grant's column met
with disaster as Confederate cavalry under Major General Earl Van Dorn
sacked his advance base of supplies at Holly Springs. In west Tennessee,
Brigadier General Nathan Bedford Forrest led a successful raid against
the railroads vital to Union operations. The raids compelled Grant to
abandon his maneuvers and fall back on Memphis.

On the same day as the raid on Holly Springs, December 20, Sherman's force, unaware of Grant's misfortune, boarded transports in
Memphis for the push down river.

December 20th

We were ordered aboard the transports to proceed against Vickburgh. Our regiment embarked on the transport Duke of Argyle. Lieutenant [Silas] Wagoner was the officer in charge of the detail of men who were loading our traps on the boat. He was a very small man in a very large body. He was very over bearing and abusive. His little authority seemed to hurt him. He cursed and abused the men at a terrible rate until the colonel had to reprimand him. One would have thought from his talk and actions that he would tear the confederacy all to pieces in a little while but I noticed that he was one of the first to resign when we got where rebel bullets begun to sing around in a careless manner.[1]

December 21th

Having all aboard by 2 pm we started down the Mississippi River with flags flying, bands playing and the men cheering. Our fleet of gunboats and transports, some 75 or 80 in all made an imposing sight as we floated down the river. We proceeded down the river to a small town called Friors [Friars] Point in Mississippi where we tied up for the night and throwed out pickets.[2]

December 22th

At an early hour a lot of our boys got off of the boats and strolled off down into the town. Where it was reported to them that the rebel citizens had caught some of our men a short time before and had nailed them up in sugar hogsheads and rolled them into the river. So the boys thought it was their duty to retaliate by raiding the town which they did in good shape by raiding the stores and firing a good many buildings. Then a lot of them dressed up in the dry goods which they had taken from the stores and came marching back to the boats looking like a lot of Indians. The officers had seen the fire and sent a guard to arrest the perpetrators and as the men came up they were arrested and marched up to headquarters in their fantastic uniforms where they were ordered to pile up their calico and were sent to their regiments under guard which ended their punishment as far as the 77th was concerned at least. We soon shoved out and

1. Lt. Silas J. Wagoner from Elmwood enlisted in Company I on September 2, 1862. Unable to cope with the horrors of the battlefield, as experienced at Arkansas Post on January 11, 1863, he resigned from the service on March 17, 1863. *RH*, 81; *AG*, 4:675.

2. Friars Point is located south of Helena on the Mississippi River in Mississippi.

proceeded down the river. That night we tied up at Halls Point Miss and throwed out pickets.[3]

December 23th
We shoved out at an early hour and proceeded down to a place called Gasters [Gaines'] Landing where we pulled up at 2pm to procure wood for the boats and remained there during the night.[4]

December 24th
We proceeded down the river to Milikens [Milliken's] Bend and tied up for the night.[5]

December 25th
Our first Christmas in the army. Our regiment was ordered to march out some 12 or 15 miles from the river to take up a railroad. The regiment marched out and tore up a lot of the road and returned to the boat. I was on guard on the boat and did not go.[6]

December 26th
Our regiment was sent out on another expedition to try to capture a squad of rebel caverly that had been following our fleet and watching

3. The exact location to which Wiley refers is uncertain. The armada tied up for the night along the Arkansas shore, several miles below the mouth of White River. Thomas B. Marshall, *History of the 83d Ohio Volunteer Infantry* (Cincinnati: Gibson and Perin, 1912), 49.

4. Gaines' Landing, where the armada next tied up for the night, was situated about thirty miles below Napoleon, Ark. The Federals set fire to the town. *The War of the Rebellion: A Compilation of the Official Records of the Union and Confederate Armies*, 128 vols. (Washington, D.C.: GPO, 1880–1901), ser. 1, vol. 17, pt. 1, p. 605. Hereafter cited as *OR*. Unless otherwise indicated, all citations are to series 1.

5. Milliken's Bend is situated on the Louisiana side of the Mississippi River just north of Vicksburg. Throughout the winter of 1862–63 it would be the Federal base of operations against Vicksburg.

6. The objective of this march was to tear up the tracks of the Vicksburg, Shreveport, and Texas Railroad. Chartered in 1852, by the eve of civil war the railroad, despite its grandiloquent name, only stretched from De Soto (opposite the Mississippi River from Vicksburg) to Monroe—a distance of eighty miles. During the winter of 1861–62 floodwaters had washed out most of the bridges along the line between Delhi and Delta. Burbridge's brigade was given the task of ensuring that the railroad could not be put back in service. The men of the 77th marched thirty-seven miles to Dallas, La., where they set to work with a vengeance tearing up tracks. The depot and several warehouses filled with corn and forage were burned. The covered bridge across the Tensas River (200 feet in length) was filled with cotton and also fired. Lawrence Estaville Jr., *Confederate Neckties* (Ruston: McGinty Publications, 1989), 61–77; *OR*, vol. 17, pt. 1, pp. 627, 629.

our movements but the rebs got wind of them got away. While returning from this trip G. A. Phillips [John G. Philips] a half witted fellow in our company got very tired and would let his musket drop backward and shot the men behind him and he and some of the men got into a rackett over it and Phillips got in a terrible fashion and was going to kill some of them and the captain [J. M. McCulloch] had his musket taken from him but he cursed everthing from the highest to the lowest. Lieutenant Colonel Webb tried to talk to him but he cursed the colonel and told him G—— d—— you. When we were in Kentucky you tryed to ride your d—— old big horse over us. So the colonel ordered the captain to tie his hands behind his back and put him under guard so they tied his hands with a gun stap and set him down on the boat to cool off. He worked his hands loose and throwed the stap in the river saying, there goes your d—— old stap. Then he began to laugh and was alright again.[7]

December 27th
We left Milikens Bend and preceeded up the Yazoo River, some ten or twelve miles where our army went ashore and was drawn up in a line of battle and lay on our arms. During the night we did not sleep very sound wondering what of the tomorrow.

December 28th
We were aroused at an early hour and fell into line and marched some six or seven miles out from the river towards the city of Vicksburg where we came upon the rebel outposts. About daylight we were on the extreme right of the union line. Our right resting on the Mississippi River. The troops on our left having encountered the rebel out works. The battle began meanest in that direction. This being our first introduction to Johnny reb and the smoke and music of the battle. We felt strange sensations crawling up our backs and out to the ends of our hairs. We were haulted a few moments and were then ordered forward. Our regiment in the advance, we proceeded for a short distance when our regiment was deployed as skirmishers and proceeded forward through the thick

7. John G. Phillips from Cazenovia enlisted on August 13, 1862. He was discharged for disability (perhaps for being "half-witted") on March 25, 1863. *RH*, 50; *AG*, 4:661.

cypress timber over what is known as the Chickasaw Swamp or flats.[8] The timber was all interlaced with vines of all descriptions which made it very difficult for us to proceed in any order but we made our way through as best we could. Driving the rebel outposts before us here our simple friend G. A. Phillips soon got into trouble again as he became very much excited and went slamming and tearing along through the brush and vines with his musket at full cocked generally about a rod or two behind the rest and would trip over the vines and fall at full length and his old musket would go off and the ball would whistle past our heads. He would get up and ram in another load and come ahead a slobering and swearing until he would incounter another vine with the same result until the boys got out of patience and told the captain that if he didn't send that d——d fool to the rear they would kill him for if they had to be shot they wanted it to be by the enemy and not by that d——d fool. So the captain sent him back with the musicicans and hospital attendants who were following up to take care of the wounded and he was soon after discharged and sent home. We drove the rebel outpost into their intrenchments and took position a short distance from their works which we held until night. The rebs making it pretty hot for us as they rained their shot and shell around us in a very careless manner cutting the tree tops off over our heads and their shot and pieces of shell barking the trees all around us. We held our ground until night when we fell back about half a mile where we lay on our arms until morning. Our company being thrown forward as pickets.

December 29th
We were ordered back to the regiment at an early hour after eating some breakfast. We fell into line and started forward again. Our regiment being deployed as skirmishers and driving the rebel outposts into their works again and taking the same position as the day before which we held until

---

8. Wiley refers to Chickasaw Bayou. The fighting that ensued was often referred to by the soldiers as Chickasaw Swamp, Chickasaw Bluffs, Walnut Hills, and even First Vicksburg. The official name of the engagement is the Battle of Chickasaw Bayou. During the advance, the 77th pushed forward along what is today known as Long Lake Road. The enemy outpost they encountered was manned by soldiers of the 61st Tennessee Infantry of Brig. Gen. John Vaughn's Brigade, posted behind a thick obstruction of felled trees. See the Battle Maps of Chickasaw Bayou drawn by Edwin C. Bearss, Vicksburg National Military Park, Vicksburg, Miss.

night. Again the rebs making it particularly warm for us making us hug our trees pretty close. No one was hurt but Joeseph Pots of company K who had his finger shot off. Some were foolish enough to think that he done it himself.[9] There was heavy firing off to our left during the day. At night we were relieved by the 19th Kentucky and fell back some distance where we layed during the night in support of the 19th Ky. The ground where we layed was very low and flat and it came on a terable heavy rain during the night and the water gathered in around us and then some of us awoke we were covered with water. Our little greenbacks and every-thing in our pockets was well soaked. So we got up and leaned against the trees until morning passing jokes and ludiorous presions [impressions] to keep up spirits.

December 30th

At an early hour we built some fires as best we could with the wet wood, got some breakfast and dried our clothes and greenbacks a little when we fell in line and marched out and relieved the 19th Ky where we remained on the skirmish line for the next two days and nights exchanging leaden compliments with the Johnnies. Our men and the rebs were so close together that they could talk back and fourth. Warner Holingsworth [Hollinsworth] made some of the boys very mad by calling out to the rebs, say Johnnie the [you] will have to shoot a d——d site lower to hits any of us.[10] When Johnnie acting on the suggestion began to shoot low enough to suit even Warner.

⚞ 1863 ⚟

January 1st

We were ordered back from our skirmish line, word having been received that Gen Grant had met with disaster and failed to cooperate with Gen-

9. Joseph Potts from Rosefield enlisted in Company K on August 11, 1862. Potts's wound resulted in his discharge for disability on March 14, 1863. Cutting off a finger was not out of the question for some soldiers at the front, for they viewed it as a ticket home. Rather than be drafted and forced to serve in the Civil War, many men knocked out their front teeth or cut off their trigger finger, which eliminated them from duty. *RH,* 91; *AG,* 4:679.

10. Warner Hollinsworth from Rosefield enlisted in Company K on August 9, 1862. He evidently learned from this experience, as he survived the war and was mustered out with the regiment on June 10, 1865. *RH,* 90; *AG,* 4:679.

eral Sherman and we could hear the trains coming in almost constantly from the east bringing back the troops that had been operating against Gen Grant and we were evacuating them out after us. So we fell back some distance and spent that new years day cuting and carrying logs and building breast works. That night our company we sent forwards as pickets it was a terable dark night. We were ordered to be on the elert and maintain the greastest vigilance as they were expecting the rebels onto us at any moment. We could not see our hand before our face but had to defend our ears and every twig that snaped we could hear the click of the hammer as every musket was cocked for buisness along about midnight after I had been placed out infront some distance as a vidette for some time I heard stealthy steps approaching from the rear and right of me. I did not know whether to think that Johnie had got around in the rear of me or what but as the steps approached closer I heard the order given in a whisper vidtts fall back to the reserve very quietly. I obeyed the order and found the reserve drawn up in line. We fell back to the regiment which we found in line teams hitched and everything ready for the retreat and we retreated hastely back to our boats on the yozoo river some 7 or 8 miles where we arrived about daylight. The rebel cavelry came after us in force but the gun boats kept them at bay until we got out into the mississippi river about the time we started on the retreat. I took terable sick with filious malarial feavor but had to march back to the river and when I got to be carried aboard the boat and did not hardly know what was going on for the next two weeks.

January 2nd

We passed on up the Mississippi River to Milikens bend where we remained until Jan 5th during which time the command of the army was transfered from Gen W. T. Sherman to Gen John H. [A.] McClernard* [McClernand] under whom we then preceeded against Fort Hinman Ark.[11]

11. Fort Hindman at Arkansas Post was situated 25 miles above the mouth of the Arkansas River (117 miles below Little Rock). The earthwork was a "square, full-bastioned fort, whose exterior scarps between the salient angles were each 100 yards in length. The parapet's superior slope was 18 feet, the ditch 20 feet across on the ground level, and 8 feet deep." Fort Hindman's complement of artillery consisted of two 9-inch columbiads, one 8-inch columbiad, four 10-pounder Parrott rifles, and four 6-pounder smoothbores. Edwin C. Bearss, *The Vicksburg Campaign*, 3 vols. (Dayton, Ohio: Morningside, 1985–86), 1:350–1.

*   *   *

McClernand named his command the Army of the Mississippi and in January directed his force up the Arkansas River to capture Arkansas Post. Strategically situated to defend the interior of Arkansas, it was also a point from which Confederate gunboats could operate against the Union supply line on the Mississippi River. In the ensuing fight, the 77th Illinois suffered its first loss in battle. Fortunately for William Wiley, the malarial fever he had contracted at Chickasaw Bayou rendered him unfit for duty and he was not exposed to the carnage, which claimed the lives of many of his comrades.

January 5th
We left Milikins Bend and proceeded up the Mississippi River, stopping frequently to procure wood for the Boats until we reached the mouth of the white river in Arkansas up which we proceeded until we came to a cut off which led into the Arkansas river through which we passed into and up the Ark. river until within about three miles of the town of Arkansas Post where the rebs had erected strong earth works which they called Ft. Hinman.

January 10th
Our army left their boats again and proceed to surround the rebel works which they had acomplished by ten o'clock that night where they lay on their arms during the night waiting for the morning and the mornings battle (I say they as I was laying aboard the boat so sick and delerious with feaver that I did not know what was going on).

January 11th
Was the sabath, clear and beautiful but not to be sanctified by a holy rest but by carnage and death. Our army alert at an early hour and lay in terable suspence mometarily expecting the order to advance against the rebel works until about one p.m. When the gun boats and land batteries opened on the rebel fort and soon after the infantry was ordered forward and the clear ringing voice of Colonel Grier was heard commanding attention 77 forward guide center march at first the 77 was in the second line in support the 19th Kentucky but in a few moments they were ordered support the 83 Ohio they had now got within clear range of the rebel works and the shot and shell were flying around them altogether to thick for comfort. Men were falling killed or wounded on all sides.

They would be ordered forward on double quick for aways and then they would be ordered to halt and lay down until other parts of the line would come up and then they would be ordered forward again. The lead hail from the rebel works getting thicker and more deadly all the time. About this time the 83 Ohio being ordered forward again failed to respond and the 77 being ordered forward charged right over them and took the lead for the rebel works. Our color bearer, John Hornbaker being knocked down by a piece of a rebel shell, Lieutenant Jenkins of Co C grabed up the flag and ran for the rebel fort and planted it upon their works just as the rebs ran up the white flag and the 77 scaled the rebel fort and was the first to enter the fort and was given the post of honor to guard the fort and prisoners.[12] The inside of the fort presented a terable site. The ground was litteraly covered with dead men and horses all cut to pieces and strewn in every direction where our gun boats and batteries had done their deadly work. The 77 lost sick, killed or badly wounded. We took 7,000 prisoners, 8,000 stand of arms and a considerable amount of other stores including 20 cannon.[13] That night the 77 guarded the prisoners. The prisoners were mostly Texans[14] and were pretty wiry chaps. They demonstrated strongly against being sent north they thought they would freeze to death. The next two or three days was spent in sending the prisoners away destroying the rebel works and burying the dead of both sides.

The men of the 77th had at last "seen the elephant." Those who had survived now considered themselves soldiers in every sense, and approached the next campaign with the confidence of battle-hardened veterans. William Wiley, however, had yet to face the test of battle. Throughout the winter of 1862–63, he struggled with a more immediate enemy as he wrestled with the debilitating effects of malaria.

12. Several regiments claim the honor of being the first to scale the parapets and plant their colors on the fort. The fact that the 77th was given the post of honor to guard the fort and prisoners lends credence to the claim made here by Wiley on behalf of the regiment.

13. In this, the first action in which the 77th suffered casualties, the regiment lost 6 men killed, 2 officers and 37 enlisted men wounded, for a total of 45 men. The men and property captured at Arkansas Post included 4,791 men, 17 cannon, and 7 flags. *OR*, vol. 17, pt. 1, pp. 708, 716.

14. The Confederate garrison at Fort Hindman consisted of two brigades, the troops of which were from Texas, Arkansas, and Louisiana. Bearss, *Vicksburg Campaign*, 1:418–9.

4

WINTER OF FRUSTRATION

The winter of 1862–63 was a miserable experience for Wiley and the men of the 77th Illinois, as it was for all Federal troops involved in the Vicksburg campaign. McClernand's army, fresh from its victory at Arkansas Post, moved to Milliken's Bend, Louisiana, where it was merged with the Army of the Tennessee under Grant's command. Determined to capture the river fortress, Grant orchestrated a series of ill-fated Bayou Expeditions during the winter months, but the only result of his operations was an ever-lengthening casualty list. The Confederate citadel remained defiant, seemingly impervious to capture by Union land and naval forces. The northern press ridiculed Grant and clamored for his removal. Even members of the Cabinet urged President Lincoln to find a new commander for his western army. The president, however, answered Grant's critics by saying, "I can't spare this man, he fights. I'll try him a little longer."[1]

As Grant contemplated his next move, Union soldiers struggled to survive the harsh environment in which they lived. The camps in Louisiana were situated along the levees to escape the flood water of the Mississippi River. Cleanliness and sanitation were impossible; the men lived in a vast sea of mud. Freezing rains added to the sufferings of the troops,

---

1. Cognizant of the criticism swirling around him in both military and political circles and aware that even the president's patience had limitations, Grant appeared stoic, but confided the torment he felt to his wife, Julia. Determined to persevere, he ignored his critics and remained focused on his objective—Vicksburg. John Fiske, *The Mississippi Valley in the Civil War* (New York: Houghton Mifflin, 1900), 225.

who sickened and died by the hundreds. Among those faced with death was William Wiley. Although not fully recovered from malaria, he returned to duty only to be stricken by a more severe illness. His physical condition worsened, and he was confined to Van Buren Hospital at Milliken's Bend, where he feared that the Angel of Death awaited.

It was truly a winter of frustration, as Wiley fought to live and his comrades waited for the arrival of spring when the roads would dry, enabling them at last to march on Vicksburg.

January 14th
They got up terable wet, it having rained hard all night. That day they went abord the boats again and that night there fell several inches of wet, slushy snow and the men that had to be exposed on pickett and other drill suffered terably and the enclosure of the past month was beginning to tell on the men and we had a great many sick on the boats beside what had been sent away to the general hospitals. Our boat had considerable of the apearance of a hospitial boat as we had about 40 wounded besides the many sick. I had goten barely able to leave my bed by this time and as the cabin of the boat was so badly filled up with the sick those of us that were at all able had to go out on the guards of the boat with their company and the rain and snow blew in on us and wet our blankets and clothing and a great many of us caught terable colds. I could not speak above a whisper for several days and from the effects of the feavor and enclosure I became so stiff and sore that I could hardly walk about and remained in that condition for the next three or four months until the weather got dry and pleasant the next spring and I got so poor I would hardly make a shadow as the saying is and I began to think that I would sell out my chances pretty cheap.

January 15th
Remained on the boat the weather was very disagreeable.

January 16th
Remained on the boat during the day. That night a part of the regiment had to go on picket in the snow and mud and put in a terable disagreeable night on the pickett line.

January 17th
We left Fort Hinman and driffed down to the mouth of white river where our fleet of boats tied up again.

January 18th
We layed at the mouth of white river where we burred one of Co C.[2] I well remember how in my weakened condition I shuddered at the thought of being burried in such a dreary and forbiding spot. Some of the boys went out and confiscated some chickens and we had some chicken soup for a change.

January 19th
Our fleet started down the Mississippi River again. We stopped in the evening to cut wood for the boats where some of the boys stayed off and got a lot of beef and we had fresh beef for supper.

January 20th
We passed on down to the mouth of the Yazoo River where we remained until the 23, some of the troops going ashore and others remaining on the boats. The 77 remaining on board.

January 23rd
We droped down to youngs point on the Lousiana shore where we disembarked and bid farewell to the old Transport Duke of Argyle, which had been our quarters allmost continuosly since Dec 20.[3] We were glad to get ashore again but felt sad to part with the old Transport and her good natured crew. Altho our life upon the waters was begining to tell sadly on the health of the regiment as we had at that time present sick 195, absent sick 240, being more than one half of the regiment. The regiment marched down the river some three or four miles and went into camp nearly oposite and in plain view of the rebel strong hold of Vicksburg. I being barely able to walk and carry my traps I did not march with the

2. Possibly Pvt. George M. Lay from Cazenovia, who had enlisted on August 14, 1862. He is the only member of Company C listed as having died near Arkansas Post, on January 10, 1863. *RH*, 49; *AG*, 4:661.

3. Young's Point is located in Louisiana on the Mississippi River upstream from Vicksburg and between the Confederate fortress and Milliken's Bend. Throughout the winter of 1862–63 Union troops used Young's Point as a base.

regiment but in company with J. H. Pinkerton of my company and other convalescents of the regiment. We formed a slow brigade of our own and ploded on as best we could haulting quite frequently to rest. J. H. Pinkerton and I kept together night coming on we crawled up into the loft of an old barn where some of our cavalry was camped and laid down on some corn tops and slept til morning. At daylight we crawled down and started on our slow march again down the leavee stoping where some regiment was camped we got some coffee from the boys and eat some hard tack and coffee and went on until we found our regiment which we found in camped in a low flat corn field just outside of the leavee from the river. The furrows between the corn rows was standing full of water not a very cheerful location but here was our position and here we had to stay and make the best of it.

January 24th
We spent the day draining our camp we had to dig a deep ditch on each side of our rows of tents and between each tent to drain the water away from the tents and throw the dirt inside of the tents to raise us above the water line and gather old corn stalks, weeds, brush and whatever we could find to lay on to keep us out of the mud and everytime it would rain our ditches would stand full of water and all the surrounding country would look like a vast lake. At such places the leavee had to be built very high to keep the water in the river from spreading all over the country in time of high water front of our camp was some 15 or 20 feet high and the water in the river at that time was some 10 or 12 feet higher that the ground on which we were camped and continued to rise for the next month until the water was nearly to the top of the leavee. All the water we could get to use miserable stuff and to add to our other discomforts all the wood that we could get was green cifreso [sic] gum and the like which would hardly burn when it was dry and worse when it was wet and we could hardly get fire enough to make our coffee and it was almost impossible to get even that kind of wood as it had to be hauled from the swamps about a mile away and the gound was so wet and soft that the wagons would sink down to the hubs in many places. There was a great many swales running up through the fields and these were all full of water and the boys in going to and from the pickett line would have to wade these swales and either take off their clothes and wade the cold water almost waist deep or wade through with their clothes on and stand

pickett all day and night in their wet clothes. The duty here came very heavy on those that were able for duty as aside from all other duty there was heavy details made every day to work in what was called Butler canall as our oficer had coinceived the idea of trying to cut a canall across youngs point which was a point of land about a half mile wide oposite Vicksburg caused by a sharp bend in the river which striking the bluffs blow the city made a short bend almost running paralell to its self for quite a distance causing a long narrow point of land in the bend.[4] Thinking that they could turn water enough through this canall while the water was high to float their gun boats and transports through and get some of them below the city and cut off their suplier below for our army and to assist in crossing our army over the river below the city as the intention was to march the army below the city cross over the river and come around in their rear. But afer working through rain and mud for some two months they had to abandon the undertaking as the water began to fall in the river before they got the canall finished and they had to run

4. Although referred to as Butler's Canal by Wiley, it is more properly known as the Williams-Grant Canal. On June 27, 1862, as the ships of the West Gulf Blockading Squadron under Flag Officer David Glasgow Farragut bombarded the Vicksburg river defenses, a 3,000-man infantry brigade commanded by Brig. Gen. Thomas Williams began work on the canal, hoping to create a channel for navigation that would bypass the Confederate batteries at Vicksburg. The scouring effect of the Mississippi River's current, it was thought, would keep the canal open. It was also believed by some that the man-made channel might catch enough of the current's force to cause the river to change course, thus leaving the city high and dry and rendering Vicksburg militarily worthless.

Yet the canal proved a daunting task. Men died by the dozen of heat exhaustion, sunstroke, or disease. "The labor of making this cut is far greater than estimated by anybody," confessed General Williams. In spite of the adverse conditions, the canal was excavated to a depth of thirteen feet and a width of eighteen feet—but it was still impractical for navigation. On July 24, work on the canal stopped when Farragut withdrew from Vicksburg to safer waters, accompanied by Williams's weary soldiers.

In January 1863, work on the canal was resumed by troops under Grant's command, which included the 77th Illinois. Initially rapid progress was made, but a sudden rise in the river broke through the dam at the head of the canal and flooded the area. The canal began to fill up with backwater and sediment. In a desperate effort to rescue the project, two huge, steam-driven dipper dredges, *Hercules* and *Sampson,* were put to work clearing the channel. The dredges, however, were exposed to Confederate artillery fire from the bluffs at Vicksburg and driven away. By late March 1863, Grant had determined on a bold change in operations and work on the canal was abandoned. For additional information on the Williams-Grant Canal, see Edwin C. Bearss, *Rebel Victory at Vicksburg* (Little Rock: Pioneer Press, 1968) and Bearss, *Vicksburg Campaign,* 1:431–50.

the blockade with their boats past the rebel batteries in the darkness of the night and all theses things told terably on our men and many a noble boy gave up his life there in that forbiding spot for the cause of friends and country. Our doctors has taken posession of two or three old log houses that stood near our camp as a regimental hospital. These were full all the time with the sick of the regiment and almost every day during the last few weeks of our stay there, there was from one to three or four laid out in front of the hospital to be burried and toward the last there was hardly an hour in the day but what we could hear the drums beating the dead march as some pour comrade was carried to his last resting place and as the ground was so full of water about the only place we could find that was dry enough to burry the dead was in the side of the leavee and before we left there the leavee was lined with the graves of our dead for miles up and down the river.[5] All this time I was just moving around hardly able to be on my feet and by times confined to bed having to return to the doctors every day for treatment and to be excused from duty until I got so tired of the whole business that I wished they would bring out my rebel and let us fight it out and be done with it. I tried to keep up spirits knowing that it would not do to give up but when I would hear the drums beating the dead march in all directions the thought would come unbiden how soon will they beet for me but there was some bright spots in all this gloom our cheering letters from kind friends at home whom we tried to keep the knowledge of our surroundings and also the 28 of Jan when Mr. Rugg and others from Pearice Ill. came to

5. In the years after the winter of 1862–63, when thousands of Union soldiers died from disease and exposure in Louisiana, the annual spring rise of the river opened many of the levee graves that Wiley mentions. In Vicksburg, it was common to see corpses or human bones floating past the city. In addition, graves throughout the region were dug up by cattle or wild animals. The situation became so unsightly and unhealthful that local citizens petitioned the federal government to establish a central burial location for these remains. Congress responded in December 1866 by establishing Vicksburg National Cemetery. Throughout the region, bodies of Union soldiers were disinterred and taken to Vicksburg for permanent burial. By late 1869, approximately 17,000 Union soldiers were interred at Vicksburg, 13,000 of whom are listed simply as "Unknown." Richard Meyers, *The Vicksburg National Cemetery: An Administrative History* (Washington, D.C.: GPO, 1968), 1–22. Twenty-one of the identified soldiers were members of the 77th Illinois, two of whom were members of Company C. James Drake from Panola enlisted in Company C on August 22, 1862, was wounded in the May 22, 1863, assault against Railroad Redoubt at Vicksburg, and died on June 6, 1863. He is interred in Section G, Grave 5360. Sgt. James H. Drennan is buried in Section G, Grave 5337. *RH,* 47–8; *AG,* 4:661; Burial Records, Vicksburg National Cemetery, Vicksburg, Miss.

us bringing a lot of sanitary goods for the regiment also on march 10 Rev P. H. Drenen of Woodford County Ill came down with a lot of good things for company C and again on April 1 Mrs. Hansel and Doup came down from Peoria with a lot of sanitary good for the regiment which cheered our spirits to know that our friends were so throughful of us and their good things done our iner man a world of good, also on March 7 the pay master came around for the first time and cheered our pockets with some of Uncle Sams greenbacks and again on April 5 we were paid all arears up to the first of March. On march 13 we received a box of good things including socks, mittens, needle books which was very acceptable to us in our sad plight and went a long ways in reviving our spirits and failing health.[6]

March 9th
We broke camp at Youngs Point and went aboard the transport Hiawatha and went up the river some 15 or 20 miles to Milikens Bend where we arived about noon and marched out aways from the river and went into camp in a very wet flat cornfield but little if any better than the camp we had left at Youngs Point and had to go through the same work of ditching and fixing up again.

March 10th
I was taken worse and was taken to the regimental hospitle which was in an old house near the camp. I remained in the hospitle some two weeks.

March 14th
Thomas Patton returned to the company he having left at the hospitle at Evinsville Ind on Nov 14 1862.

March 22th Sabath
Chaplain [William G.] Pierce preached to the regiment having just returned he having been absent sick for some time. He made quite a stirring up among the doctors who had got rather abusive with some of sick who they thought were playing off to try to get a discharge. When the chaplin heard of it he went to the colonel and made complaints against

---

6. Needle books were commonly known as "housewives" by the soldiers because they contained needles, thread, cloth patches, buttons, and a thimble so that the troops could mend their uniforms.

the doctors and the colonel gave him charge over the hospitle and he straigthen things out generally.

March 24th
Having recovered my health somewhat I returned to the regiment.

April 7th
Things began to look like business again as the regiment was ordered out to be inspected by Gen A. J. Smith.

April 8th
The 13th Army corps was ordered out to be reviewed by Gen Grant but Gen Grant not being present the corps was reviewed by Gen J. A. Mc-Clernard [McClernand] our corp commander.

April 9th
The corps was ordered out again and reviewed by Gen Grant.

5

THE CAPTURE OF GIBRALTAR

The campaign of spring 1863 would be the most significant one in which Wiley and the men of the 77th Illinois participated. It was focused on the fortress city of Vicksburg, which President Lincoln referred to as the "key to victory." On March 31, Major General Ulysses S. Grant began the campaign by boldly launching the Army of the Tennessee on a march south from his base camps at Milliken's Bend and Young's Point, Louisiana. Anxious to take to the field, the men shouldered their knapsacks and rifle-muskets and took up the line of march confident of victory.

Wiley, however, still suffering from the effects of malaria, remained in the hospital. He only slowly regained his health and did not rejoin the regiment until June, when the soldiers of the 77th manned the siege lines around the Confederate Gibraltar. Most of Wiley's diary entries from this period were later gleaned from his comrades or culled from Bentley's regimental history.

April 16th
Our 13th Corps broke camp at Milikens Bend and started on the great march around Vicksburgh. Myself with others not being able for the march we were aboard a hospitle boat and taken to the Vanburen hospitle at Youngs Point[1] where we remained until we were able to rejoin the regiment in the seige of Vicksburgh. The weather becoming warm and pleasant and having a better chance to take care of myself. I soon

---

1. Van Buren Hospital was located at Milliken's Bend, not Young's Point.

recovered my health to such an extent as to be able to rejoin the regiment as soon as a way was open so I could. After leaving Milikens Bend the regiment marched some 12 miles on the road leading to Richmond La where we went into camp.

April 17th
The 77th marched some 13 miles to a place called Holmes farm where we went into camp and remained until the 24th.[2] While at this place a lot of the boys went on an aligator hunt and was liken to get into trouble when they came back to camp but got off with a lecture.

April 24th
Broke camp at 8 o'clock at night, marched 7 or 8 miles by two o'clock and then laid down until morning where we remained until the 26th.

April 26th
Left Smith's plantation after dark.[3] Marched about five miles it raining hard all the time. It was terable slipery and many a soldier got a fall in the mud that night. Stoped about 4 o'clock and laid in the mud until morning not knowing what minute we would be ordered forward.

April 27th
Put in the day marching about 5 miles it raining all the time making the roads so heavy that the artilery and wagon trains could hardly be moved at all and making it very hard on the troops as it kept them on their feet all the time as it was so wet and mudy that we could not sit down. When we did stop and our clothes got soaking wet.

April 28th
Moved on at daylight. Marched on until about nine o'clock marching about 7 miles where we remained until 4 o'clock. When we resumed the march going about 7 or 8 miles to Joseph Lake [Lake St. Joseph] where

2. Trinidad plantation, the home of T. H. Holmes, was located eight miles south of Richmond. Many of the Federals mistakenly believed that it was the home of Confederate general Theophilus Hunter Holmes. Bearss, *Vicksburg Campaign,* 2:27.

3. The Pliney Smith plantation, known as Pointe Clear, was located along Bayou Vidal near New Carthage. Grant had intended to use New Carthage as his staging area, but due to the flooded condition of the countryside, it proved inadequate. The march south continued.

we went into camp for the night. This was a very pretty place. An old reb by the name of Ruth King, Ruth as he was called owned a large plantation on St. Joseph Lake.[4] He was very wealthly. It was said he owned 18000 acres of land and 200 negroes. He had a very fine mansion finished up in grand stile and grandly furnished but he skipped out at the approach of the union army and some bad yank set fire to his house during the night and it was all destroyed.

April 29th

Left lake St. Joseph at daylight and marched to the Mississippi River oposite Grand Gulf where the rebels had strong earthworks.[5] A fleet of gunboats and transports which had run the blockcade at Vicksburg under the command of Admiral [David Dixon] Porter* came down the river. The gunboats attacked the rebel forts and after bombarding them for sometime they with drew until night. When they engaged the rebel works again while the transports run past the rebel forts to carry the troops across the river below their works.

April 30th

The 77th Regt with the entire 13 corps crossed the Mississippi River on the transports and attacked the rebel works driving them out of their works and followed them up towards Port Gibson. Until about 2 o'clock

4. Ruth King cannot be positively identified, as no one by that named lived along Lake St. Joseph. A wealthy planter named Routh owned considerable acreage around the lake and a large number of slaves. It is likely that Wiley is referring to this man. See Bearss, *Vicksburg Campaign*, 2:288.

5. Grand Gulf, situated on the Mississippi River twenty-five miles below Vicksburg, had been selected by Grant as his landing site, for there was a good all-weather landing and roads radiated from the town into the interior of the state. However, two powerful forts, Forts Cobun and Wade, towered over the landing and posed a major obstacle to Federal plans. Fort Cobun was situated forty feet above the river, dug into the side of Point of Rocks near where the Big Black River empties into the Mississippi. Protected by a parapet nearly forty feet thick, the fort contained four guns manned by Company A, 1st Louisiana Heavy Artillery. A double line of rifle-pits and a covered way led south from Cobun three-quarters of a mile to Fort Wade. The lower fort, erected behind the fire-gutted town, was on a shelf twenty feet above the muddy Mississippi. Fort Wade contained four large guns and several light field pieces manned by the skilled artillerists of Capt. Henry Guibor's and Col. William Wade's Missouri batteries. Ibid., 2:307.

the next morning where we came upon the rebels in strong force posted in a ravine behind the timber and canebrakes.[6]

May 1st
Gen McClernard advanced against the rebels with the 13 corps and drove them from their position and driving them for several miles.[7]

May 2nd
The 13 corps pushed forward after the rebels, the 77 was in the advance line. They drove the rebels for some distance back across Bayou Pierree [Pierre] taking their works and the town of Port Gibson. The boys looted the town going through the stores and taking whatever suited them best. We remained at Port Gibson until the next morning.[8]

May 3rd
Fell in line about 10 o'clock and marched out to Bayou Pierree where we remained until the seventh. The rebels having burned a bridge at that place which had to be replaced before the army could cross.

6. Wiley writes without personal knowledge of the events that followed the Union landing at Bruinsburg and the march on Port Gibson. The advance was not contested by the Confederates until the Federal vanguard reached the Shaifer house on Rodney Road, approximately twelve miles from the landing site and four miles west of Port Gibson. The battle began shortly after midnight (May 1) and continued until 3 A.M., when, due to darkness, both sides settled down for the night.

7. The Battle of Port Gibson resumed around 5 A.M. when McClernand's corps advanced in force along Rodney Road from near the Shaifer house toward Magnolia Church. A second column was sent from the Shaifer house north along a connecting plantation road toward the Confederate right flank along the Bruinsburg Road, which was anchored on high ground overlooking Bayou Pierre. The battle raged throughout the day, during which the Confederate left, manned by Brig. Gen. Martin E. Green's brigade, was driven from its position near Magnolia Church. The gray-clad brigades of Brig. Gen. William E. Baldwin and Col. Francis Cockrell arrived late in the morning and reestablished the Confederate left flank along the White and Irwin branches of Willow Creek. Cockrell's Missourians unleashed a vicious counterattack, to no avail; by late afternoon the Federals advanced in overwhelming numbers and forced the Confederates to flee the field. Landram's brigade, to which the 77th was attached, saw limited action late in the day and suffered only 31 casualties. The 77th reported no losses. *OR*, vol. 24, pt. 1, p. 583.

8. Wiley incorrectly implies that the Confederates had field works in the Battle of Port Gibson. They did not. The diarist continues to write without foundation when he states that the soldiers "looted" Port Gibson. Measures had been taken by the Federals to prevent such activity and, for the most part, private property was respected by the victorious Union army. Bearss, *Vicksburg Campaign*, 2:410.

May 7th
Having the bridge rebuilt we crossed over and marched to Willow Springs Miss where the rebels made a stand but were soon dispersed.[9] We remained at Willow Springs until the 9th.

May 9th
We left Willow Springs that afternoon and marched to a place called Big Sandy [Big Sand Creek], some three miles distant.

May 10th
Left Big Sandy that afternoon, marched to Kayuga [Cayuga] some three miles where we remained until the twelveth.

May 12th
Left Kayuga in the morning, marched some eight miles towards big Black River where we remained until morning.

May 13th
Marched some eight miles to a place called Auburn where we were halted to guard a supply train where we remained until the fifteenth. On the fourteenth Co C was sent out on picket duty.[10]

May 15th
Co C was called in off picket duty about noon to resume the march towards to Vicksburg. Marched some fourteen miles ariving at Raymond

9. The events described by Wiley in this entry occurred on May 3. Having crossed Little Bayou Pierre, the Federal column marched to Big Bayou Pierre, only to find the suspension bridge on fire. After repairing the bridge and crossing the stream, the soldiers pushed up the hill toward Willow Spring, where they encountered the Confederate brigades under Col. Arthur Reynolds and Brig. Gen. Stephen D. Lee. In quick order, the southerners were driven from their position by the troops of the 17 Corps with few casualties on either side. No troops of the 13 Corps, including the 77th Illinois, were involved in the action at Willow Springs. Ibid., 2:423–8.

10. Auburn, situated northeast of Cayuga, was a strategic crossroads from which roads ran north to Edwards, northeast to Raymond, and south to Utica. The 13 Corps, on the army's left, wheeled north at Auburn. Contrary to popular belief, Grant did not cut himself loose from his supplies. Wagons laden with supplies rolled out of Grand Gulf every few days; escorted by a brigade-size unit, they pushed to join the army in the interior of Mississippi.

Miss at midnight where some of our troops had a [battle] the day before, taking a lot of prisoners.[11]

May 16th

Left Raymond before daylight, marched about eight miles to Champion Hills where a great battle was fought. That day the 77 being in reserve was not actively engaged but were run about from one position to another all day where support was needed. The day being very warm we were badly exhausted and suffered for want of water. At one time we were ordered to pile our knapsacks to charge a battery but the order was counter-manded. The fighting on the left [Union right] of the line was terrific. The rebels held a strong position and fought stubborn to hold our forces back until we [they] could get our [their] trains across the big Black River. The ground was covered with a considerable growth of timber which was literaly cut to pieces by the artilery and infantry fire. In passing over the same ground a couple of months after [en route back to Jack-son] it was fearful to behold large oaks trees were literaly cut to pieces with canon balls. Large white oaks two and three feet through were pierced through with the solid shot of the artiley and the bodies of the trees were literaly barked by the musket balls. I could not lay my hand on the body of a tree without covering one or more bullet holes. But the long rows of graves told the fearful tale, our loss was estimated at 429 killed, 1649 wounded and 189 missing. Hovey division of the 13 corps sustained the heaviest loss. The rebels gave way and we persued them

11. The Battle of Raymond was fought on May 12 between the 17 Corps under Maj. Gen. James B. McPherson and a lone Confederate brigade led by Brig. Gen. John Gregg. The weather was warm and the roads dry. Due to the dust kicked up by the soldiers and the smoke of battle, neither commander could discern the force in his front. Gregg, convinced that he faced a small flank force, attacked the Federals. Due to the ferocity of the attack, McPherson feared he faced a larger force and yielded the initiative to Gregg. By early afternoon, both commanders realized the true situation and McPherson counterattacked, driving Gregg from the field. In the engage-ment, northern casualties totaled 68 killed, 341 wounded, and 37 missing. Confederate losses numbered 73 killed, 252 wounded, and 190 missing.

The Battle of Raymond convinced Grant of the need to march on Jackson, the state capital. Using the 13 Corps to screen his movement, the Union commander directed his other two corps to advance on Jackson. Confederate Gen. Joseph E. Johnston arrived in the city late on May 13. Rather than fight for Jackson, he ordered the city evacuated. On May 14, when the Federals struck, they faced only token opposition. The Battle of Jackson cost Grant only 300 casualties. Bearss, *Vicksburg Campaign*, 2:515–7, 557.

with the bayonett and they were routed in confusion. That night our men slept on the battlefield.[12]

May 17th

Advanced some eight miles towards Vicksburg. Gen Austerhauses division (Gen Austerhaus* [Osterhaus] was wounded the day before so he couldn't ride his horse but they got him in a carriage and he continued to command his divison) was in the advance. He had considerable fighting and skirishing during the day. The rebels contesting every foot of ground. But we drove them back across Black River taking a good many prisoners and some artilery. Our divison charged across the Black River bottom and captured a Tennisee regiment.[13] A good many of them had been neighbors of our young Tennisee refugee Dudly Lindville who came to us at Marssails Ky and when they recoginized him the rebels made some big threats as to what he would get if he came back to Tennisee and as we never heard form him after his return. It may be that they carried out their threats. (Have lately learned that he died of heart disease some years after the war leaving a wife and three or four children). The trophies of this days work was 1700 prisoners, 18 canon besides small arms. Our men drove the rebels from their works at the point of the bayonett. They retreated across Black River and burned the bridge so that our men had to lay a pontoon bridge before they could cross which they did by morning. The rebels having retreated back toward their works at Vickburg. Our troops had got very short of rations having been cut loose from their base of suppiles for so long. Infact we were almost

12. The Battle of Champion Hill was the most significant action of the Vicksburg campaign. Federal troops advancing over three parallel roads encountered Confederate Lt. Gen. John C. Pemberton and his field army east of Edwards. The salient of the southern line rested on the bald crest of Champion Hill. Brig. Gen. Alvin P. Hovey's division of the 13 Corps, advancing along the Jackson road (the uppermost of the three roads), swept the Confederates from the crest of Champion Hill. His success, however, was cut short when the Confederates counterattacked and reclaimed the hill. By midafternoon, the Federals had regrouped and Grant ordered his troops to press the attack on all three roads. The Confederate line collapsed and the southern soldiers fled in disorder back through Edwards to the line of the Big Black River. The 77th Illinois, which advanced on the southernmost road (the Raymond road), saw limited action late in the day and sustained only one wounded. Ibid., 2:625–7, 647.

13. Probably the 60th Tennessee led by Lt. Col. Nathan Gregg. The two other Tennessee regiments that fought at Big Black River, the 61st and 62d infantry, also lost heavily in the number of men captured. Ibid., 2:676, 689.

without rations. That night we captured some meal and had some mush which made by mixing our meal in water without salt and cooking it in our tin cups.[14]

May 18th

Our army crossed Black River and having their lines form by eleven o'clock. We advanced towards Vicksburg marching some ten miles without encountering the enemey. We formed our lines [within] four miles of the rebel works at Vicksburg.

May 19th

Our army advanced on the rebel works. The 77 was in the advance line companies. We was deployed as skirmishers. The ground over which we had to advance was very rough being a sucession of hills and hollows and when we would reach top of the hills or ridges we were exposed to a murderous fire from the rebel forts. When one part of our line was exposed the rebels would consentrate their fire on them from all directions. When our men would charge forward on the run until we would reach the next hollow where we would reform our lines and advance again over the next ridge and at each advance the rebels fire became more deadly. Thus we continued to advance until we got within some five or six hundred yards of the rebel works where we halted and held our ground until night. When we fell back over the brow of the first ridge where we laid on our arms during the night. Several of the 77 was wounded during the day but none very serious. Van Robins of Co I was struck on the cartridge box by a piece of shell and thought he was badly hurt but found he was only bruised.[15]

14. Following his defeat at Champion Hill on May 16, Confederate general Pemberton fell back to the line of the Big Black River, where he attempted to hold the bridges long enough for the division of Maj. Gen. William W. Loring to cross. (Unbeknownst to Pemberton, Loring had been cut off from the retreating army by rapidly moving Federal troops and escaped to the southeast.) The Battle of Big Black River Bridge was a short affair as the 13 Corps drove the Confederates from a strong defensive position. Southern soldiers fled across the river in panic and confusion. Fortunately for Pemberton and his men, Maj. Samuel Lockett, the army's chief engineer, set fire to the bridges, preventing pursuit. Federal casualties were fewer than 300 men. The 77th Illinois was not engaged at Big Black River.

15. Anxious for a quick victory, Grant ordered an assault against the Vicksburg fortifications on May 19. Of his three corps, only one (Sherman's) was in proper position to make the attack. Although the Federals succeeded in planting several stands of colors on the exterior slope of

May 20th

Held our position during the day. There was several wounded during the day as the rebels kept dropping their shells among us.

May 21th

The 77 was in reserve and got a little rest althro we were exposed to the rebel fire more or less all day. Our officers having learned the formible nature of the rebel works. We had wisely decided to take time to get our forces all up and batteries in position before they attempted the final assault, which it was ordered by Gen Grant that it should take place the next day. Promptly at ten o'clock the orders were that the whole line was to move steadily forward at the firing of the signal gun with fixed bayonetts without firing until the outer line of the rebel works were carried.

May 22th

Promptly at ten o'clock the firing of the signal gun was given. The assault on the rebel works commenced. At the command, forward 77th, every man in his place pressed forward to the deadly assault. Determined to enter Vicksburg or die in the attempt. When we reached the top of the ridge we encountered a terible fire of shell and shot from the rebel forts which made sad morale in our ranks but we pressed steaily forward leaving a path strewn with our dead and wounded. On over the ridge and down into the abatis of fallen trees,[16] brushes and brambles and through which we crawled and strugeled as best as we could in face of a most deadly fire from the rebel works but on we went up the steep hillside in our front catching hold of the brush and briers to pull ourselves up until

---

Stockade Redan, Sherman's men were driven back with the loss of almost 1,000 men. The Thirteenth Corps was checked by artillery fire before it closed on the enemy's work.

Van Robins is not listed on the regimental roster. Possibly this was Cpl. Benjamin F. Robbins, Co. E, who enlisted on August 14, 1862, was taken prisoner on August 8, 1864, and died a captive in Savannah, Ga., date unknown. *RH*, 58; *AG* 4:665.

16. An abatis is an obstruction of felled trees toppled toward likely avenues of enemy advance. The limbs are stripped and sharpened and an entanglement of telegraph wire is strung in front of or among the fallen limbs, in order to disrupt approaching lines of infantry. If the Union army advanced in the conventional format of the time, with man touching man two ranks deep, all along its front the soldiers would encounter the abatis. If the Federals attempted to maintain their alignment, many men would trip over the entanglement of wire and impale themselves on the sharpened limbs. At best, the northern soldiers would be able to filter through the obstruction singly or in small groups. Once on the other side of the obstruction, they would be easy targets for Confederate riflemen posted behind the Vicksburg defenses.

within a few rods of the rebel works where we were halted to let other parts of the line come up but some of the regiment not hearing the order to halt, dashed forward into the ditches outside of the rebel works.[17] Some scaled the works and were either killed or capture. The other seeing the regiment had halted stopped in the ditches and waited for the regiment to come up. The color bearers planted their colors on the side of the rebel works and the other parts of the line failing to come up. The 77 with other regiments held our ground all that long and terible afternoon until dark defending our flag and comrades in the ditch and many a daring rebel lost his life in trying to pull in that flag. Our men in the ditch had a fearful time. The rebels lit handgrenades and fuse shells and threw them over among them which exploded and killed a great many of them until our men got to grabing them up and throwing them back before they would exploded which made them a little more careful how they throwed them over.[18] But they would cut the fuse short that some would explode before our men could throw them back. When our men seen one was going to explode they would lay down flat with their faces on the ground and a good many saved their lives in this way as the fragments of the shells would fly over them. Thus our men in the ditch put in a dreadful afternoon fearing to try to fall back toward the regiment as it would be almost certain death to attempt it. The only protection the men in the ranks had was to make it so hot for the rebels that they were afraid to raise their heads above the works to fire. Towards night the

17. The work toward which the 77th Illinois advanced was known as Railroad Redoubt, since it guarded the Southern Railroad of Mississippi. Situated on the south side of the tracks, the fort, shaped like the letter "J," was divided into three sections by two parallel traverses and mounted three field guns. Bearss, *Vicksburg Campaign*, 3:742; Edwin C. Bearss, *Texas at Vicksburg* (Austin: Texas State Historical Survey Committee, 1961), 8.

18. Hand grenades were used freely by the Confederates at Vicksburg. These devices were mainly of the Hanes and Ketchum varieties, but glass bottles filled with powder and balls were also used. The Hanes grenade, patented in August 1862, consisted of a cast-iron sphere with an inner and outer shell. The inner shell contained the powder and had fourteen nipples, upon which were placed regular musket percussion caps. The two halves of the outer shell were then screwed together and formed the hammer to the percussion caps. When thrown, at least one of the fourteen caps was sure to explode the shell. The most commonly used grenade was the Ketchum, patented in August 1861. It was slightly larger than an egg, and had a small tube of soft metal with a flange at the outer end. A nipple for holding a percussion was inserted at one end. A stick with four wings of pasteboard, to be used as a guide, was inserted in the other end. These grenades weighed approximately one pound apiece. Francis A. Lord, *Civil War Collectors Encyclopedia* (Harrisburg: Stackpole, 1963), 116–7.

rebels massed a strong force in our front and attempt to charge out and capture our small force and our men in the ditches. But our men in the ditches hearing the rebel officers giving their orders and knowing what they were going to do jumped out of the ditches and ran back to the regiment and the rebels soon came charging out over their works but our men made it hot for them that they were glad to retreat within their works and our men held their ground until night when they were ordered to fall back to their position of the night before. What was left of them as their loss had been very heavy. The 77 having lost 130 men in killed, wounded and missing.[19] Just one half their number. Darkness never was more accepatble than to our little band up there at the front as they felt that they were not acomplishing anything as other parts of the line had failed to come up and they were exposed to the greatest peril. There was many acts of herosim performed on that day and none shown more brightly then that of Chaplin Pierce of the 77 as he was seen everywhere that duty called him regardless of danger carrying got the wounded and dying. Helping carrying ammuinution to the men and encouraging the men by his noble words and actions which raised him very much in the estimation of the oficers and men of the reigment and gave him the name of the fighting chaplain. One of the sad features of the days operations was the loss of the regimental colors which had been planted on their works and defended there during the day until the rebels charged out in the evening and were driven back they carried the colors back with them and the 77 had no flag for a time but one that had been presented to Co C before leaving Peoria.[20] A little incident ocured during the afternoon which showed the ludicerous side of some mens dispostion. Warner Holingsworth of Company K during the hotest of the fight when men were falling all around him acosted the colonel who came

19. The counterattack to which Wiley refers was launched by Col. Thomas Waul's Texas Legion, which drove the Federals from inside Railroad Redoubt and the ditches which fronted the fort, thus sealing the breach in the Confederate works. In this action, the 77th lost 19 killed, 85 wounded, and 26 missing. Bearss, *Vicksburg Campaign*, 3:862.

20. Both the national colors and state flag of the 77th were lost that day. Described by Confederate colonel Thomas N. Waul as "a rich and heavy silk flag and finely decorated," the national colors of the regiment was taken from the parapet by members of Waul's Texas Legion. The state flag was ripped from its staff by a member of the 77th to prevent its capture and partially buried in the ditch fronting Railroad Redoubt, where it was found by the Confederates. Thomas Waul to William T. Rigby, letter of March 10, 1903, Regimental Files, Vicksburg National Military Park, Vicksburg, Miss.

near were he was thus say colonel doesent thee think we are making a d——d site of widowers today. As ordered the 77 fell back beyond the brow of the hill where they had started from when the assault was ordered.

May 23th

Held our position during the day and that night we were at position more to the right. The assault of the 22th having failed and finding the rebel works very formidable Gen Grant decided to besiege them and starve them out as we had them completely surrounded by the troops on land and the gunboats on the river.[21] So thus commenced the Siege of Vickburg which was to last until July 4th. The time was now employ in geting our forces into position and strengthing every part of our lines by throwing up breastworks, planting batteries and diging rifle pits.

May 26th [25]

A truce was aranged between the contending armies for the purpose of burying the dead which fell of the 22th. When large details from each army was sent out to collect and burry the dead. These details form the Union and rebel armies mingled together in a friendly way, shook hands and talked of their experiences and complimented each other on their fighting qualities and in a little while they were back in their respective positions trying their best to kill each other again. A good many of the rebels wanted to come over to our lines and take the oath of alegence but our officers told them they could not receive them during the truce but to go back and watch their chance and come over to our lines during the night which they did and continued to do so all through the seige and every once in awhile we would hear a rebel from between our lines and the rebel lines calling in a suppressed voice, say yank don't shoot I want to come over and surrender and the officer in charge would answer all right come ahead and word would be passed down the line not to shoot and mr reb would come hustling in over our works looking pretty badly scared as he felt he was exposed from both sides.

21. Grant's decision to besiege Vicksburg was not made until the night of May 25, when the Union commander asked for a truce to remove his wounded and bury his dead, many of whom had been lying exposed since the May 19 assault. Once the encirclement of Vicksburg was completed, the city and its Confederate garrison were virtually cut off from supply and communications with the outside world.

June 1st

I return to the regiment having been left behind sick when the regiment left Milikins bend on the march around Vicksburg.[22] Harvey McCullough[23] and others of the regiment had been left back also. We were taken to the Vanburen Hospitle at Youngs Point where we remained for some time. When I had recovered my health to some extent I was appointed ward master over one of the wards of the hospitle composed of a number of tents ocupied by those that were convalescent but still in need of medical attendance. My duties was to over see and report each day the condition of the ward and those that needed attention and see that they all got their medicine and provision. But Harvey and I soon got very tired of the place and very anxious to get to the regiment. So after we had been there some three weeks we reported as being able for duty and asked to be discharged from the hospital to return to our regiment. They did not want to let me off but after considerable insisting and finding another man to take my place they gave us our papers and we went and reported to the provost martial. He said he could not send us to our regiment just then but he gave us a tent and rations for a few days and then told us that he could not send us to our regiment as there was no communication open with the army but would have to send us to a convalescent camp to await an oportunity to get to our regiment. After we had been in this camp a week or two they decided to send a lot of the men to their regiments by way of Grand Gulf and as that would be along march. They decided that I was not able to go but took Harvey. They got to Grand Gulf but had to stay there a week or more before they could get to their regiments and after remaining in the camp at Youngs Point for some two weeks longer I came across the sutler of the 77 and we found some of our men that had been captured in the assault on Vicksburg and paroled[24] and sent across the river and we learned from them about what

22. This is another example of the irregularities of Wiley's diary. Although dated June 1, this entry describes events which did not happen until June 22 or later.

23. Harvey McCullough is possibly Thomas H. McCullough from Woodford County who enlisted on August 14, 1862, and served in Company C until mustered out on July 10, 1865. *RH*, 50; *AG*, 4:661.

24. Rather than holding prisoners, with the attendant responsibility of feeding them, the Confederates paroled a number of the Federal soldiers captured in the May 19 and 22 assaults. In signing a parole, a soldier made an oath that he would not take up arms against the Confederacy until properly exchanged—that is, until an equal number of southern soldiers were released from prison or from their paroles. Boatner, *Civil War Dictionary*, 619–20.

position our corps ocupied at the time and the sulter determined to start to the regiment the next morning and wanted me to go with him. So I went back and reported to the commander of the camp and asked permission to return to my regiment with the sulter but he gave me a regular scaring and ordered me to my quarters and told me that when he got ready to send me to my regiment I could go and not before it. So I concluded that he was just wanting to keep us there so he could get to stay himself. So I concluded that I would go inspite of him so the next morning before daylight I gathered my traps and lit out down the leavee to where the sulter was and we were soon on our way and arrived at the regiment the second day in the evening. The position which the 77 ocupied while in their quarters was a pretty secure one as we were quartered in a large hollow with a high blough [bluff] between us and the rebel works. Althro they would drop an occasional shell down amongst us and an occasional solid shot would rebound from top of the hill and come tearing down through our camp. Samuel Sharkey of Co K had his head taken off by a solid shot just as he was rising from his bed in the morning.[25] But if was a rather unhealthly place for the yank that exposed his head above the hill as he would soon hear the rebel lead singing about his ears. But we would keep low in daytime and work at night diging rifle pits and planting batteries. Working parties would be sent out after dark which would follow up some hollow to some point as near to the rebel works as they thought best where we would start our rifle pits below the brow of the hill and run them up towards the rebel works in such a shape that the rebels could not rake them from their batteries and these main trenches we would cover with boards and fence rails and throw dirt back over top of that so that the rebels could not see our men as they would be going back and fourth.[26] And when we would reach some suitable point of the rebel works we would start side trenches from these which we would dig parllell with the rebel works throwing the dirt out in front of us towards the rebel works diging them in such a zig zag shape that the rebels could not rake them from any part of their line and when these were finished all around the line and our batteries brought up and

---

25. Samuel Sharkey of Company K was killed on June 22, 1863, and is interred in Vicksburg National Cemetery, Section G, Grave Number 4804. Burial Records, Vicksburg National Cemetery, Vicksburg, Miss.

26. Such trenches are known as "covered ways."

planted in favorable positions in rear of these trenches. Then we would extend our main ditches up still farther and start a new line of trenches or rifle pits still closer to the rebel works and would bring some of our batteries up still closer and were bringing up heavy siege guns and planting them in favorable positions. At first the rebels made it pretty hot for us as their forts were so situated that they had the range of all the hills and country around and when anyone would exposed themselves they were mightly sure to catch it from some direction. And we would very often have quite a tussle with them as our men would be trying to get some battery or siege gun in position and the rebels would try to prevent them when the infantry in the ditches and the batteries already planted would have to keep the rebels down until they would get the guns in position. Our aim would be to keep up such a rain of balls and grape and schapnell from the batteries over the top of their works that they did not dare to raise their heads above their works. But they were gritty and would give us the best they could and many a man lost his life or sustain terable wounds in those ditches. At such times we were in almost as much danger from our batteries in our rear as from the rebels. As our batteries had to fire so close over our heads that the iron bands from grape and schapnell would break and fly all around us and a stray shot would strike among us or a premature explosion of a shell would rain death amonght us but our duty was to stand to our works come what there might. But thus in time we got our rifle pits extended to within a few yards of the rebel works and our batteries so well placed that the rebels darest not to show themselves. Our batteries got the range of their batteries so well that if one of their guns opened on us a dozen or fifteen of our guns would let loose on it and soon disable it. By times some parts of our line of trenches owing to the lay of the ground was so much exposed to the rebels fire from their forts that we could not work at them in the day time but would have to dig such parts during the night and they would take a lot of us out with spades and picks and deploy us out along where the ditch was to be dug just as close together as we could work to good advantage and this right in front of the rebel forts and but a few yards from them and they would place another line of men with their guns between us and the rebels work to keep the rebels down while we dug and if is needless to say that we needed no overseer to keep us at work until we got a hole dug deep enough to protect us. But very often the rebels hearing us diging would raise up and fire a volley into us in spite of our guards in front and would kill and wound a good many of our men. Some of our men that were generaly inclined to try to play off a little when on fatigue duty were ready to acknowledge that these were occassions that they did not try to play off. During the first part of the seige in particular our duty was pretty heavy as we had to keep a strong picket line in our rear in addition to our duties in front as the rebel Gen [Joseph E.] Johnston* with a portion of their army who had got seperated from [Lt.] Gen [John C.] Pemberton's main army and failed to get into their works at Vicksburg was hovering in our rear and we were expecting him to attack us from the rear and try to raise the seige.[27] But when Gen Grant had got suffifient reinforcement, two divisions under General Austerhause and [Francis P.] Blair* were sent to the Black river later which rendered our rear safe and relieved us from picket duty in the rear. But heavy details were made each day to work in the trenches and do picket duty in the trenches already dug. We soon got our trenches up so near to the rebel forts that they could fire down on our workmen from the top of their works. But our yankey ingimuity over came this dificulty by making long rollers or tubes of bamboo canes about as large as sugar hogheads but longer and filling them with cotton and rolling them in front of us as a breast work.[28] These they would first tried to knock out of the way with solid shot but failing in that they took to loading their guns with wads of cotton suturated with turpentine which would take fire when shot. These they would shoot into our rollers and set them on fire. Then we would throw dirt and water over them so they would not take fire and we proceded in this way until we got within a few feet of the rebel works when the miners set to work to dig tunnels from our trenches under the rebel forts for the purpose of blowing their forts up.

27. Having evacuated Jackson, Johnston moved to Canton, where he began to assemble what became known as the Army of Relief. His force swelled to 31,000 men by June 3, but still he would not move, claiming a lack of transportation, men, and supplies. Finally, under tremendous pressure from the authorities in Richmond, Johnston began a movement on July 1, by which time it was too late. The vanguard of the relief force reached the Big Black River on July 3. Unable to cross north of the railroad, Johnston ordered his columns south when he realized the firing in Vicksburg had stopped. Realizing what this meant, he beat a precipitate retreat to Jackson. Bearss, *Vicksburg Campaign*, 3:chap. 58.

28. Known as sap rollers, these devices were pushed by hand in front of the fatigue parties to protect the men with picks and shovels who were digging the approaches.

June 24th

Our reigment was called out shortly after midnight with orders to prepare to march back to Black River with two days rations as they were
expecting an attack by Johnston's army on our rear but after waiting
sometime for orders to march, the orders were countermanded.

June 25th

Gen [John A.] Logon's* troops on our right having succeeded in tunnel-
ing under the rebel Fort Hill and having everything ready for blowing
up the fort.[29] The troops were all drawn up in line. The trenches were
filled with men and everything looked very much as if we were going to
try to carry the rebel works by assault again. As our trenches had been
filled up here and there and road ways made for the artillery to pass over
and the infantry such as could not get in the trenches were massed in the
hollows and all available places as near the rebel works as they could be
got without being observed by the rebels. Our regiment was marched
some distant to the right and up a hollow not far from Fort Hill, when
at about three or four o'clock in the afternoon the mine was sprung
under Ft Hill and the air was filled with debris. Men, timbers and dirt
was flying in all directions and the blowing up of the fort was a signal
for all the artillery around the line to let loose on the rebel works. For
about an hour it sounded like all pandermorinum had broke loose and
while the rebels attention was drawn by the attack all around the line a
bridage of Gen Logan's troops dashed in and after a pretty hot hand to
hand fight got possession of Fort Hill and the surrounding works. But
as we was not ordered to assault the rebel works as we expected, we fell
back to our camp. But then we were ordered to remain in line and lay
on our arms that night as they expecting the rebels to try to retake the
fort, but they did not make the attempt. Very frequently during the seige
we would be called into line at all hours of the night. As some picket
officers would think that he seen indications that the rebels were massing
their forces on some part of the line to try to cut their way out or something of that kind. At such times Colonel Grier would step out of his tent

29. Fort Hill refers to the Third Louisiana Redan, one of two forts that guarded the Jackson
Road entrance into Vicksburg, which was the objective of Logan's approach. A redan is a trian-
gle-shaped fortification, the apex of which faces the enemy. On June 25 and again on July 1,
Federal forces detonated mines beneath the Third Louisiana Redan but failed to gain access to
Vicksburg.

and call out in that peculier voice of his, fall in 77th. When every man would jump to his feet, grab his gun and acoutrements and be in line in a moments time no matter how soundly he may have been sleeping. In fact some would come into line with gun and traps all on who were aparently sound a sleep and would have to be shook and wakened up. After the blowing up of Fort Hill the rebels got into our trick and began to dig counter tunnels under one of their forts and thinking that they were close enough to our tunnel they fired their charges but not being as close as they thought it did not harm our men but blowed out the other way and simply caused our men to have to go back a ways and start in the new [direction].[30]

June 30th
We were mustered for pay.

July 3rd
The rebel Gen [John S.] Bowen* and [Lt.] Colonel Montgomery[31] came out of their works in our amediate front under a flag of truce to stipulate for terms of surrender. They were received by the officer in charge of the pickets. When they were blindfolded and escorted to the headquarters of our division commander Gen A. J. Smith. When the paper they bore from Gen Pemberton was sent to Gen Grant who returned answer that an unconditional surrender was the only term that he would consider and that he would meet Gen Pemberton at a certain tree between the lines the next morning at a certain hour to make farther arrangments for the surrender under these terms.

July 4th
A meeting was held between the lines early in the day by Generals Grant, McFerson* [McPherson] and A. J. Smith of the union army and Generals

30. The Confederates placed light charges in front of their works which, when exploded, would pulverize the dirt and hinder Federal approach operations. The loess soil for which Vicksburg is famous has the amazing capacity to hold a vertical cut indefinitely. One can even tunnel into it without shoring. But one cannot dig into it once the dirt is pulverized.

31. Lt. Col. Louis A. Montgomery was a member of Pemberton's staff who rode with Bowen to request a meeting with Grant on the morning of July 3. Later in the afternoon, he again accompanied Bowen and Pemberton to meet with Grant between the lines to discuss the surrender of Vicksburg.

Pemberton, Bowen and Col Montgomery of the rebel army.[32] When arrangements was made for the surrender of the rebel strong hold of Vicksburg to take effect at ten o'clock of that day July 4th 1863. When the white flag was hoisted over the rebel's works a shout went up from all around the union lines that fairly made the old hills around Vicksburg tremble. The cheering would die away for a little time, when if would break out again in some part and be taken up all around the line until our throats was sore from cheering. To say that we rejoiced and felt very much releaved in putting it very mild as we felt that we had accomplished a great victory. One of great importance to the union cause as it opened up the Mississipi to the Gulf and cut the confederacy in two. And we felt very much relieved as everything for the last few days seemed to indicate that we were getting ready for another assault on the rebel works and we had no particluar desire for any more of that kind of works. General Grant tells us since that it was his intentions to assault their works again on about the fifth or sixth if they had not surrendered. As Joe Johnston who had been trying to raise the siege at Port Hudson,[33] was concentrating a large army in our rear to try to raise the siege of Vicksburg. Shortly after the surrender the 17th corps under Gen Logan after the rebels had marched out side of their works and stacked their arms, marched down into the city and took formal possession. We were all very anxious to go inside and examion the great stronghold that had withstood us so long but were very much disappointed when our oficers got orders not to alow any of their men to leave camp but to be ready to march amediately against Joe Johnston army. But Colonel Grier learning that we would march before six o'clock that evening and thinking that it was too bad for the boys not to get to see the place after battling so long for its possession, he told the boys that if they would all be back before that time he would take responability to let them go and see the town. So we started out in squads and took a general view of the town and forts and caves in the hills. The rebel citizens that had remained in the city had dug great caves under the hills and bluffs back of the city to get out of reach of our

32. The conference was held at 3 P.M. on July 3 and not on the Fourth of July as Wiley states.

33. Johnston made no effort to raise the siege of Port Hudson, which was besieged by the Army of the Gulf under Maj. Gen. Nathaniel P. Banks. The Confederate garrison under Maj. Gen. Franklin Gardner was compelled to surrender to Banks on July 9, 1863. The fall of Port Hudson gave the North undisputed control of the Mississippi River.

shells from our gunboats and batteries. They had carried their carpets bedding and furniture in there and was living in as much comfort as the circumstances would permit of. But we noticed that they were mighty glad to get some of our hardtack and sow meat. We were all back at camp promptly on time but did not march until the next morning. The rebel prisoners after stacking their arms were marched away some distance and rations issued to them and they took hold as if they enjoyed the change from mule meat to Uncle Sam's rations. The next few days was spent in parolling them and sending them away. We felt that this was about the biggest fourth of July that we had seen. That night we had quite a demonstration over the fall of Vicksburg with fireworks included.

❧ 6 ❧

ON TO JACKSON

It had been a glorious Fourth of July for William Wiley who, for the first time, was able to personally celebrate a victory with his comrades. Five days later, when Port Hudson, Louisiana, fell to Union forces under Major General Nathaniel P. Banks, the federal government reestablished control of the Mississippi River and President Lincoln declared that "the Father of Waters again goes unvexed to the sea."[1]

Although the fruits of victory were bountiful, there was still serious work to be done by the men of the 77th, who shouldered their knapsacks and took up the line of march east toward Jackson. With Vicksburg in his possession, Grant moved to drive Confederate general Joe Johnston and his Army of Relief from the state.

Despite the men's buoyant spirits, the march got off to a poor start for Wiley, who soon discovered that physically he was not yet up to the rigors demanded of soldiers during active campaigning.

July 5th
We were called out and started on the march toward Black River at an early hour. We were marched at a very rapid pace as Gen Sherman was trying to steal a march on Gen Johnston before he learned of the fall of Vicksburg. As the day got very hot and the road terable dusty and water was very scare and the boys being rather soft on the march after laying

---

1. Henry Steele Commager, ed., *The Blue and Gray: The Story of the Civil War as Told by Participants,* 2 vols. (Indianapolis: Bobbs-Merrill, 1950), 2:677.

in the trenches around Vicksburg so long. By the middle of the day a great many began to give out and fall out of ranks. The officers told the men that if they could not keep up they would have to fall out but to come on as fast as they could. A great many of us took the benefit of that permishion and fell out of ranks during the afternoon to save our wind. Lieutenant Harkness of Co K who had given out was left to gather the straglers and bring them on by slow march.[2] By the middle of the afternoon he had a great deal larger regiment then Colonel Grier. The rest of the officers and about one third of the men arrived at Clear Creek near Black River about four o'clock where they went into camp. Company C just had three men in line when they went into camp and Captain McCullock was considerably out of humor. Lieutenant Harkness and his stragler bridage came into camp in good shape before night.

July 6th
We laid in camp at Clear Creek until four pm when we fell in and marched some four or five miles crossing Black River and went into camp on the east side of the river near the ole rebel fortifications from which our brigade had driven the rebs at the point of the bayonett some six weeks before.

July 7th
After sending our knapsacks back to Vicksburg and taking our ruber blankets in a roll around our sholders we started at an early hour in presuit of Johnston's retreating army. We had another very hot days march as we marched some 14 or 15 miles passing through the little town of Edwards station and over the battlefield of Champion Hills where our forces had fought a hard battle with Pemberton's rebel army on May 16 driving them from the field. The long rows of graves of our comrades told the sad cost as which that victory was won but the poor boys on fames external camping ground, their silent tents are spread where glory guards with solumn round the bivaoc of the dead.[3] But having little time

2. Marcus O. Harkness of Elmwood enlisted on August 13, 1862. He was promoted to second lieutenant on October 21, 1862. Transferred upon consolidation of the regiment with the 130th Illinois, he was mustered out of service on June 15, 1865. *RH*, 87; *AG*, 4:678.

3. The last part of this sentence is taken by Wiley from "Bivouac of the Dead" by Theodore O'Hare, a Mexican War veteran who later served in the Confederate army. The remains of Federal soldiers buried at Champion Hill were later reinterred in Vicksburg National Cemetery.

to spend in regretts over the dead we pushed on after the enemey. Passing through the little town of Bolton Miss we marched on until after night turned around and marched back aways and went into camp in a corn-field. We cut up the green corn to bed ourselves with, laid down on it and drew our ruber blankets over us. That night came a terable heavy rain and we got well socked. We had to crawl up out of the furrows onto the ridges to keep from drowning.

July 8th
We remained in camp in our mudy cornfield until 4 pm. The sun came out and we built some fires and got our clothes a little dry. At 4 o'clock we fell in and marched some three or four miles and went into camp in another cornfield.

July 9th
We fell in at daylight and marched some five or six miles passing through Clinton Miss. We filed out off the road and formed in a line of battle where we remained until the next morning.

July 10th
We resumed the march at an early hour. The 77 was detailed to guard the wagon train. The rebels fell back inside of their works at Jackson Miss where they made a stand and our forces closed in around their works.

July 11th
Colonel Grier being in command of the brigade, Major Hotchkiss was left in command of the regiment and perhaps thought that was his chance to gain a little glory so he fussed around until he got the regiment ordered to the front which did not please the boys very much as we thought we were going to have a soft thing for once in our lives guarding the train back out of reach of the rebels guns and knowing Colonel Grier had placed us there because he had no more confidence in Major Hotch-kiss than we had been taking the brunt of everything we felt that we were as much entitled to a soft thing that day as some other regiment. But some other regiment was sent to take our place and we were ordered to the front and the officers and men were all out of humor and felt a little like taking the wind out of the major's sails if opportunity presented. So when the major marched us up to the front giving his orders with a

terable flourish and the shell and shot from the rebel guns began to sing around our ears pretty lively, Colonel Grier came riding along not far from our regiment, the boys all along the line began to call out, Colonel Grier, Colonel Grier and the colonel rode over to the regiment to see what the men wanted and the boys called out to him, colonel if we are going into battle we want you to command us, we don't want to go into battle under Hotchkiss and the colonel said, never mind men if you go into battle I will not be far from you. The boys set up the cheer for Colonel Grier and the little major looked like his wings were clipped rather short. The major could not handle the regiment on drill without getting us all double up and we did not care to be doubled up in the face of the enemy. But having asertained the rebel's postion in our front we were ordered back aways and formed our lines some little distance from the rebel's lines. We were not so far away but what the balls from the rebel's muskets would sing around our ears when they would fire on our front line which was posted in rifle pits some little distance in front so that we had to take fence rails and fix up baricades. That night a part of our regiment was detailed to go on the skirmished line in front where we had a pretty hot time of it for the next twenty-four hours where we were posted in a narrow tip of timber between our line and the rebel works. The rebel skirmishers and our were only about twenty rods apart, each posted behind the pine trees which in many cases were hardly large enough to cover our bodies and thus we stood each man hugging his tree and making the bark fly around each others ears and woe to the head or arm that showed its self past the tree. One in our regiment got a ball through his arm.[4]

July 12th

There had been a sharp fight off to our right a day or two before as our trops were closing in around the rebel works and a good many were killed on both sides.[5] During that day the rebels asked for a truce to bury

4. The units of A. J. Smith's division, which included the 77th Illinois, were positioned west of Jackson, between Raymond road on the south and Robinson road on the north. Also positioned between these two roads were the divisions of William P. Benton on Smith's right, and Osterhaus on his left. Battle Map of the Siege of Jackson drawn by Edwin C. Bearss and contained in his book, *The Battle of Jackson/The Siege of Jackson* (Baltimore: Gateway, 1981), 71.

5. Wiley refers to the assault of Jacob Lauman's division made on July 12. Lauman's men advanced north from Bailey's Hill, across Lynch Creek, and closed on the Confederate fortifi-

their dead which was granted and during the truce we left our trees and took a look around and talk with the rebel pickets. After a little, some of the fool yanks who had more curiosity than discretion sountered off towards the rebel lines when the rebs fired off their guns to warn them off. When not knowing what they meant by firing on us during the truce, every man jumped to his tree and let it fly at the rebs and it sounded for a little while like all pondimonium had broke loose and the bark from the trees was flying until the air was full of it. Our officers got us to hear the orders to cease firing then all was quiet again and we crawled out from behind our trees and called out to the rebs, say Johnie what the thunder did you mean by that? Well says the Johnies back, we don't want your d——d yankeys coming over here till after the truce then let them come all they want to. We answered back, allright Johnie we'll come (and let me stop right here to remark that we had some yanks that so much curiosity and foolhardiness that they would walk straight into Hadees if the door was left open just to see what it looked like) and thus continued to gibe one another until the truce was off. Then we went to pecking away at each other again. When the firing commenced during the truce, Gen A. J. Smith our division commander who headquarters was about a mile back in our rear hearing the firing and thinking perhaps the rebels were trying to take advantage of us in some way, he mounted his horse (Old Billy) a thorough bred Kentucky racer, ordering his staff and orderlies to follow him. He headed Old Billy for the front and give him the spurs and the boys in the rear that seen it said, they thought they had seen wild riding before but they thought the General and Old Billy broke all past records on that ride. His staff and orderlies urged their horses to the top of their speed to try to keep up but could hardly keep in sight when the General reached our front lines. They had not made much more than half the distance when the General reached our skirmish line, the firing had ceased. He came dashing right up to the skirmished line with his hat in his hand and his old white hair streaming back in the wind. He rode up to the officers of the skirmished line and said what the

---

cations, where they were roughly handled and driven back with the loss of 68 men killed, 302 wounded, and 149 missing. The colors of the 28th, 41st, and 53d Illinois regiments were also lost. Maj. Gen. Edward O. C. Ord, commander of the Thirteenth Corps, furious over the manner in which this assault was made, relieved Lauman of command. The truce to which Wiley refers did not occur until July 14 and lasted from noon until 4 P.M. *OR*, vol. 24, pt. 2, pp. 547, 604–8, 654–7.

Hells up? When the officers explained to him the cause of the firing and the boys began to laugh the General said, Heck boys I thought all Hell had broke loose! Cautioning the officers to see that such a thing didn't happen again he rode off to Corp's Headquarters to report. We kept behind our trees pecking away at the Johnies until dark when we were relieved by some other troops.

July 13th
There was considerable skirmishing all around the line. Our brigade was marched to the front and some distance to the right where we remained untile returned to our former position in the seckond line.

July 14th
We were called into line three or four times during the day as the rebs were making considerable demonstration in our front. But I presumed it was to draw our attention while they were getting their trains and supplies away.

July 16th
There was considerable firing all around the line. Major Hotchkiss with fifty men from the 77 was sent back to the rear some distance to guard a bridge. That night the rebs evacuated their works crossing Pearl River and retreated to the east.[6]

July 17th
All was quite around the rebel line. At daylight the skirmishers were ordered forward to reconoiter and found their works deserted. Our cavelry followed the retreating rebels for some distance capturing quite a number of prisoners and returned to Jackson. Our forces took possession of the city and hoisted the stars and stripes over the capitol building. The capitol of Mississippi was in the hands of the yanks for the seckond time in the past three months as a part of Grant's army had taken possession of it on their way to Vicksburg. When we learned that Johnie wasn't at home we strolled down and took a look at the city and concluded that it was not very much of a city to be the capitol of the great soverign State

6. Three pontoon bridges spanned the Pearl River just north of where the Southern Railroad of Mississippi had crossed the stream. At 9 P.M., Johnston's force began the evacuation of Jackson and marched toward Brandon. The Confederates fired the bridges behind them.

of Mississippi. That evening our division marched back some three miles and went into camp.[7]

July 19th

The 77 Ill. and ninty sixth Ohio was ordered out some distance to the south to destory a portion of the New Orleans, Jackson and great northern RR.[8] We marched south 6 or 7 miles and finding the RR destroyed and it being late we went into camp for the night. We got alot of roasting ears from a field nearby and had roasting ears for supper and breakfast.

July 20th

We marched some 7 or 8 miles farther down the RR to a little station called Byram where we went to work and tore up some two or three miles more track, burning the ties and bending the rails which was pretty heavy work and by night we were very tired.[9] That evening our quartermaster with a squad of men went out aways with a couple of wagons and loaded them with peaches and roasting ears. That evening we feasted on peaches and corn and stretched our weary bodies on mother earth thinking that we would have a good night sleep after a hard days work but we were doomed to dispointment for just as we were getting into a sound slumber, orders came for us to fall into line and march back to Jackson some 15 miles that night and be ready to take up of line of march for Vicksburg with the ballance of the army at daylight and some of the boys seemed to think that this was a little rough and expressed their thoughts in terms that was a little more forceable than polite. But as a soldier can do nothing but obey, we simply obeyed and tramped back to Jackson. The night was very warm and water was scare and we had a very

7. Much of Jackson had been destroyed by Sherman's troops on May 14 and 15 when the capital was neutralized militarily to render it useless to the Confederates. Rail lines were destroyed, telegraph lines cut, machine shops and factories set on fire. The flames, fueled by strong winds, quickly spread to residential areas, and much of Jackson was left a smoldering ruin. It was known thereafter as "Chimneyville." Bearss, *Battle of Jackson/Siege of Jackson*, 30–4.

8. The railroad connected Jackson with New Orleans. During the course of Grierson's Raid, conducted by the Federals in the opening stage of the Vicksburg campaign, the railroad was so badly damaged that it was not put back in operation until after the war.

9. The rails were placed atop stacked ties which were then set on fire. Heated by the fire, the rails began to bend and were then twisted around trees to render them useless. Such rails were known throughout the South as "Sherman neckties." Bearss, *Vicksburg Campaign*, 2:550.

hard nights march. We arrived at Jackson about two o'clock. When we got within two or three miles of where the ballance of our corps was incamped, the boys thought it would be a good idea to let the general know that we were coming so they set up the most unearthly yell I ever heard and kept it up for about an hour until we arrived in camp at Jackson. I shall never forget how we waked the echoes through those old hills and forests of Mississippi that night. Some of our troops there hearing our racket and thinking they were about to be surpised by the Johnston's army were drawn up in line when we arrived and went back to bed muttering something about damnfool idiots, etc. After finding our place in line we were soon stretched on the grouns trying to get a little rest but had not long to rest as we were called up at an early hour to start on the march towards to Vicksburg.

July 21th
Started on our march back towards Vicksburg. We marched hard all day. When we left Jackson they ordered each man to carry one hundred rounds of cartridges. We could not see any reason for the order unless it was that they wanted to load the wagons with cotton and make the men carry the ammunition. So we concluded that we would not be made pack mules of. So about the first time we halted to rest the most of us laid the cartridges carefully away under the leaves by the roadside, all except what our cartridge boxes would hold, the traditional 40 rounds. These were kept for a case emergency. That night we encamped at Mississippi Springs.[10]

July 22th
We resumed the march at an early hour and marched hard all day. They rushed us through as if we were on a forced march. We could not see any particulas use in it as we had driven the enemy all out of the country and was simply going back to Vicksburg to go into camp. But as we learned afterward some of our head officers had got too much Mississippi rum aboard to know what they were doing. Our boys had got to calling themselves Gen Smith's greyhounds on account of being run

10. Mississippi Springs no longer exists. In Wiley's day, the town stood midway between Raymond and Jackson, near the present-day intersection of Spring Ridge road and the Raymond-Jackson road.

about so much and on this march when ever Gen Smith would come in sight they would set up the most unearthly howling like a pack of hounds. At one time the Gen rode up to our Col and asked him what the H——ll his men meant by howling that way when ever he can near. The Col told him he guessed the boys thought he was trying to make hounds of them by running them so hard. Huh sais the Gen d——n them I give them enough to do without howling that way and he put us through all the faster from that to Vicksburg and the harder he marched us the harder we yelled. That night we camped on the battle ground at Champion Hills. After going into camp a couple of old darkies who were cooking for some of the officers in the regiment for want of something better gather up a couple of long friction shells not thinking in their inocence that they might still be loaded and laid one on either side of their fire to set their camp kettles on and then they hunkered down by their fire to watch their coffee boil and presently one of their side stickes becoming hot it exploded with a terable roar and sent their coffee pots away heavenward out of sight. But luckily no one was hurt. But our two darkies were so surprised at the way their coffee pots acted that they did not take time to get on their feet but ran several rods on all fours before they attempted to get or look back and they could not be gotten near that fire again and our officers had to borrow some coffee for supper and had to get some new coffee pots.

July 23th

We were called up at an early hour but John Hill[11] of Co I had failed to get up when reveilee sounded and when the rest were in line ready for the march Hill was just ready to eat his breakfast and seated himself on a log and proceeded very leasurely to grind his hardtack and drink his coffee regardless of the order to fall in. When the Colonel was about to give the order to march he discovered Hill setting on the log and wanted to know what he was doing there. Hill told him he was eating his breakfast. The colonel asked him a few questions as to how his breakfast come to be so late and then gave the order for the regiment to rest in place

11. John C. Hill of Salem enlisted in Company I on August 18, 1862. Despite the gibes of his comrades, Hill served faithfully until mustered out with the regiment on July 10, 1865. *RH*, 84; *AG*, 4:676.

until Hill got his breakfast eat and poor Hill munched away very leasurely amid the taunts and jeers of the boys and it was a good while before poor Hill heard the last about that breakfast. After Hill had finished his breakfast and found his place in line we preceeded on our march. We crossed Black River about 2PM and arrived at our old camp in the rear of Vicksburg about 9 o'clock that night. When it began to get dark we were still some four or five miles from Vicksburg and when we found we had march to Vicksburg that night we thought it would be well enough to let Vicksburg know we were coming so we set up the most unearthly yelling and kept it up until we got to camp. Some of our men that had remained in Vicksburg said they heard us when we were five miles away. Being very tired and foot sore we soon found a place to lay down.

July 24th
Our Division was marched down through Vicksburg and went into camp about one mile below the city on the river bank where we remained until the 25th of August. While there our duty was light but the weather was terable hot. I think I never experienced such hot and oppresive weather as we had. While there we had to fix up frames and cover them with brush to make shades to lay in during the heat of the day. While there we had company drill in the morning and dress parade at night. A good many was taken sick and was given furlows for sixty days. The most of our officers went home on leave of absence. Capt Stevens of Co E was left in command of the regiment.[12] Gen A. J. Smith our division commander was sent to other fields of service and Gen [Stephen G.] Burbridge* was placed in command of the division. We spent a good deal of our time when not too terable hot in visiting the city and the surrounding fortifycations, our old battle grounds etc and visiting friends and aquaintances in other regiments. We had preaching services on sabath day by our chaplain W. G. Pierce. He adminstered the Sacrament of the Lords Supper to quite a congregation of bonzed [bronzed] veterans on the sabath Aug 2nd in front of the colonel's tent. The members of the Christian Commission preached a fine thanks giving sermon on Aug 6th in the

12. Edwin Stevens from Princeville was mustered in as captain of Company E on September 2, 1862, and served in that capacity until mustered out on July 10, 1865. He was commissioned major on July 24, 1865, but was not mustered. *RH,* 57; *AG,* 4:665.

Walnut St Presbyterian Church.[13] On Aug 19 a lot of us were detailed to load a boat (The City of Madison) with amunition at the Vicksburg warf and while laoding it we were placing boxes of pecussion shells on hand barrows and carrying them onto the boat and some careless one dropped a box of the shells and exploded them which ignited the powder and blowed the boat to attoms. A great many were killed and a great many others badly hurt and a good many other boats that lay near it was badly injured. I was on shore at the time and escaped unhurt.[14]

13. During the Civil War, the First Presbyterian Church stood on the northeast corner of Walnut and Clay Streets but was later moved and now stands on the southeast corner of Cherry and South Streets. The historic site of the church is now occupied by The Vicksburg, luxury apartments.

14. Built in Madison, Ind., and launched in 1860, the *City of Madison* weighed 419 tons. Prior to the Civil War, the vessel ran between Cincinnati and New Orleans. Converted to military use, the boat served in the campaigns against Forts Henry and Donelson, at Shiloh, and on the Mississippi River in the operations focused on Vicksburg. On August 18, 1863, while being loaded with shells, the boat was destroyed by an explosion. Capt. W. W. Collins dove from the roof to safety. Others were not so fortunate, and the official death toll was placed at 156 persons. It is interesting to note that although Wiley states that several men of the 77th were involved in loading the boat with shells, not one man in the regiment is listed as having been killed in the explosion, nor is the incident mentioned in Bentley's regimental history. Records, Old Court House Museum, Vicksburg, Miss.

7

The Department of the Gulf

After a well-earned and much-needed rest in Vicksburg, Wiley and the men of the 77th shouldered their rifle-muskets and boarded transports for the journey down river to New Orleans. The soldiers from Illinois were now attached to the Department of the Gulf, under the leadership of Major General Nathaniel P. Banks. The politician-turned-soldier had no clear objective, unlike Grant at Vicksburg, so Wiley and his comrades would spend the next several months wandering aimlessly in Louisiana and Texas.

August 25th
Our corps having been transferred to the department of the gulf[1] we went aboard the transport Atlantic and sailed for New Orleans passign Port Hudson Batton Rouge and other historic points on the way. Ariving at New Orleans on the 27th and went into camp at Corrolton [Carrollton] just north of the city where we remained until the 3rd of Oct.[2] Our encampment at Corrolton was a great deal more plesant than at Vicksburg as the heat was tempered by the breeze from the Gulf of Mexico. Our duty here was very light. We spent considerable time visiting the

1. Departments were the basic territorial organization used by both the United States and Confederate War Departments for control of military operations. The Department of the Gulf was organized on February 23, 1862. Headquartered in New Orleans, it consisted of areas of the Gulf states occupied by Federal forces. Boatner, *Civil War Dictionary*, 234, 364.
2. Carrollton, now part of New Orleans, encompassed the area now occupied by Tulane University and Audubon Park.

city of New Orleans, Lake Ponchartrain and other points of interest. The hucksters of all kinds colors and nationalities visited our camp each day with their pies, cakes and hashes of all kinds of which the boys would buy to a limited extent as a change from the regular army ration of hard-tack and sow bosom until they found out that they were gathering up the scraps and refuse from the camps and bringing it back the next day in the shape of mince pies, pudding etc after which none that had much respect for the inner man would invest. During our leasure hours some of Co C took up the art of drawing at which they got to be quite proficient and we soon had a blank book filled with pictures from the hand of such authors as T. S. Patton, Wm Wright, Duff and others which laid the old authors all in the shade. Among the happenings of the Corrolton camp was the finding of his Grandmother by W. H. Stevenson and Major Hotchkiss trying to ride his horse over Dennis Duff and others and his learning that little Duff had been drilled in the art of guarding against caverly, Wm Wright apointment as corporal and his speech on the occasion how he told us that if he should be killed he wanted us to walk right over his body just the same as if he had been a private and the raiding of the provost martials office while he was upstairs asleep. Soon after going into camp a lot of the boys sauntered off as soldiers will to see what they could find and coming across the provost martial's office and finding it deserted as they supposed and foolishly concluding that it was some seceshes office that had been abandoned and following their soldier's instinct they helped themselves to what suited them best in his line such as paper pens ink blank books etc. Some even carried off easy chairs light writing desks etc to the camp. Others coming in a little late and finding the supply exhausted went upstairs to see what could be found and found the provost martial laying on a cot asleep and would have carried him off I suppose but he awoke and let them know who he was and ordered them out of there in a hurry and they didn't stand on the order of their going but got out of there and mixed up with other soldiers in a hurry for fear of being identified and in a very short time the provost guard were going the rounds of the camp looking for men and materials and the poor luckless soldier that was caught with any of the confiscated goods on hand was arrested and taken to Division headquarters and had a heavy stick of cordwood put on his shoulders and was made to march back and fourth through camp for an hour or two and then they were drawn up in front of Gen [Michael] Louler's* [Lawler's] tent and he put them through the manual of arms for a while with their cordwood muskets and then ordered them to break ranks. Also the guarding of a regiment of Vermont caverly who had been dismounted for some misdemeanor and who had refused to take muskets as infantry and were in a state of mutiny and were put under guard and starved into submission. During our stay there a certain brewery co would send out a load of fresh milde beer every day and company entered into a agreement that someone was to furnish the beer each day when on company drill commencing with the captain and going down according to rank the captain and two lieutenants each set up the beer in their turn. But when it come to orderly seargent Wright he refused to set up so that spoiled the arrangement.

August 29th

We appeared in grand review before Gen Banks* and again on Sept 4th before Gen Grant. After the latter was over we were shocked by hearing the Gen Grant had been thrown from his horse and killed but we shortly after learned that he was not killed but pretty badly shaken up. He and Gen Banks had been doing some fast riding after the review was over and Gen Grant's horse had run into an ambulance and throwed him heavily to the street from which he was laid up for several days.[3]

October 3rd

Having received marching orders we went aboard the transport North America and droped down the river some ten miles and dismarked at

---

3. The incident occurred on September 4, 1863. Grant was incapacitated for weeks afterward and had to be lifted into and out of the saddle. So severe were his injuries that Grant traveled with crutches strapped to his horse during the Chattanooga campaign. In his *Memoirs,* the Union commander describes the incident: "During this visit [to New Orleans] I reviewed Banks's army a short distance above Carrollton. The horse I rode was vicious and but little used, and on my return to New Orleans ran away and, shying at a locomotive in the street, fell, probably on me. I was rendered insensible, and when I regained consciousness I found myself in a hotel nearby with several doctors attending me. My leg was swollen from the knee to the thigh, and the swelling, almost to the point of bursting, extended along the body up to the armpit. The pain was almost beyond endurance. I lay at the hotel something over a week without being able to turn myself in bed. I had a steamer stop at the nearest point possible, and was carried to it on a litter. I was then taken to Vicksburg, where I remained unable to move for some time afterward." Ulysses S. Grant, *The Personal Memoirs of U. S. Grant,* 2 vols. (New York: Charles L. Webster, 1885), 1:487.

Algiers on the oposite side of the river at nine o'clock PM. Where we remained until eleven o'clock PM. When we took cars for Brashear City some eighty miles west on Burwicks [Berwick] Bay.[4] Our acomodations were not the best, our cars were simply flats. They loaded us on as thick as we could set around the edge of the flats with our feet hanging over the sides and then filled the center of the cars as close as men could set together and when they got the cars all filled in this way some of the officers came along and gave orders to put at least one third more men on each car. But Lieutenant Colonel Webb objected saying that his men was piled on then as thick as they could posably ride. But the officers insisted that he should put on more men. When Webb got his mad up and swore that he would not put another man that his men were not hogs and he would nave them treated like hogs. The officers fuss around and threaten to have Webb arested but the more they threaten the harder Col Webb swore and they went away directly and let us ride one deep. The wind was blowing from the west and the smoke and cindars blowed back over us from the engine and almost sufiicated us and burnt our clothes and blankets full of holes and our nights ride was not a pleasant one. We had to go very slow and look out for bush wackers and obstructions.

October 4th
We arrived at Brashear at daylight and went abourd the transport Starlight and crossed over Burwick Bay and went into camp at what was Burwick City before it was burned where we remained until the 7th waiting for the rest of our force to come up and put in our time hunting aligators and the like.

October 7th
Left Burwick Bay at daylight and marched out over a road built through the swamps and canebrakes passing lemon and orange orchards by the way. Seeing some very fine looking large oranges on the trees near the road some of us fell out of ranks and grabs our hands full of them but when tasted them they were as bitter as soot and we passed them around and let the boys all have a taste. We struck the Bayou Teche during the

4. From Algiers, opposite New Orleans, the regiment traveled to Brashear City on the Opelousas & Great Western Railroad.

day and followed up that stream passing through Pattersonville and camped for the night at a place called Camp Bislen where the rebs had a small earth fort which had been taken by Gen Banks forces the spring before.[5]

October 8th

Started at sunrise passed on up Bayou Teche passing through Franklin La about noon and marched on towards New Iberia taking a near cut across some abandoned plantation leaving New Town [New Iberia] to the right camped that night on the prarie some two miles fron New Town.

October 9th

Started at daylight marched some sixteen miles and camped for the night within three miles of New Iberia.

October 10th

The 77 Ill 19 Ky and 48 Ohio having got orders to march back to Franklin. We marched back some 19 miles and camped for the night within four miles of Franklin.

October 11th

Marched into Franklin and went into camp just outside of the town where we remained until Nov 11. We spent a very pleasant month at Franklin. Our duty was not very heavy and the country had not been picked very lately and we found plenty of sweet potatoes and fresh meat.[6]

5. Fort Bisland was located on Bayou Teche a few miles west of Pattersonville. In the spring of 1863, Union forces under General Banks pushed up the Bayou Teche toward Alexandria with the intention of clearing the west bank of the Mississippi River of Confederates, thus turning the enemy's position at Port Hudson. Confederate general Richard Taylor had a force of 2,700 at Fort Bisland to oppose Banks's 15,000. In the action that took place on April 12–13, Taylor was forced to evacuate his position, since Federal troops moving by boat on Grand Lake to Irish Bend threatened to cut his line of retreat. To extricate his command, Taylor struck the Union force at Irish Bend on April 14 and then skillfully withdrew. Boatner, *Civil War Dictionary*, 426–7.

6. As William Bentley wrote, "We found the country along the Bayou Teche, one of the richest and most beautiful portions of Louisiana we had yet seen. Large and fertile plantations reached back as far as the vision extended, while handsome residences, almost hidden behind the dark green foliage of trees peculiar to the south, fronted on the bayou, and long rows of orange trees, at that season of the year, almost bending under their loads of luscious fruit, lined the road along which we passed. Cattle and sheep, as well as the agricultural products of the country abounded." *RH*, 206–7.

We tore the siding from some old buildings and built us some very comfortable quarters. Col Grier, Lieutenant [Charles F.] McCullock [McCulloch], Wm Pinkerton and others who had been home on furlow returned to the regt. Col Grier brought us a new stand of colors in place of the ones we had lost at Vicksburg presented by the women loyal liege and missed [misses'] aid society of Peoria which was acompanied by a letter of presentation which was read to the regiment at dress parade and a committy was apointed to draft a reply which was done and sent to the doners.[7] Franklin La was at the time but a small town situated on the Bayou Teche about one hundred miles west of New Orleans surrounded by a very rich productive country. The great sugar producing district of Louisiana. The buildings and other improvements had been very fine before the war but were principle distroyed at that time some of the sugar houses were left and was being run under goverment control. There was no railroad through the valley at that time and all their freight was transported by water. Their warehouses were built on the Bayou at some convenient place for loading boats where the sugar and molases was stored until they got ready to ship it to market. We could tell by what was left

7. Two flags were presented to Colonel Grier, a state flag and a national flag. In presenting the colors, Mrs. A. G. Curtenius, president of the Woman's National League of Peoria, wrote: "In replacing the Flag lost under circumstances of so much daring and peril, the members of the 'Woman's National League' feel that they are in part fulfilling their pledge, and are making to you and your Regiment, the most acceptable expression of their sympathy with, and appreciation of your valor. Accept it then, accompanied with the earnest prayer of the league to the God of battles, even He who ruleth supreme over all, that He will ever be with you, giving you in conflict the victory over our country's enemies, protecting you in the hour of danger, assuaging suffering, if suffering there must be, and fitting each by His Spirit, through the merits of His crucified Son, for mansions in Heaven."

Colonel Grier formed a committee to draft resolutions of appreciation, which read in part: "We tender our grateful thanks—that we appreciate the gift and the spirit of patriotism and kindness that prompted it, and we promise as we hope for Heaven and as God is just, that never, by one cowardly act on our part, shall these banners be dishonored, but that we will ever be true to our country and our colors, and will do and suffer in their defence until 'Old Glory' waves in triumph over every stronghold of treason and rebellion, and as we can only feel that the colors are entrusted as a memento of confidence and respect—not given, so we promise that when our country shall be reunited and peace shall reign from ocean to ocean, from the Lakes to the Gulf, to bring back these banners, and then only will we accept them in full, when each star represents a loyal State. Then we can feel that these flags are fit to take the place of the old ones, which, though faded and worn by service on the well-fought fields of Post Arkansas, Port Gibson, Champion Hills, Black River Bridge and Vicksburg, nevertheless were dear to every one of us." RH, 208–12.

of the buildings such as the foundations fine marble steps, coping walks [walls], fountains, statues etc that they had been on a grand scale. But were then but sad evidences of the horers of war. Orders were very strict against foraging but the boys could generaly find a weak place in the picket lines to get outside especialy by agreeing to divide with the pickets and to make it right with the officers a choice piece was left at their mess and the officers wanted to go out on larks of their own and wanted to keep solid with boys for fear of getting into trouble at the picket lines. There was an old widow lady that lived out some distance from camp by the name of Madam Porter a war widow or otherwise. She owned a large plantation and a lot of slaves and in order to get protection for her property she was in the habit of entertaining some of our officers very nicely when they would go out to her place which they did frequently when she would get them up fine dinners etc. On one occasion shortly before we left Franklin Col Grier, Lieut Tracy[8] and several others of the younger officers rode out to pay their respects to the maddam and while they were being entertained at supper some of the maddams darkeys who had been on the lookout came running in and said, scuse me massa colonel but I guess you all had better look out a little I sees a lot of fellers acrossing ober de bayou in skifs and I think dey is rebels. So our officers thinking that perhaps it was time to look out a little left the table rather abruptly and mounted their horses and started for camp at the top of their speed supposeing that the widdow and the rebs had laid a trap for them and that she had given them the signal and they were sliping into capture them and they rode for dear life until they reached our picket line. I was on picket at the time near the road where they come in. We heard them coming when they were a mile or two away and thought from the noise they made that a brigade or two of rebel cavelry was coming on to us. The reserve pickets were all ordered into line and drawn up near the road ready to receive them and word was sent to camp to arouse the camp and when our officers reached our line, Hault Hault Hault came from every side and their wild flight was brought to a suden stop and the reply came in a shakey voice, friends with the counter sign and at the order advance friend with the officer of the picket and sliped off to camp as

8. Charles C. Tracy from Peoria enlisted as a private on August 6, 1862. He was promoted to first lieutenant of Company B on January 16, 1863, and mustered out on January 25, 1865, when the 77th and 130th Illinois were consolidated. *RH*, 41; *AG*, 4:658–9.

quitely as they could and perhaps would not have told the joke if they had not made the thing so public by there abrupt return. At one time during our stay there I was detailed with several others to guard a steamboat that was going up the bayou to take on sugar and molases from the rebel warehouses along the bayou. We had a great time as the trees hung over the bayou in such a way that our boat could hardly get through. We would have to stop and cut trees out of the way and cut limbs off of others before we could get past. One night myself and T. H. McCullough [McCulloch] had made our bed and laid down on the deck oft behind the wheelhouse and was just getting into a dose when we were awaken by a terable crashing and knowing what it meant we jumped and ran just in time to see the wheelhouse come rolling over where we were laying which would have ground us to mince meat if we had not got out of the way in time. A large limb had caught the wheelhouse and swept it clean off even with the deck. On several occasions as we were going up and down the bayou the old rebel bushwhackers dashed in on us on their mules until they would get within gun shot and give us a charge of buckshot from their shotguns and then whirl and ride away as fast as their old mules could carry them and we would let loose on them with our muskets and make the dust fly all around them. We proceeded this up the bayou quite a distance and finding a place in the bayou wide enough to turn our boat we started back down the bayou loading the sugar and moleses at each warehouse as we passed along. The countrebands would gather in from all sides to get away from massa. At one place a little colored child just big enough to run a little belonging to colored woman who had so many she could not take care of all of them ran in front of a sugar hogshead that they were rolling down the slope onto the boat and was mashed as flat as a pancake. Its mother grabed it up and began to scold it for being so foolished not knowing it was dead until someone told her some of the soldiers dug a grave and burried the child. And after being gone several days we returned to Franklin with quite a load of sugar and darkies.

November 11th
We got orders at ten am to be ready to march for New Iberia at two pm. We started at two pm and made a forced march of some twelve miles that evening as the rebels were threating an attack on our forces at New Iberia and we were wanted to reinforce them.

November 12th

We started as soon as it was light and continued our march at a rapid pace arriving at New Iberia at two PM. The rebels came in sight and reincounted our position for a while but withdrew without making an attack. Gen Burbridge was in command of the post and he forced all the male citizens of the place to turn out and work with the darkeys digging rifle pits and throw up breast works for us while we were drawn up in line to receive the rebels if they made an attact. The citizens were very bitter rebel sentiments and objected very strongly against working with the niggers to build fortifycations for the yanks but the general ordered the guards to trot them out and give them the bayonette if they didn't work. So they had to come to time which pleased the boys so well that Gen Burbridge was a great favorite with them afterwards. When the rebels had withdrawn the under officers and some of the men turned out one evening and suenaded the general and they had composed a song for the occassion in reference to his making the citizens work. The chorus was General Burbridge hes the man grab a root O heres your mule. We remained at New Iberia until Dec 7th. While there the regiment was seent out on two different forageing expeditions on Nov 20th. We went out some eight or ten miles north and loaded our wagons with corn fodder, beef, hogs, chickens, etc. and returned to camp. Gen [William B.] Franklin who was in chief command of the expedition up the Teche had given very strict orders against forageing, pilfering, etc. So when we went to start our expeditiion Major Hotchkiss who was in command of the regiment, Col Grier in command of the brigade reported to General Burbridge for orders. The gen read gen Franklin orders to him and told him to observe those orders but to tell his men that if they caught any chickens or geese or anything like that to be careful and not get bit. So we understood that to mean help yourselves but don't give the general away. So we acted accordingly and came back to camp pretty well loaded and again on Nov 27th we were sent out on another foraging expedition. We went out some 15 miles to a large plantation where there was plenty of forrage. As we approached the place we seen a squad of rebels ride away from the house and the darkeys said that massa went away with them and some of the men went into the house and found a fine dinner on the table which had been prepared for the rebs but was eaten by the yanks. They also found a rebel flag in the house. So we cleaned the ranch pretty effectualy and loaded our wagons with forage for both man and beast and returned to camp with out getting bit. While there we tore the siding off an old mill near our camp and fixed us up very comfortable quarters. While at New Iberia the regiment having become so provoked with Major Hotchkiss, both officers and men on his overbearing way and his incompetency, the other officers got up a petition asking him to resign couched in as respectful terms as they could and all went up to his tent one evening and presented it to him and the Major got in a terable rage and stormed around and gave them to understand that he would not resign but they would have to walk very strait after that or he would make it hot for them. So they went back and wrote out a statement of the facts in the case and all signed it and sent it to the war department in Washington asking for his removal.[9]

December 7th
About 11 O'clock AM we got orders to be ready to march at one PM. Before we started the boys from some other regiments that were going to stay there came and asked our boys for the lumber in their quarters and we told them to take it. But when they began to tare the shanties down an officer came from some other bridage and ordered the boys away in a very rough haughty manner saying, that his bridage was to be quartered there and he had orders from General McGinis* not to alow anything to be taken off the ground and he was so haughty and abusive that he made our boys mad. They thought they had a right to give their shanties to who they pleased and they told the other boys when the officer went away to take the lumber and they would help them. But the officer soon returned with a guard which he placed around the camp with orders not to alow a man to come on the ground. Then our boys began tearing the shanties down and pitching the boards over the guards heads and the other boys carried them away. The officers forbid our boys to touch the lumber and their officers and our boys and some of our under officers got into a squabble over it and they sent a whole regiment or two and placed them between our camp and the other regiment three or four lines deep and had them to load their guns and ordered them to shoot anyone that dared to throw a board but our fool boys set up the yell and just hurled the air full of boards so that their guards had to dodge

9. In response to this petition, the War Department requested Hotchkiss's resignation, which the major tendered on February 2, 1864. *RH,* 31; *AG,* 4:654.

and run out of the way to keep from being hit and just hooted their guards and dared them to shoot and cussed any of their officers that said anything to them. General McGinis and some of his staff rode in among our boys and tried to deter them but they had got so mad by that time that could cuss a general just the same as anybody else and he rode away and ordered Col Grier to quiet his men. The colonel was busy at headquarters and sent some of the other officers to see what the trouble was but them and the other officers soon got into a rumpus. Our officers told them to withdrawn their guards and there would be no more trouble but they swore they wouldn't do it. Our officers went back to report to the colonel and the others put guards on all the shanties that was left and ordered them to shoot any man that dared to touch them. Then some of our fool men lit torches and threw them into the shanties and burned them under the guards. Colonel Grier learning how things were going called for the blowing of the call to fall in line and every man fell into line and the colonel marched us away some distance and halted us until everything was ready for the march. We marched some ten miles that evening and went into camp. Colonel Grier, Captain [Edwin] Stevens and one enlisted man from each company being detailed to go home to enlist recruits for the regiment.[10] Major Hotchkiss took comand of the bridage and Capt McCullock of the regiment.

December 8th

We resumed the march at daylight marching some eighteen miles and camped for the night near Franklin. That night some our men went out and confiscated a lot of fresh meat etc. The owner came to camp in the morning and laid complaints to Colonel [William J.] Landium* [Landram] who was in command of the division. But the colonel told him that he must be mistaken for his men never stole anything. He remarked to Captain McCullock when the man was gone that he would bet a hundred dollars that the 77 Ill. and the 19 Ky. got their share of it. At daylight some rebel bushwackers sliped up on the other side of the bayou and tried their hand on some of our pickets but failed to hit them.

10. In addition to the officers mentioned by Wiley, the enlisted men were: Cpl. Charles Arms, Co. A; Sgt. James Wier, Co. B; Sgt. Joseph Hutchinson, Co. C; Sgt. James Bender, Co. D; Sgt. Benjamin Robbins, Co. E; Sgt. James Hammers, Co. F; Cpl. Moses Burt, Co. G; Cpl. David Murdock, Co. H; Cpl. Austin Aten, Co. I; Sgt. John Yinger, Co. K. These men recruited 192 new members for the regiment. *RH*, 218–33.

December 9th
Marched through Franklin and on through Centerville and camped for the night having marched fifteen miles.

December 10th
Marched on through Pattersonville and arrived at Burwicks Bay at ten AM. The 48th Ohio was in advance and tried to run us down but we kept up with them. We remained at Burwick City until the twelvth.

December 12th
We crossed over Burwick's Bay where we remained until the next day. Wm M Wright was taken quite sick at this time and was carried off the boat on a stretcher and laid down and a shelter of some kind placed over him and as it happened as it was liable to happen once in a while Lem Wiley[11] got very full of old comisary [whiskey] and as Wright belonged to the band, Lem concluded it was his place to take care of Wright and got oficers and would come fussing around him and would fall down over him and when the other boys would try to keep him away he would get terable mad so the Drs placed a guard over Wright to keep Lem away. Then Lem got it into his head that it was time to blow the fall in call and he kept that up until they had to take his bugle from him and put him under guard until he got sober again.

December 13th
We took the cars for Algiers where we arrived about dark and went into camp where we remained until the 17th getting ready to take the ship for Pass Cavalla [Cavallo] Tex.[12]

December 17th
We embarked on the steamship Demola [De Molay] and pushed out from Aligers about dark and passed down the Mississippi river, passing

11. Lemon Wiley of Elmwood, principal musician, entered service on August 5, 1862. Although he was cantankerous, disliked authority, and often got drunk, he remained with the regiment until mustered out on July 10, 1865. *RH*, 34; *AG*, 4:655.

12. Pass Cavallo is the entrance to Matagorda Bay. Situated along the Texas coast, midway between Louisiana and the Mexican border, Matagorda Bay was guarded by Fort Esperanza (also called Fort Debray or the Saluria). Confederate forces evacuated the fort on November 29, 1863, prior to the arrival of the 77th Illinois. George B. Davis, Leslie J. Perry, and Joseph W. Kirkley, *The Official Military Atlas of the Civil War* (New York: Arno Press, 1978), Plates 26-1, 65-10.

Forts Jackson and Fort Stfillips [St. Philip] during the night and cast anchor at the mouth of the river until morning. It was quite stormy and the waves were rolling high on the Gulf and we did not like the looks of things out there very much and began to think we would rather go round by land if they would let us.

December 18th

We were piloted out over the bar into the Gulf. The water was getting very rough. The waves were rolling almost as high as our ship and making a terable noise which appeared pretty bad to us poor land lubers and when they let our pilot down over the side of the ship in his little skiff to go back we thought good bye old chap. We would not give much for your chances and we watched him for a long time and could see him and his frail bark every once in a while riding up over some big wave and as we got out more into the open sea the water got rougher and a great many of us got seasick and began to heave Joner.[13] Our company and others were quartered on the hurricane deck and when some of the officers who had quarters in the cabin and eat at the ships table got sick and came running out to the guards of the ship to heave Joner. The boys would forget their own troubles at the fun of seeing the officers heaving and would gibe them with there goes your fifty cents and such like. As night came on the storm grew worse and made the old ship groan and creak in every joint and they put us down in the hold of the ship for fear we would be washed overboard by the waves and that soon became a terable palce as nearly all the men was vomiting and the ventilation being poor the stench became terable ane to help matters the upper berths fell down letting the men down on the men below and we had a good time generally. Sometime during the night when the storm was at its hight I crawled out on deck thinking that I would like to see what it looked like outside. I stood there and held to the mast for a while and I thought it was a pretty wild old sight. The great waves were rolling about twise as high as our ship and each one looked like it would roll right over our ship but she would ride up over the wave and down into the trough between that wave and the next and up again over the next wave. The next day and night was not quite so rough and we got out on deck again

13. "Heaving up Jonah" was a popular expression used to describe vomiting. Bentley states that the expression means the soldier "vomited most majestically." *RH*, 234–5.

but still continued to be very seasick. When the storm was on, some of the men got very badly scare thinking they were going to be shipwrecked espically the harder class. They did not seem to think that they were ready to go down just yet. Some of them pulled their cards and such things out of their pockets and throwed them overboard. I suppose they did not want to go to judgement with those things in their pockets. But our ship Demola weathered the storm and carried us safety to our destination but our ship being so large and the water so rough we could not go within a mile of shore. We arrived off pass Cauollo early in the morning of Dec. 20. But I had to lay aboard the Demola until evening waiting for the water to get calm enough so they could take us off on lighter boats. They could not bring the vescels near enough together to transfer us and out traps from the one to the other without danger of them knocking together and breaking so they had to wait for the water to calm down. But when they took us the water was still so rough they could not bring the boats nearer than eight or ten feet of each other and after a good deal of time and toruble they got them stayed in that position and a narrow gand plank fastened form one to the other. But our boat being so much larger and higher than the other our gang plank sloped down at a angle of fortyfive degrees or worse so that we could not walk down but had to set down and slide with our knapsacks and accoutraments and our muskets swung round out necks by the straps and thus we shot down on after another with the boats a rolling and pitching with the waves and woe to the luckless yank that might have fell off that narrow board. He wouldn't have been worth looking after but we got a cross safely and was taken over the bar into Matagorda Bay where our lighter boat could get within about twenty rods of shore where by another sliding process from our boat down onto a barge and from that onto a temperary landing, we proceeded to shore over some temperary foot walks made by driving stakes in the bottom, nailing strips across and laying boards on them which gave way before the regiment all got ashore and some had to wade out. But we got on firm land once more and felt very much relieved after our rough experience on shipboard but for quite a while the earth seemed to keep up the same motion of the old ship and we went stagering and steping unecessary high but in course of time we regained our land legs and all was well again. The narrow strip of land on which we landed was called Decrows [Decros] Point.[14] It was a narrow strip of land or

14. Situated on the western tip of Matagorda Peninsula, Decros Point commands Pass Cavallo.

rather sand varying from one half to one mile wide and some sixty miles long between Madagorda Bay and the Gulf of Mexico. We never could see the object of landing us on such a God forsaken looking place but we took it for granted that some one knew. But we were glad to get ashore even on that sand bar and as we had learned to take things as they came we proceeded to make ourselves as comfortable as posable, which was poor enough at best. A good many of the men were very loud in their declarations that they would never go on the water again but I thought perhaps I would go where I was ordered to whether that was on water or land. That night we layed on the sand near where we landed.

December 21

We marched back about half a mile up the sandbar and went into camp and put up our tents. We did not find Decrows Point a very plesant camping place as there was nothing in sight but sand and water, no vegetation whatever. The sand was piled up in great heaps and ridges like great snow banks by the action of the wind which had a pair sweep from all directions. All the fuel we could get was driftwood that had washed ashore from the Gulf and was so badly soaked with the salt water that it would hardly burn when we got it dried out. All the water we could get was so brackish we could hardly use it and we did not need to salt the army bean very much that we cooked in it. When the wind was blowing the sand it would sift into everything that we tried to cook so that we could not eat it. We concluded afterwards that they just sent us to Decrows Point to get sand enough in our crows to go with Banks on his famous expedition up Red River as we could see no other reason for sending us there.[15] For the first week or ten days after we landed there it was very warm and pleasant. We celebrated Christmas by going a swimming in the Gulf and bay.

≈ 1864 ≈

January

But on the day before New Years we were struck by what the southerners call a northerner. Our old friend Borielus [Boreades] came down from

---

15. Wiley again anticipates events. The Red River campaign did not begin until March 10, 1864.

Illinios to see us and he came with power and lots of him.[16] It blowed for three or four days from the north and as it had a fair sweep over our sandbar and was made damp and piering by passing over Matagorda Bay on its way to us. It became very cold, the wind blew our tents all down the first nights which raised a terable upore and yelling in camp as the wind was blowing so hard we could not set our tents up again. So we pulled the tent poles out and drew the tent canvas over us and lay there until morning. When by all hands taking hold we got out tents set up again and by driving the stakes down in the sand full length and piling sand on the bottom of the tents we got them to stand and for the next three or four days we kept from freezing by piling up in the tent like a lot if pigs and piling all our blankets over us all. The way we make any fire to make coffee was to dig a hole down in the sand and throw the sand on the wind side and build a fire down in the hole and then the sand would blow down on our fires so that it was almost imposable to keep them going long enough to get our coffee boiled and we generally took soaked coffee. Some tried to keep warm by building fires in their tents and by the time the storm was over their tents, clothes, blankets and everything was as black as soot could make them and they themselves looked like negroes. Altogether we thought we had a pretty rough experience while the storm lasted some nights those on the outside of the pig pile would wake up pretty nearly froze and we would have to get them in the middle of the pile and warm them up and to help out discomfort the storm lasting so long and the water being so rough they could not unload any supplies for us and our rations ran very short and crackers and water not being very good diet to keep up the animal heat and as a military necessity to tide us over they issued us a little comisary and some of the boys got rather hilarious. Our Harvey got a little to much abroad and some of the boys played rather a rough joke on him. His coat which he had worn for a long time and had gotten rather thread bare and greasy and the boys had been thinking that he should draw a new coat so some of the boys engaged Harvey in conversation and got him very much interested while some of the others took knives and riped the seams of his old coat so that when he went to get up it fell off him and Harvey had to go round with a blanket round him like an Indian

16. Boreades are figures of Greek mythology, the wind gods Zetes and Calais, sons of Boreas and Oreithyia. Reference is made to Boreades to indicate the intensity of the storm.

until the storm was over and he could draw another coat.[17] On Jan 1st S. M. Hart and J. C. Dunbar and others returned to the regiment, Hart and Dunbar had been wounded at Vicksburg, May 22 1863 and had been absent from the regiment since that time. J. C. Dunbar was wounded in the forearm and disabled for service and was soon after discharged and sent home. When the storm abated it soon became warm and pleasant again and we resumed our bathing in the Gulf and Bay. Some of the boys amused themselves and the rest of us by trying which could go the farthest out into the Gulf and beat their way back against the outgoing waves. One evening T. S. Patton and Wm Wright had gone away out so they could just touch bottom with their toes and had been working hard for some time to make their way back but were not making much headway as the outgoing waves would carry them back about as fast as they could go forwards. When some of us on shore discovered a big porpous coming right up behind them and we hollowed to them to look out that a porpous was coming for them and they looked around and seen the thing not more than twenty feet away coming right towards them and not knowing what the thing might try to do with them they kicked and paddled for dear life. The rest of us being considerably concerned for them and having no guns with us to shoot with, we set up a shout to try to scare the thing away. But it didn't scare but come right up to them and rubed it cold nose against them and if two chaps ever worked lively they did for a while until they got where the water was so shallow the porpous couldn't follow them. They were so exhausted they had to lay there in the shallow water for quite a while before they could come to shore. Our hollowing brought a hundred or so of the boys from the camp to see what was up and Tom and Bill got it from all sides and it was considerably amusing to hear Wright tell his experience when he got to camp. Captain McCullough had a young darkey called Mark who he kept as a body servant and he was a very sassy chap.[18] He had been a body servant to his young massa, a young southern highblood before the war and had learned several things and thought he was very sharp and as he was the captain's servant he soon began to think that he outranked a private soldier considerably. One day he came to our tent putting on quite a swell and Tom Patton began to gie him and among other things

---

17. Harvey is probably Thomas H. McCulloch of Company C. *RH*, 50.
18. While in the South, many Federal officers hired or "adopted" blacks as servants.

Tom was explaining to him how they made rubber blankets such as we carried in the army. He told him that they took young darkeys like him and skinned them and made the rubber blankets out of their hides and was explaining to Mark about how they tanned them and fixed them up when Mark straitened himself up on his dignaty and waved Tom off with an imperious wave of his hand saying, Massa corprel, Massa corprel I wish you wouldn't talk to me any moah. All your conversation this long time hadn't done amounted to nothing. At which Tom colopsed and rolled off his cracker barl into the sand and we laughed til our sides ached, while Mark marched off towards the captain's tent with all the dignity of a major general. But poor Mark's imperious ways soon got him into trouble. He got very sousy and quarlsome with the boys and the captain seemed to think the boys were imposing on him and would take Marks part which made him a great deal worse and he got into several scraps with the boys especially one Wm Carson[19] of company C, a big thick necked quarrelsome chap who had made up his mind that he was going to thump the darkey the first chance he got and in order to get a chance, Carson played off and did not go on dress parade one evening and not long after the regiment had gone out Carson and Mark got into it in good shape. Carson was a good deal bigger than the darkey but the darkey's head was a good deal the hardest and he used both head and feet for all they were worth. When the regiment came in off dress parade they were still at it in good shape pretty evenly matched. Carson was hammering and Mark was butting and kicking and when John McGowen[20] and some other Irish men in Company D seen the fight they broke out of ranks and ran with their muskets clubed crying kill the dam nager, kill the dam nager and the captain had to pull his sword and rush in to save his nager and things got pretty exciting for a little while. The Irish seemed to think that any nager that would fight a soldier ought to be killed and the captain seemed to think not especially if the soldier was Carson and while they were discussing the matter Major Hotchkiss sent a guard and had Carson and the nager both arrested and taken to head-

19. William F. Carson of Cazenovia enlisted on August 13, 1862, and was mustered out on July 10, 1865. *RH,* 48; *AG,* 4:661.

20. John McGowan from Lacon enlisted on August 12, 1862, and was mustered out on July 10, 1865. *RH,* 56; *AG,* 4:664.

quarters and put them in the guardhouse together until morning. He give them a good lecture he shamed Carson for stooping to fight with a negro and telling the nager that if he did not carry himself pretty strait after that and show the soldiers proper respect he would put him out of camp. Mark was pretty docile after that and seemed to be a little afraid some would kill the d——m nager. But Carson felt rather sold out as he was sent calculating on things terminating as they did he expected to handle the darkey pretty easily. After we had been there some time each regiment was ordered to have regimental drill each day. Major Hotchkiss would get the 77 out each afternoon and try to drill us but would soon get us all mixed up and get mad and abuse the men and company officers and bluster around a while and then he would have to get Captain Mc-Cullock to take command and get us straitened out again. Things went on in this way from day to day until the men began to loose all respect for the major and disipline was getting to a pretty low ebb in the regi-ment. When the major would go dashing off towards one end of the regiment to give some luckless officer or company a blessing some of the more reckless men of the other wing would whistle like if they were call-ing a dog and hollow out here Major when the little major would whirl his horse and come dashing back and demand of the company officers to know who it was that done the whistling and hollowing but no one knew and after making some big threats as to what he would do if such a thing happened again he would start off again and wouldn't get far when the whistle sounded again and here major would come again from all along the line and the major was getting about to the end of his string when the higher officers learning how things was going, issued orders for the 77 to discontinue regimental drill. In a day of two an order came to the major from the war department to send in his resignation, which he did. This order came in answer to the petetion which our company officers sent up from New Iberia La. The major before leaving made us a little speech and told us how much he thought of the regiment and how sorry he was to leave us but he had a little wife in Illinois that he thought a little more of and he had concluded to got to her. He suppose that every man in the regiment knew why he was going home. Captain McCullough took command of the regiment and everything went off smooth again. During our stay at Decrows Point the chaplain of the 67

Indiana, Rev [Lyman S.] Chitenden[21] a methodest minister held a series
of revival meetings and quite a number of the men from the different
regiments were converted and a number of them was immersed in Mata-
goria Bay. They joined hands and waded out into the bay singing a himn
to where the water was about waist deep where they halted and continued singing while the minister took them one at time and layed them
backwards under the salt water. When they would raise up and join in
the singing again. It was an impressive sight. When we landed on Decrows Point the only way they could get the horses and mules from the
ships was to shove them overboard into the bay and had men in sciffs to
drive them to the shore but the salt water would blind them so they were
just as apt to go the wrong way as the right and some of them swam
nearly across the bay (which was three miles wide) before they could get
them turned back. It looked pretty tough but it was a military necessity.
While there James Wedley of Co C stole a blouse from the quartermasters
department and was cortmarsheled and sent to the Dry Tortugas.[22] During our stay there our cavelry would make a trip up the point towards
the main land and gather up a few cattle and sheep from the range and
drive them down to us but they were generally so poor that they would
not make very rich soup but by cracking the bones and utaliying the
marrow we could make it taste a little soupy and by soaking our hardtack
in it did for a change.

21. Rev. Lyman S. Chittenden of the 67th Indiana was commissioned on September 18, 1863,
but one week later was transferred to the 24th Indiana. As William Bentley noted, "The Rev.
Mr. Chittenden, of the 67th Indiana was, emphatically, the right man in the right place, and
the boys of the 77th can never forget his kind services. He was faithful in season and out of
season—faithful all the time." *Report of the Adjutant General of the State of Indiana*, 8 vols.
(Indianapolis, 1865–69), 2:236, 614; *RH*, 239–40 (quotation); *AG*, 4:654.

22. James H. Wedley of Woodford County enlisted on September 27, 1862. For his crime,
he was sent to Fort Jefferson in the Dry Tortugas, off the Florida Keys—the same prison that
Michael O'Laughlin, Samuel Arnold, Ned Spangler, and Dr. Samuel Mudd were sent to in 1865
for their alleged roles in Lincoln's assassination. Wedley returned to the regiment after serving
his sentence and was mustered out on July 10, 1865. *RH*, 52; *AG*, 4:662.

≋ 8 ≋

RED RIVER

Months of aimless wandering and useless activity in Louisiana and Texas convinced William Wiley and the soldiers of the 77th Illinois that the leadership within the Department of the Gulf was inept. They longed for a general such as Grant and suffered under the leadership of General Banks, whose movements were governed more by political aspirations than by military logic or necessity.

In the spring of 1864, Banks launched the ill-fated Red River campaign. Without a clear military objective, his columns began the long march north along Bayou Teche to Alexandria and on toward Shreveport. The campaign began promisingly, as the Federal troops marched almost the length of Louisiana without serious opposition. However, near Mansfield, the enemy suddenly turned and savagely attacked the lead elements of Banks's column, which included Wiley and his comrades. The Red River campaign would result in a congressional investigation and the official censure of the army's high command.

February 22th
Having received marching orders we embarked on the steamship St Maries [St. Mary] for the Mississippi river and Algiers. The 77 Ill, 19 Ky. and part of the 67 Ind. embarked on the same vescel about fifteen hundred men about as many as could find room to lie down and I expect if it had been as stormy on this voyage as it was when we came over some of us would have went over board. We did not like the looks of things very much as we had nothing to do but submit we submited and as the water

was very calm we got back to the Mississippi River in good shape althro some of us was just as sea sick as we were going over in the storm.

February 24th
We arived at the mouth of the Mississippi River at 10 o'clock AM and passed on up the river reporting at Ft Jackson and Fort St. Philips and arived at Algiers Miss [sic] at 10 PM where we disembarked and lay on shore until morning.

February 25th
We took the cars at eleven AM for Brashear City where we arived at four PM and crossed the [Berwick] Bay on the streamer Starlight and marched out aways and camped for the night.

February 26th
We marched up the Bay about half a mile and went into camp where we remained until the sixth of March geting ready for the great Red River Campain. While there Captain McCullock's nager and Captain [Robert H.] Brock's nager got into trouble with some hoodlum soldiers at a negro house not far from camp and they came back to camp and got Captain Brock's revolver and went back to the house and shot at some of the soldiers and hit a negro wench and the worthies were arested and sent to work on the fortifycations with a ball and chain to their leg. And the captain lost his nager and I fear the boys didn't shed many tears over him. We seen him but once afterwards with some cavelry regiment.

March 6th
We left Burwicks Bay at daylight and marched 17 miles passing through Pattesonville [Pattersonville] and camped for the night at Camp Bislin [Fort Bisland].

March 7th
We resumed the march at daylight. Marched 13 miles passing through Centerville and Franklin and went into camp about three miles beond Franklin where we remained until the 16th while General Banks and Gen Franklin were organising their great Red River Campain or foraging expedition and formulating their famous orders against marauding pilfering etc. for the violation of which every man was to be shot or otherwise

severly were purnished and a lot more to numerous to mention which gave us western troops a very unsavory opinnon of our commanding generals. It rained a great deal while we were there and we had a rather disagreeable time. Lieutenant Colonel Webb who had been on detached service at New Orleans had resumed command of the regiment.

March 16th
Resumed the march at daylight. Marched some 17 miles and encamped within some 7 miles of New Iberia.

March 17th
Marched about 11 miles and encamped on Spanish Lake.[1] Some of our boys went out that night and captured a lot of beef not with standing Bank's orders but they laid a choise piece on Lieut Col Webb's mess chest and Banks was none wiser and no one was shot for the crime.

March 18th
We marched some 16 miles and encamped on vermilion Bayou.[2]

March 19th
Marched some 16 miles and encamped on Carrion Crow Bayou where a brigade of our men had been surprised by the rebs sometime before. The rebels had thrown our dead into a big trench that had been washed out and threw a little brush and durt over them. Some of their arms and legs were sticking out above the durt.[3]

March 20th
Marched some 18 miles passing through Opoluses [Opelousas] and Washington and encamped on Bayou Catablo [Courtableau]. As we passed through Opolouses and Washington the negroes had gather in from all directions and demonstrated their joy at the sight of the yankeys.

1. Spanish Lake, listed on many period maps as Lake Tasse, lies along the main road between New Iberia and Vermilionville.
2. Vermilion Bayou was also referred to as Bayou Vermilion or Vermilion River, near Vermilionville, present-day Lafayette.
3. Wiley refers to the Battle of Bayou Bourbeau. On November 3, 1863, a body of Confederate soldiers attacked the Union division commanded by Brig. Gen. Stephen G. Burbridge. In this spirited action, Burbridge lost 680 men. *OR*, vol. 26, pt. 1, pp. 360–1.

In all maner of ways some of the younger ones would look at us very curiously and say to one another, why de yankeys haint got no hons like massa said da had. Some of the religiously inclined would invoke all kind of blessing on our heads and one very old negro woman in particular attracted our attention. She looked to be about two hundred years old. A little old dried up looking thing. Some of the others had carried her out near the road and were holding her up and she seemed to be perfectly frantic. She was throwing her arms around and hollowing out with her weak squeakly voice, bress de Lord, bress de Lord, is liked to see de day of jubilee. Some seem to be very curious to know all about what we were going to do. They would ask where is you all agoing? The boys would tell them that we were after the rebels and they would say, is you jus goin to hunt a fight? That night we encamped on Bayou Catablo.

March 21th
We remained at Bayou Catablo to give the 19 corp time to get out of our way. It rained all day and night. The seckond night some terable yank set fire to a shed full of cotton that stood a little ways from our camp and it was all burned. Gen Banks got in a terable rage about it and said he would have it assessed against our brigade and take it out their pay but we got our poor little $16 all the same.[4]

March 22th
We marched 20 miles and encamped on a plantation belonging to an old Rebel bushwhacker. His darkeys told us that every day or two some man would come riding up to massa house as hard as his mule could go den massa would come out and blow his big haun and men would come on der mules from all directions with their shotguns and massa would get on his mule with his shotgun and away dey would go. From which we understand that massa was a leader of a band of bushwhackers but he had the masonic sign of the square and compass on his front gate which seemed to make him all right with Gen Banks.[5] For wherever we seen

---

4. Wiley is in error. In March 1864, the standard pay for a private in Federal service was $13 per month. The pay was increased to $16 a month on June 20, 1864, three months after Wiley "penned" this entry. Boatner, *Civil War Dictionary*, 624.

5. Wiley is referring to the Free and Accepted Masons, a secret society that enjoyed widespread membership in both the North and the South. Many prominent Union and Confederate civil and military leaders were Masons.

that sign there was always guards placed to guard their property. That night guards were placed over all the old chaps property and buildings with very strict orders not to alow anyone to come near the property. I was placed to guard a corn crib with three or four others. We stood around until everything was quite in camp and then we crawled into the corn crib and went to sleep where we slept the sleep of the just until the revielee sounded before daylight. We crawled out and went to guarding the corn cribs again in good shape. But we did not take invoice to see how much corn was gone.

March 23th

We marched some 22 miles passing through Holmsville and camped that night on Bayou Beouf [Boeuf]. During the afternoon some of the boys got into a good old masonic rebel's gardon and pilfered some onions. When we went into camp near by he went and complained to Gen Banks and the gen sent some of his staff officers with orders to Col Webb to find out who it was that done the pilfering and have them arested and sent up to his headquarters. But the Col got on his ear and told them that they could go back and present his complaints to Gen Bank and tell him that he would do no such damn thing. But the officers told him that wouldn't do that he certainly knew what kind of trouble he would get into that the general would have him cortmarshalled and likely dismissed from the service. But the col only got mader and told them to go and tell Gen Banks to arest and be damned that his men done just right that he would have arested every damn one of them if they hadn't took the onions and the officers seeing they could do nothing with him they rode back and reported to the Gen and the Gen sent an officer and had Col Webb arested and taken to his headquarters. Some of our officers that followed up said the col just cussed everything from the Gen down and swore he would leave any of his men arested that wouldn't disobey such damn unmanly orders. The Gen seeing he had got hold of a bad westerner he ordered him back to his regiment and that was the last of it.

March 24th

We marched 16 miles passing through Cheneville [Cheneyville]. It rained terable hard during the afternoon and our clothes were soaked through. Col Webb having filled up with whiskey to keep the water out got pretty drunk and made us marched right in the center of the road where the mud was the deepest and we thought he had forgotten how much he thought of us the evening before but we charged it up to bad whiskey and plouted through. Before we went into camp it cleared off. We camped for the night on Bayou Beouf. When we went into camp the colonel lined us up facing a high rail fence and after stacking arms he ordered us to charge on the fence which we did with a will each company geting all the cypress rails we could and built big fires which we kept going during the night and got our clothes pretty well dried. After going into camp they issued us some comisary on account of our wetting and some of the boys after drinking their portion and borrowing from them that did not want much got pretty full especialy Harvey and [James] Crow.[6]

March 25th
We marched 15 miles our regiment guarding the train that night. We encamped within 6 miles of Elxandria [Alexandria] La.

March 26th
Marched some 8 miles passing through Elxandria where we came up with the 16 corps commanded by Gen A. J. Smith our former division commander.[7] Here we met and compared notes with the 47 Ill. regiment which had been organized at Peoria.[8] They belonged to the 16 corps. We marched on through Elxandria and went into camp about two miles beond. We got some mail at Elxandria, signed the pay rolls and got some pay that night and had a pleasant chat with Wm Paton and others of the 47.[9]

March 27th
We remained at Elxandria, wrote letters and sent some money home by the returning boats.

6. James Crow Jr. from Limestone enlisted on August 12, 1862, and was mustered out on July 10, 1865. *RH*, 48; *AG*, 4:661.

7. Smith assumed command of a detachment of the 16th Corps on March 7, 1864, and led it throughout the Red River operations. Boatner, *Civil War Dictionary*, 768.

8. The reader will recall that Col. John Bryner of the 47th was in command at Camp Lyon when the 77th was mustered into service.

9. William Patton of Smithville joined the 47th Illinois on August 16, 1861. He was mustered out on December 17, 1864, after his exchange as a prisoner of war. As the 47th was also organized at Peoria and mustered into service on August 16, 1861, Wiley would have known several men in the regiment. *AG*, 3:412.

March 28th

We resumed the march at six AM. It rained all the forenoon. We marched some 20 miles and encamped on Bayou Rapidees [Rapides].

March 29th

Marched some 18 miles through the pine timbers and encamped on Cane River. Our company C was detailed for pickett duty.

March 30th

We were relieved from pickett duty at daylight and remained in camp waiting the completion of a pontoon bridge across Cane River.

March 31th

Marched at six AM crossing Crane River. Marched 18 miles crossing Cane River again in the evening on another pontoon bridge and camped for the night near the bridge.

April 1st

Marched some 19 miles and encamped on Cane River that day. Our advance cavalry had quite a little fight with the rebs near Nachitoches La.[10] The third division of our 13 corps was ordered up to support the cavelry and made the march of 22 miles in five hours.

April 2nd

We marched to Nachitoches some five miles where we went into camp and remained until the 6th geting supplies from the boats on Red River at Grandecore.

April 4th

Gen A J Smith commander of the 16 corps who had commanded our division for a long time came to visit us. The division was drawn up on line to receive him. Generals Banks and Franklin accompanyed him to the division and received him with cheers long and loud.

10. The skirmish referred to by Wiley took place on April 2, when Brig. Gen. Albert Lee's Union cavalry division struck Col. Xavier Debray's regiment of Texas cavalry near Crump's Hill. Ludwell H. Johnson, *Red River Campaign* (Kent, Ohio: Kent State University Press, 1993), 116–7.

April 5th

Rev J. S. McCullock came to our regiment. He had been commissioned as chaplain of the 77 in place of chaplain W. G. Pierce who had resigned on account of failing health.[11]

April 6th

We marched 18 miles and encamped in the pine timber. That night we had prayer meeting in the woods, God's first temple. Chaplain McCullough spoke a short time to the men. That evening our cavelry had enother skirmish with the rebels.

April 7th

We started marching at 5:30 AM. Marched 20 miles and encamped at Pleasant Hills.

April 8th

Our brigade was called up at two o'clock to go forwards some 10 miles to assist the cavelry in dislodging a fource of rebels who had made a stand in the timber and hills and the cavelry was unable to dislodge them. We marched at 3 AM. The night was very dark, we could hardly see the man a head of us. But we made the march in good time ariving on the scene of trouble just as the sun was coming up. Shortly after the 23 Wisconsin and the 67 Indiana were deployed and advanced on the enemy, supported by the 19 KY and 77 Ill. After a sharp little fight during which quite a number of our men was carried back past our line on stretchers which began to look like business again once more. The rebels gave way but kept up a runing fight making a stand at every convenient position and waiting for us to come up then giving us the best they had. The rebels were persuded in this order for two or three miles when our regiment took the front supported by the 19 Ky. The rest of the brigade keeping in supporting distance. We drove the rebels from one position after another for several miles through the pine timber along the course of the Shievesport [Shreveport] Wagon Road. The rebels were mounted and when we would press them too hard they would fall back to their horses,

11. Pierce resigned on January 7, 1864. His successor, John S. McCulloch, was mustered in on April 5, 1864, and provided for the spiritual needs of the men until mustered out with the regiment. *RH*, 33; *AG*, 4:654.

remount and ride away until they would find another good position where they would make another stand and wait for us to come up and then give us the best they had in store. Soon after we took the advance, Lieutenant Colonel Webb who was allways full of vim and aparently fearless became very much depressed and came to Captain McCullock and told him that he had a premonition that he would be killed that day and that thought over came him that he was unfit to perform his duty and that he thought of asking the brigade commander to have the regiment relieved from taking the front. Captain McCullock said he tried to talk him out of the premonition idea but the colonel told him it was no use to talk to him that way that he knew it just as well as he knew that he breathed and for the captain to hold himself in readyness to take command of the regiment. A short time after that the colonel rode foward to where Colonel Landrum, the brigade commander was and looked up to speak when a musket ball struck him just below the eye and killed him instantly. His body was carried into a vacant house nearby.[12] Captain McCullough took command of the regiment and we were hurried forward to dislodge the rebels. All was excitement after the colonel fell. Lem Wiley had got pretty full and went taring around and falling down over roots and brush until he mashed his bugle as flat as a pancake. At one time a company of Ny cavelry[13] was ordered forward for some purpose and camed dashing up through our lines and had not gone but a little ways in front of us when the rebels let loose on them from the brow of a hill killing their leader a young lieutenant and wounding several other men and horses. The lieutenant had on a very nice pare of hightop boots and on of the rebs seemed to covet them for when the lieutenant fell the rebel ran out in the road in plain view of us and pulled the boots off of him and ran away with them. We made dirt fly all around him but he got away with them. An old irishman in the cavelry company had his horse shot under him and he pulled the saddle off of the horse and came back through our lines with the saddle swung over his sholder. The old

12. As Bentley wrote, "A brave man, a good soldier, and a gentleman in every sense of the word, Col. Webb fell with his face to the foe, universally respected and regretted." Jacob H. Snyder of Company I wrote in similar terms of Webb: "An excellent officer, eminently courteous and social, he commanded the respect and esteem of all who came into contact with him, and his loss is deeply felt by his comrades." *RH*, 250, 259.

13. Possibly the 14th New York Cavalry, which was the only mounted unit from the Empire State involved in the action at Mansfield.

horse had been shot through the head just below the eyes and when the man pulled the saddle off him the horse come too and got up and followed him back with the blood streaming from his nose. The irishman was running to try to get away from the horse but the old horse was keeping close up to him and paddy was waving his hand back to try to scare the horse away and hollowing byes byes, driving the bloody horse away. I don't like to see the blude but we made way and let the horse follow his master to the rear. After we had drove the rebels for several miles the 19 Ky took the advance and we followed up as support. The 19 crowded the rebs and kept them on the go for some time until near the little town of Mansfield La. where there was a big hill extending to our right and left in a horse shoe shape behind the brow of this hill. The rebel generals Dick Taylor* and Kirby Smith* had a large army in line and were apearantly just trying to keep us back until they got everything ready for us. They drew us right into the center of the horse shoe. Gen Banks didn't seem to have any idea what a trap he was geting into but coming into an open field a little ways from the brow of the hill we were ordered into camp and pickets were detailed and sent out and the teams of the cavelry force and of the 13 army corps (which for some reason unknown by us was pushed right up to the front with us) was being parked in the open field. When the rebels advanced on us our pickets commenced firing and we were ordered to pile our knapsacks and were rushed forwards to the edge of the timber just at the brow of the hill. Just as the rebels were coming up the hill in our front we made a stand in the edge of the timber and poured such a withering fire into their ranks that they gave way and fell back in our front but they swung around and flanked the left of our line doubling it back onto us. When we were ordered to fall back across the open field and form a new line in rear of our Chicago Mercantile Battery which had taken position in the edge of the open field which we did in not the best of order perhaps but we got there.[14] The ballance of our division had come up and taken position to our right but were flanked like ourselves and compelled to fall back. As we fell back out of

---

14. The Chicago Mercantile Battery had been organized at Chicago and mustered into service on August 29, 1862. Commanded by Capt. Patrick White, the unit participated in Grant's Central Mississippi campaign, the battles of Chickasaw Bayou and Arkansas Post, the Vicksburg campaign, and the siege of Jackson. During the Red River campaign the battery was attached to William Landram's division, which is the reason Wiley refers to it as "ours." Dyer, *Compendium*, 3:1044.

the edge of the timber our flag caught on a limb of a tree and was jerked out of the color bearer's (Corporal Black) hand.[15] When Seargent Curd of Co E who was right behind him grabed it up and carried it back and was made color bearer afterwards.[16] Nims NY [*sic*] Battery[17] which was posted to our left engaged the rebels so strongly that it drew their attention from us as we fell back across the open field or perhaps we would have been roughly handled but we got back with but slight loss. The rebels consentrated their fource on Nims Battery to take it but the New York [*sic*] boys stood bravely by their guns and worked them for all that was in them loading with grape and srapnel and as the rebels came closer filling their six guns to the musle with minie balls [canister] they mowed the rebels down by the hunderds and continued the fight until they were driven from their guns at the point of the beyonette.[18] The other boys were somewhat amused at myself as we retreating across that open field as I had on a pair of boots that had become badly run over at the heal and were not the best thing for fast running which we were practicing just at that time so I sat down in the middle of the field and pulled those crooked boots off and made the ballance of the race barefoot. We fell back to our battery and formed a new line supporting the battery until the rebels flanked us out of that position also and captured the battery after a desperate fight.[19] The lieutenant in command of the battery seeing

15. To lose the regiment's colors was considered a disgrace, and Cpl. James P. Black was relieved of his duties as flag bearer and reduced in rank. *RH,* 47; *AG,* 4:661.

16. George F. Cord [also listed as Card] from Medina enlisted on August 22, 1862. Elevated to sergeant, he was mustered out with the regiment on July 10, 1865. *RH,* 60; *AG,* 4:666.

17. Wiley refers to the 2d Battery of Light Artillery from Massachusetts commanded by Capt. Ormand F. Nims. Organized at Quincy, the battery was mustered into service on July 31, 1861. Although the battery lost its guns in the Battle of Mansfield, three of them were recovered at Yellow Bayou several weeks later. Dyer, *Compendium,* 3:1243.

18. In his report of the action at Mansfield, Col. Landram praised the artillerymen from Massachusetts, writing: "It is proper to say that Captain Nims' Battery displayed during the whole fight an example of coolness and true courage unsurpassed in the annals of history. They are entitled to the highest commendations, and although they lost their guns it is due to them to say that they could not have prevented it, and that the damage they inflicted upon the enemy was such as to entitle them to the thanks of the whole army." *OR,* vol. 34, pt. 1, p. 293.

19. Brig. Gen. Thomas Ransom noted in his report that the Chicago Mercantile Battery "went promptly into action and behaved with great gallantry. When the second line was broken, notwithstanding their great loss in men and horses, they would have brought off their guns in safety had it not been that our line of retreat was blocked by the train of the cavalry." Ibid., p. 267.

his horses shot down and seeing that he could not save his guns refused to leave his battery and jumping onto one of his guns with a revolver in each hand fought until the rebels came up and killed him. When we fell back from this position all was confusion. Our lines were so doubled up that the men of the different regiments were all mixed up and the regimental officers could not get their men together. The ballance of our corps had come up but too late to affect anything. The rebels soon brought their lines around and had us completely surrounded and the narrow road through the pine timber was completely blocked up with our trains. The teamsters in their frantic attempt to try to turn around in the narrow road and get to the rear had upset their wagons, broke the wagon longs [tongues] off and finding impossible to get their wagons away cut their saddle mules loose and rode away through the woods. The road being thus blocked it was imposable to get our artilery up to the front or get that away which had been goten up and was not already captured by the enemy. So that we lost almost everything in the way of trains and artilery. At this time a good many of our officers gathered as many of their men together as they could find and advised them to stop and surrender as we were surrounded would most likely loose their lives in trying to get away. But a good many of us having visions of Andersonville and the like fliting through our minds thought we would take our chances a little longer hoping that the 19th or 16th corps might come to our rescue in time to help us out.[20] So we continued to fall back and make a stand here and there as some of our officers would get a lot of our men of all regiments in line and try to hold the rebs in check until reinforcements would arive. We were rewarded for our perseverance as along about dusk the 19th corps which had been ordered into camp some eight or ten miles back came up on the double quick. The rebel cavelry which had swung around us gave way before them and when they met

20. Andersonville did not then have the reputation for being a notorious prison. Named Camp Sumter, the prison, which came into existence in February 1864, was located near Andersonville, Ga. A log stockade enclosed 26 acres in which more than 32,000 Union soldiers would be imprisoned at one time in the summer of 1864. Poor sanitation, exposure, inadequate diet, and overcrowding led to a staggering death rate among the prisoners. By September 1864, the daily death toll averaged 102 men. In all, nearly 13,000 of the Federal prisoners held at Andersonville died. At the time Wiley made this entry, he would not have heard of Andersonville, let alone fear being sent there. Boatner, *Civil War Dictionary*, 15; William Marvel, *Andersonville: The Last Depot* (Chapel Hill: University of North Carolina Press, 1994), 204.

our retreating fources they whirled into line in gallant stile with their
bands playing and waited until our men all got back through their lines
and then they opened on the rebs such a withering fire that they soon
checked their advance and night coming on the Battle of Sabine Crossroads came to an end and we retreated back to Pleasant Hill some twenty
miles where we had started from at three o'clock the morning before.[21]
Sometime after the retreat began myself and two or three others of Company C had kept together came across S. M. Hart of our company who
had been shot in the foot and had become so lame that he could not
walk any further and we tried to get him in an ambulance but they were
all full of the wounded. We were some what bothered to know what to
do with Hart as we had no notion of leaving him there. When a young
boy belonging to some of the regiment came dashing up on a horse
which he had caught runing loose. We stoped him and persuaded him
to give up his horse and started on the run for the rear. We got Hart
on the horse and continue the retreat tramping all night and ariving at
Pleasant Hill at daylight feeling pretty blue as it was the first time we had
to retreat before the enemy. We were a pretty sorry looking set. We were
black with the powder smoke and a good many of us were bareheaded
and some had their clothes badly torned. I was both bareheaded and
barefooted as I had lost my hat when we first started to retreat out of the
edge of the timber. I discarded my boots as we crossed the open field
and had retreated all night in my bare feet and my feet was geting terable
sore and I went limping along looking pretty badly dilapidated. The 16th
corps was encamped at Pleasant Hills and they had a laugh at our apearance when we came in. Soon after we arived at Pleasant Hills we got the
remmant of our regiment together. We had hardly men enough to form
a good company. At least one half of our men had been killed, wounded
or captured. Captain Brock of Company D took command. Orderly
Seargent J. P. Wiley was the highest officer in our company. We felt pretty
sad when we seen how many of our men was missing. We had no idea

21. The Battle of Mansfield or Sabine Crossroads was fought in three different stages, as
described by Wiley. The first took place in the clearing, where the 77th and its comrades of the
Fourth Division, 13 Corps, received Taylor's initial attack. The second occurred in the woods
along the southeast edge of the clearing, where the 77th supported the guns of the Chicago
Mercantile Battery. The third was two miles farther to the rear at Sabine Crossroads, where the
troops of the 19 Corps checked the Confederates.

how many were killed or how many was taken prisoner.[22] Soon after we got together again Gen A. J. Smith came riding up to where we were and asked boys what regiment is this, someone answered the 77 Illinois. My God is it posable sais he that this is all that is left of the 77 Illinois and the tears ran down his face. He looked at us a little and said that tells the tale there has been hot work up at the front.

April 9th

After the shattered remains of our 13th corps was got together again we were sent to guard the train back to Grandecore. The 16th and 19th corps were drawn up in line to receive the rebels when they came. The rebels followed us in fource, flushed with their victory of the day before and doubtless expecting to capture the balance of our army that day but were not expecting to meet two fresh corps at Pleasant Hills. About 8 or 9 o'clock they came in fource. The cavelry kept them in check until our officers got every thing ready for their reception when our cavelry fell back and let them come. They were met with such a withering fire from our lines that they gave way for a little but soon came on our right with a strong fource. Gen Banks ordered all of his reserve fource to the support of that wing but Gen A. J. Smith commanding the 16th corps told him he was making a mistake as they were only making a feint in that direction and would come on his right flank in a little while and try to turn his right flank.

Gen Banks contended that he was right and while they were parleying over the matter the rebels threw a strong fource on his right and would have out generaled him again and turned his right flank. Gen Smith seeing Gen Banks incapasity and fearing for the safety of the army assumed command of the army ignoring Gen Banks and ordering the reserve fources to the right to meet the onslought of the rebels and after a desperate struggle the rebels gave way in confusion and Gen Smith pressed them hard on every point and their route become as complete as ours had been the day before. Gen Smith wanted to persue the enemy but Gen Banks forbid it and ordered a retreat back to the Mississippi

22. In the actions at Mansfield and Sabine Crossroads, the regiment suffered the loss of 143 men taken prisoner, including Capt. Joseph McCulloch and 2d Lt. Charles McCulloch. The other men of Company C to be captured were: Sgt. Alfred G. Thom; Pvts. Philo W. Gallup, Clinton L. Gennoway, John Kennedy, Thomas H. McCulloch, and Joseph T. Sims; Surgeon Maj. Charles Winnie; and Chaplain John S. McCulloch. *RH,* 281–3.

River and we had the humiliating spectacle of two armies each retreating in oposite directions. We felt very sore over our defeat, it being the first time we had to give way before the enemy and what made it worse we felt that it was simply on account of the incompetency of our head officers. We felt that under the leadership of Gen Smith or any other capable officer it wouldn't have happened. In fact the great blunder that Gen Banks had made was so plain to be seen that every soldier with any inteligence could see it. Sending one brigade of infantry and a few cavelry away on so far inadvance of any support and having his supply trains right up at the front away ahead of his main army with two divisions of our 13th corps some six of seven miles back and 19th corps ordered into camp some ten or twelve miles back with the 16th corps twenty miles back at Pleasant Hills and no scouts out in front to reconoiter. Any corporal in the army could have done better and I don't think anyone could blame us for feeling that it was a give away and that we had been betraid. But such was the facts so much so that we lost all respect for Gen Banks and during our retreat he was hooted whenever he came near the 13th corps and would doubtless have been killed by some reckless yank if he had not made himself pretty scare and got back to New Orleans at the first oportunity. Which he did leaving Gen Smith to get us out of the scrape the best way he could. The rebels paid dearly for all they gained. Some of our men who were captured on the 8th and taken back over the battle ground said that it was terable to behold the slaugther we had made among their men both where they had tried to come up the hill in our front and where they had attacked our batteries. On the 9th at Pleasant Hills some of our doctors who had staid back to help take care of the wounded said they had never seen such slaughter as there was among the rebels. There in some places they were piled up five and six men deep. Chaplain J. S. McCullock who had just come to the regiment two days before the battle of the 8th was taken prisoner that evening but was short afterwards released as he was a noncombatant and came back to us. He told us of his experience on the day of the battle. He said he not having any experience in that kind of business didn't see that the rebels were all around him and between him and our lines but sauntering around he came across a rebel who had got down in a hole to get out of danger. So he ordered Mr Reb to come out of there and surrender but when his reb got out of his hole and saw the situation he refused to give up his gun as he had demanded but told him that he guessed they would just change places that he would take him prisoner and after explaining the situation to him, his rebel marched him back to the rear. After leaving Pleasant Hills in charge of the trains, we marched all that day and all night and all the next day ariving at Grandecore in the evening. We were badly worn out. I had marched for two nights and two days barefooted and bare headed. My feet were so swolen I could hardly walk during the last night. I would march quite a distance sound asleep until I would stumble over something and wake up. A great many of our wounded were being hauled back in the ambulances and wagons and the poor fellows were having a hard time of it and we could hear their moans and cryes as they were hauled along on that weary march and many one of them died that might have lived if they could have had proper care. Ariving at Grande-core we went into camp after a manner but having lost everything in the way of our tents blankets and were not in very good trim for housekeep-ing but we tryed to get some rest after our long weary struggle. We had been on the go for three days and almost three nights. And we felt very sad over the loss of so many of our comrades not knowing what their fate was how many was killed or how many was prisoner in the hands of the enemy. And as this was the first stop we had made since the battle. We had to write the bad news home to our friends and the friends of those were missing as soon as we could procure writing material which was not very easy to find as we had lost our knapsacks and everything they contained at Sabine Crossroads including among many other things (Our Best Girls Picture) which made us feel very sad but as our hearts were then young bouyent. After a good night of rest our spirits were revived. I had considerable trouble to procure some new head and foot gear as everything was in such confusion that we could not draw a Quar-termaster department. But after considerable reconoitering Brother J P Wiley procured for me a pair of silk stocking and a pair of light graters [gaiters] from some Sutler. And some of the other boys conficated a light cloth cap for me and so I was riged out once more. And went by the name of silk stockings for some time after. The rebels finding that we were retreating came after us in fource again cuting off and capturing all outposts and straglers that they could and trying to capture our Trans-port and gun boats on the red river.

April 11
We were moved some two miles to the left where we remained until the 13 the rebels began to show themselves on all sides of us.

April 13
We advanced about one mile to the front and began to throw up fortifycations by piling up logs and throwing dirt over them.

April 14
Having got our fortifycations about finished we got orders to tare them
down and build in a new place.

April 15
Tore down our fortifycations and began a new line.

April 16
Finished our fortifycations. The rebels were geting thick on all sides harrassing us in every prosable way and we were expecting attack at any
time. We remained behind our fortifycations until the 20th.

April 20
We remained behind our fortifycations until evening when we marched
out some distance to the front and lay on our arms until near daylight
of the 21st.

April 21
We started on the march before daylight, marched hard all day and all
night until 3 oclock am when we halted and laid down until daylight of
the 22nd.

April 22 [23]
We resumed the march at daylight marching 7 or 8 miles to Cane River
where we found the rebels in considerable fource. They had passed
around us during our stop at Grandecore and had crossed over Cane
River where they had thrown up fortifycations and planted bateries to
obstruct our crossing while their main force came up in our rear to try
to crush us between their two fources. But Gen Smith took care of those
in the rear with his 16th corps while the 13th and 19 corps was marched
down the river some distance where we crossed over by wading waist
deep and marching around and flanking the rebels position and after a
pretty sharp fight we drove them from their position. but while we were
engaged in front of the 16 corps was hotly engaged with the rebels in the

rear. They thought they had got us in a tight place and they made a terrific assault on our rear but they found they had something sollied to buck against when they tackled old Gen Smith and his 16th corps. We could hear the roar of battle in the rear and we pressed the rebels hard in front when our forces were all across the river and our lines formed we went in on the rebs on double quick and drove them from their works at the point of the beyonett and finding their force in the front was defeated those in the rear withdrew. After the rebels retreated we moved down to [build a] bridge over Cane River where we remained until morning.[23]

April 23 [24]
A pontoon bridge having been laid during the night the 16th corpse and the trains crossed over and we continued our retreat towards Alexandria La. The rebels following us up and harrassing us more or less day and night. That night we encamped on Bovoir [Bayou] Rapadees.

April 24 [25]
We resumed the march at an early hour reaching Alexandria in the evening before reaching Alexandria by some five or six miles we met Gen John A. McClernard coming to reinforce us with several thousand men and quite an amount of supplies. But he was ordered by Gen Banks to burn his extra supplies and retreat which he at first refused to do but insisted on proceeding against the enemy. Gen Banks being completey whiped if his army wasn't was determined to get back to the Mississippi River and after repeated orders Gen McClernard reluctantly obeyed. But Gen Smith coming along with his 16th corps put out the fires and loaded the supplies into his wagons and brought them back with him. We arived at Alexandria the water in the Red River had goten so low that our gunboats and transports could not be got past the rapids at that palce so we had to make a halt there until we could build dams or jetties to fource

---

23. The action described here by Wiley occurred on April 23 and is known as the Battle of Monett's Ferry. As Confederate forces blocked the crossing of Cane River at Monett's Ferry, Federal troops, including the 77th Illinois, moved by the right flank and crossed the river at a ford two miles above the ferry. This flanking movement compelled the Confederates to fall back, enabling the Union army to construct a bridge at the ferry and cross the river on April 24. While the action took place at Monett's Ferry, Confederates under Dick Taylor attacked the Federal rearguard near Cloutierville with little success. Johnson, *Red River*, 225–30.

the water all to one channel so as to get sufficient depth of water to float our boats past. The rebels were making a desperate effort to capture our boats and had been attacking and harrassing them all the way down the river. When ever they could escape the vigilence of our land fources they would concealed themselves and fire on our boats from some shelter and try to disable the machinery of the boat or kill the pilot and let the boat run ashore and set fire to it and thinking they could capture them. When they got to the shoals at Alexandria they pressed us hard on all sides thinking perhaps that they could force us to abandon our boats. They were mistaken in that we now had Gen Smith and Gen McClernand, two capable officers at our head and we felt that we were a match for most anything again. Our Generals formed their lines so as to protect the boats and the details that were at work on the jetties and threw up breastworks and established a picket or skirmish line some distance in front of the main line where we had rifle pits. On our part of the skirmish line we had a rifle pit dug behind a big osage hedge where we could have a good view of the open field in our front but the rebels couldn't see us until they got right onto us and we felt that we had a little advantage of them. We also had cavelry pickets or outposts in front of this.

April 28th

Our division was inspected and given a new supply of ammunition. In the afternoon firing was heard in the distance. The rebels had attacked some of our outposts. We fell into line and marched out some distance to the front of our works expecting an attack. We formed a new line a mile or so in front of our line of works in a large field which was all in ridges as most all the fields where which was making it very dificult to march over. I well remembered a little incident of that occassion a battery which was ordered into position just to our left came up on the gallop. The gunners were riding on the gun carriages and caisons and when they left the road and started across the ridges to come into line the men were all bounced off of their perch and left behind and had to come up on foot. The horses never slackened their pace but came in on the jump and the guns and caisons jumping six feet high. I expect it wasn't very funny for the men but of course we had to yell and laugh at them all the same. Before marching to the front our regiment and some others had been out of the skirmish line and when ordered to the front we had left our knapsacks and camp equipage all behind and while we were out at the front Gen Banks got scared again and sent orders for us to fall back to our line of works and ordered all our knapsacks and stuff to be burnt. But our cooks and teamsters which were left back saved our stuff by gathering it up and loading it into the wagons. Some regiments lost everything and many was the onalidictions [curses] pronounced on poor old weak kneed Banks. Gen McClernand and Gen Smith paid no attention to Gen Banks first orders to fall back but after being ordered the third or fourth time to fall back and night coming on we fell back to within half a mile of Alexandria and lay on our arms until morning.

April 29th
Our division moved about half a mile to the left where we remained until the 2nd of May. Details were made each day to work on the jetties which were being constructed under the direction of Colonel Bailey of Wisconsin.[24]

May 2nd
Our advance cavelry was attacked by the rebels and driven back some distance and our corps was ordered out to their support. We marched out some two or three miles where we came onto the rebel advance and drove them back some distance. With night coming on we fell back a mile or so formed a new line and lay on our arms until morning.

May 3rd
We remained in line at that place until evening and fell back to Alexandria.

May 5th
A part of our corps went to the front and skirmished with rebels driving them some six or eight miles and returned back to camp.

24. Lt. Col. Joseph Bailey, an engineer officer on Franklin's staff, proposed building a log dam to raise the water level from the three feet to seven feet—the depth required to float the vessels of Porter's squadron. Work on "Bailey's Dam" began on April 30, 1864, and was carried to a successful ending when the Union fleet slipped below Alexandria on May 12. Bailey, a native of Ohio, received the thanks of Congress for his actions and was made a brigadier general on November 10, 1864. Johnson, *Red River*, 248–9; Ezra J. Warner, *Generals in Blue* (Baton Rouge: Louisiana State University Press, 1964), 14–5; Boatner, *Civil War Dictionary*, 38.

May 6th

The first and third division of our corps went to the front going some eight miles without meeting much oposition where they remained until morning.

May 7th

Our brigade went to the front to where the first and third division was. The first and third division proceeding on some distance further driving the rebels across Bayou Rapidies and returning to where we were.

May 8th

Our brigade fell back about a mile where we lay until evening when the 77 Ill and the 19 Ky which was temprarily attached to our regiment was ordered back to the Opelouses road to build a bridge which having acomplished we fell back to our place at Alexandria where we remained until morning.

May 9th

We marched out to the front again and rejoined our brigade where we remained until the 13th by which time Colonel Bailey succeeded in getting all the boats over the shoals.[25]

May 13th

We started on the retreat toward the Mississippi River at three Pm. Marched some fifteen miles stopping at ten o'clock at night at a point at Red River where the river made a short bend.

May 14th

Our division was in the rear acting as a rear guard. We marched and halted and fooled along all day and night until two o'clock the next morning going about twenty miles when we halted and lay on our arms until morning.

May 15th

We did not march any distance until sundown. The rebels attacked our cavelry in the rear pretty strongly. We were drawn up in line several times

---

25. The Union boats were: *Lexington, Fort Hindman, Osage, Neosho, Mound City, Louisville, Pittsburg, Chillicothe, Carondelet,* and *Ozark.* Johnson, *Red River,* 248–9.

during the day to support the caverly but we were not actively engaged. We started at sundown and marched some 12 miles by two o'clock in the morning coming up with the advance troops where we remained until the morning. We were geting badly worn out by this time as we had been on the go day and night. When we would halt the boys would drop down on the ground and the cavelry men would dismount and lay down on the ground and their horses would lay down by their sides and they would all be a snoring about the time they would touch the ground.

May 16th

We marched about one mile the rebels were thick all around us. We could see them plainly off to our flanks marching on roads running paralel with the one we were on. Our artilery and some rebel artilery had quite a little fight on an open field or prarie near a little town called Marks-ville.[26] They made quite a noise for a while. The rebels had got round on our flank and let loose on our batteries as they were passing over the open prarie killing some of our horses and dismounting some guns. But our men wheeled into position limbered up their guns and give them all they wanted of it but the fight was pretty hot awhile but the rebs geting enough of it limbered up and left. We started on at noon marching 6 or 8 miles across the open prarie. We did know what minute the rebels would let loose on us from some point or other but they didn't. We correlled our trains and formed our lines around them and lay on our arms from eight until ten o'clock when we were called up and marched all night stoping at a little bayou at daylight and got some breakfast.

May 17th

We started on again at seven o'clock. The trains and other forces had some distance ahead of us. The rebels geting around on our flank tried to cut our division from the main army but failed in the attempt but succeeded in cutting off a division of our caverly who were bringing up the rear. But the caverly cut their way through their lines with pretty heavy loss and rejoined the army. We came up with the sixteenth and seventeenth corps about ten o'clock. The nineteenth corps had gone on

26. On May 14 and 15, there were skirmishes at Marksville (also referred to as Wilson's Landing or Avoyelles Prairie) as the Confederates harassed the Federal rear guard under A. J. Smith.

to the Atchafaliah [Atchafalaya] River after passing the sixteenth and seventeenth corps. Our reigment was deployed as flank skirmishers for the thirteenth corps. We took our position about a half mile to the right of the main line and marched along in single file about six or eight paces apart to guard the army from a flank attack or ambush by the enemy and proceeded in this way during the day ariving in the evening at Bayou Sara [de Glaise?] which we crossed on a pontoon bridge and went into camp.

May 18th
We remained in camp at Bayou Sara. The rebels pressing us hard on all sides. Gen McClernand and Gen Smith with the sixteenth and seventeenth corps had a hard fight with the rebels in the rear defeating the rebels with pretty heavy loses on both sides. Gen Smith took some two hundred prisoners.[27] Our officers had ordered a lot of transports to be brought up to the mouth of the Atchaffaloiah River enough with what we had with us to make a bridge across the river by anchoring them side by side across the river and bridging across their bows with plank.

May 19th
The 19th corps crossed over the river to guard our trains when they crossed over and our 13th corps marched down to the river some distance to guard against an attact on our bridge and our trains while they were crossing over. That evening we fell back some distance towards the boats and lay on our arms until morning.

May 20th
After the trains had all crossed over the river the 16th and 17th corps fell back towards the boats. The rebels still pressing them hard in the rear. At one time while the skirmishing was pretty heavy in the rear Gen Smith and some of his staff came riding back to see what was going on and not knowing when he came to our advance line he dashed on through our lines and right on toward the rebel lines. Our men hollowed to him to come back that was the rebel lines but could not make him hear but had

27. This engagement, the final clash of the Red River campaign, is known as Yellow Bayou or Bayou de Glaise. In this action, Taylor's Confederates lost 608 men, while the Federals suffered 350 casualties. Johnson, *Red River*, 275.

to send an orderly after him to warn him of his danger and the Gen did not loose any time in geting back inside of our lines. Gen Smith fources had to fall back across an open field or plantation which had been swampey land and had been drained by diging open ditches through it every twenty rods or so opening into the Yellow Bayou three or four deep. Gen Smith filled some of these ditches with men and had them to keep low until the rebel cavelry came in close range and then they raised up and open on them and exited many a rebel saddle before they could get out of range again.[28] This experience made them a little more cautious how they rushed up after us. About one PM the 13th corps crossed over the river. We remained near the boats until our army crossed over. Our batteries were posted along the river bank so as to have a good range of the land on the other side. The gunboats took position so they could have a good sweep of the surrounding country to take care of the rebels while the ballance of the army was crossing the river. The artilery crossed first and the infantry followed. The rebels were careful not to come within range of the yankey gunboats. When everything was crossed over in good shape the bridgeing was taken up from the bows of the boats. When the transports raised anchor and floated away towards the Mississippi River, the gunboats stood by guard until they got safely away. When they threw a few shells over among the rebels as a parting salute and weighed anchor and followed the transports. The rebels gave up the chase being badly dispointed as we afterwards learned as they had confidently expected to crush us when we came to the Atchaffaliah River and capture the greater part of our army as least not thinking that the yankey ingenuity could devise any means of geting away from them as the river was some eighty or hundred rods wide and too deep to ford at any place. They had us like the children of the Isreal at the Red Sea. The river in our front and a vast swamp on our left and a vast army on our right and rear and althro the waters were not dried up in front of us the yankey ingenuity found a way to get over it.[29] The rebels gave up the pursuit after we got across the river and as we learned from prisoners which we captured they were very much dispointed as they had confidently expected to capture or distroy Bank's army before we could get back to the Mississippi River

28. Wiley writes of the Battle of Yellow Bayou, which had taken place on May 18 and not May 20 as recorded here.

29. The ingenuity of which he speaks was once again the work of Lt. Col. Joseph Bailey.

and would no doubt have done so if we had not had some better generalship with us than Gen Banks or Gen Franklin. But Gen A. J. Smith and Gen J. A. McClernand proved themselves that they were more than a match for the rebel Gens Curby Smith and Dick Taylor by bringing Bank's Army back to the Mississippi River with but little loss excepting a few straglers, withstanding the many dificulites they had to contend with at Alexandria, the Achaffaliah River and other places. To Gen A. J. Smith was the greatest credit due as it was he infact that saved the army. We started marching towards the Mississippi River in the evening, marching and fooling along all night reaching the river in the morning.

May 21th
We marched down the Mississippi some four or five miles when we were ordered back to the landing at the mouth of Red River where we remained until the next morning. We felt very much like we had got home again when we reached the bank of the old Mississippi River on and by the side of whose muddy waters we had spent so much of our time.

May 22th
We marched down the Mississippi River some eighteen miles to Morganza Bend where we went into camp until the 25th. Here we were rejoined by Colonel Grier and the others from the regiment who had left us in December near New Iberia La to go home to enlist recruits for the regiment. With 40 recruits for the 77th, the first installment of recruits having met us at Alexandria. Each company organised their recruits into an awkward squad and set some of the vetern soldiers to drilling them.

May 25th
We went aboard the transport Colonel Cowles and floated down the river to Batonrouge La where we arrived about midnight and got our traps unloaded by daylight of the twenty sixth.

May 26th
We marched back through the town and went into camp about a mile back from the river in the eastern suberbs of the town where we had a very pleasant camp. We remained at Batonrouge until July 20th and enjoyed a much needed rest after the long weary campaign we had just gone through. Shortly after we arived there [some of] our regiment was

sent North and got a set of silver horns, drums cimbels etc and organized a regimental band which some became very proficient under the leadership of Lem Wiley. While at Batonrouge the drilling of the awkward squads was the order each company kept their recruits drilling pretty steedily. During June and July the weather was very hot. We had to get bamboo cane from the swamps and make shades over our dog tents to keep from suficating and we had frequent heavy thunder storms with some of the fiercest claps of thunder I ever heard. About the first of July the regiment moved their camp about a half mile to the left. Shortly after going into camp there Col Grier of our regiment and Colonel Moor* of the 83rd Ohio thinking that we were going to remain there for some time concluded to send for their wives to come down to remain there and to better acomodate them they took pocession of a house near the camp belonging to a rebel family by the name of Kent. Massa Kent and three sons were away in the rebel army and maddam Kent and daughter Maggie were away at that time visting them. Our colonels had myself, J. W. Jennie[30] of company A and corporal Martin[31] of Company F detailed to guard the house with orders not to alow anyone to enter the house without orders. We would stand guard time during the day and when everything got quite in camp we would go to bed in one of the out houses and sleep until morning. But not long after we were placed there the maddam and miss maggie came home. As it happened I was standing guard just inside the door and J. W. Jennie was laying in the hallway asleep. Miss Maggie was coming on a little in advance of her mother and the first thing I hear was Miss Magie saying mama our door is open and she came a little closer. She discovered Jennie laying in the hall and she jumped back with a very refined little scream saying O mama there is a terable soldier laying in our house and she fell in the rear and the maddam came to the front. She was a large pompous looking woman, a regular She Schivelry and as she came forward I steped to the door with a musket in my hand and the maddam steped back a little but sumoning all of her southern dignity and her ears began to get red and if any poor yank ever got a blessing it was me. Sir how dare you enter my house in my absence!

30. E. Winthrop Jenney of Galesburg enlisted on August 9, 1862, and was mustered out with the regiment on July 10, 1865. *RH*, 38; *AG*, 4:656.

31. James T. Martin of Low Point enlisted on August 22, 1862, and was mustered out on July 10, 1865, as sergeant. On July 24, 1865, he was commissioned second lieutenant but not mustered at that rank. *RH*, 64; *AG*, 4:668.

I will have you arested sir, I ordered you to walk right out of my house this minute. Excuse me maddam sais I you are only waisting your breath. I was placed here by Colonel Grier and Colonel Moor with orders to alow no one to enter this house without their orders and I have to obey those orders and consequently I will niether go out or you come in without their orders. A pretty story indeed that I can't enter my own house without the consent of some insignificant yankey colonel. Stand aside sir and alow me to come in and attemping to come in I had to bring the beyonette down in front of her gentle breast saying no maddam you hear what I say you can't come in without the orders of either Colonel Grier or Colonel Moor. Well sais she if it has come to that will you be so kind to direct us to where we can find those lordly colonels. So I called to J. W. Jennie who was laying back in the hall having a good laugh at my expense and requested him to direct the ladies to Colonel Moors tent which he did and Colonel Moor came back with them and told us to let them have full possession of the house but to remain there and not alow anyone to interfere with anything about their place. So we still remained and the ladies seeing they could not drive us away concluded to be very friendly and make the best of the situation. But as the propect begin to look favorable for a forward movement the colonels ladies did not come and after remaining there some days longer we were ordered back to our regiment.

9

GUARDIANS ALONG THE GULF

Still reeling from the fiasco of the Red River campaign, Wiley and the men of the 77th were directed to Alabama in an effort to seize the Confederate forts that guarded the entrance to Mobile Bay. Under the command of a new general, Gordon Granger, an officer far more aggressive and capable than Nathaniel Banks, Federal forces moved with a vengeance against Forts Gaines and Morgan in an effort to close the last major Confederate port on the Gulf of Mexico. It would be a memorable campaign for Wiley, who watched in awe as the ships of the West Gulf Blockading Squadron commanded by David Glasgow Farragut steamed into action on August 5, 1864. In one of the most celebrated naval actions in American history, Farragut's fleet of monitors and wooden ships boldly passed the forts and destroyed the Confederate fleet in Mobile Bay.

July 20th
We broke camp at Batonrouge and went aboard the Transport Tamaulipas. Colonel Grier was in command of the regiment and wanted to make a little show as we marched down through the town and wanted our band to play at the head of the brigade. But Lem Wiley had been drinking to freely and couldn't play but after trying to play a time or two they had to give it up and the colonel ordered Lem under arrest and we marched down without music. At 4 o'clock PM having all aboard we proceeded down the river running all night.

July 21th

We arived at Algiers at 5 AM landed just below the city and went into camp where we remained until the 30th. One evening while there the Largent boys Mat and Henry of company K[1] had been over in Newolreans and were coming back to camp pretty full and as they came up through the camp of the 19th Ky they ran out onto some of the 19th boys that were about as full as they were and each took the others for some of the 19th corps or blue bellied yankeys as we called them (as there was quite an antipithy between the eastern and western troops) and they began to gibe one another pretty rough and soon got into a fight as that was one of the Largents hobbies. After the battle was over they came onto camp and was telling the other boys about their scrap when the others boys told them that it was not the 19th corps boys they were fighting but that it was the 19th Ky. Then in a terable way they had been fighting their best friends and thought it was the damn old Blue bellies. So they got some of their commrades to go back with them to apologise to the 19th Ky. Some of the other boys followed after them to see the fun and the 19th boys thought they were fighting blue bellies too. So they got it all explained out and was all so terable sorry that such a terable mistake had been made and shook hands and slobered over one another for quite awhile and then all came back to camp happy once more.

July 24th

Chaplain McCulloch who had been taken prisoner at Mansfield La came back to the regiment and through him we learned the fate of our missing comrades and were glad to learn that so few of them had been killed or wounded and that there condition as prisoners was not likely to be as bad as we had feared.[2]

July 26th

We were ordered aboard the Transport Alice Vivian to go to Morganza Bend, the seckond brigade of our division having allready gone. But after

1. Henry and Madison Largent from Limestone had enlisted on August 9 and 15, 1862, respectively. Both survived their term of service. Madison was mustered out on June 17, 1865; his brother was mustered out with the regiment on July 10, 1865. *RH*, 90; *AG*, 4:679.

2. The men captured at Mansfield and Pleasant Hill were taken to Camp Ford, near Tyler, Tex. Bentley's regimental history contains a wonderful chapter on the experiences of the men of the 77th Illinois who were imprisoned at Camp Ford. *RH*, chap. 15.

remaining aboard awhile we were ordered a shore again and when we returned to our camp again we found that the jayhockers had been there and carried everything off.

July 27th

We turned over our Enfield muskets which we had carried about two years and drew new Springfield muskets. While at Algiers the hiwaters [peddlers] visited our camp and among the rest was a very nice manly young boy who came to camp almost every day with something to sell. One day he came to camp with a lot of pocket knives to sell. He had them fastened on a board so he could show them to better advantage. He got along allright and sold a good many of his knives to the boys of the diferent companies until he came to Co E where a lot of their meaner kind (of which Company E had a full share) gathered around him and began to abuse him and take his knives and run off with them and one of them give his board a kick and scattered his knives all on the ground and then they all gather his knives up and run off with them. The little fellow began to cry and beg them to give his knives back when Orderly Seargent Parr ordered him out of camp.[3] The little fellow started off crying and as he went past Company K quarters some of the K boys seen him and asked him what was the matter and he told them how the E boys had used him and it made the K boys so mad they all gather up and marched over to company E quarters and told them in no gentle terms that if they didn't give the little boy's knives back to him every one of them, they would whip the hell out of the whole company from the orderly seargent down. E company knowing that K meant just what they said and was able to carry it out they poneyed up the knives and the little fellow went on his way rejoicing and company E heard all they wanted about pocket knives for sometime after.

July 30th

We embarked on the Transport Saint Charles for Mobile Bay. Late in the afternoon we started down the river.

3. James Parr from Logan enlisted on August 9, 1862, and was mustered in as sergeant one month later. He served at that rank throughout the war and was mustered out on July 10, 1865. Parr was commissioned a second lieutenant on July 24, 1865, but not mustered. *RH,* 58; *AG,* 4:665.

July 31th

We passed Forts Jackson and St Phillips about 8 AM and arived at the mouth of the river about noon but the water being too rough to venture out onto the Gulf we cast anchor in the southeast pass until morning.

August 1st

We weighed anchor at daylight and passed out over the bar into the Gulf and proceeded on our way towards Mobile Bay keeping pretty close to the Mississippi shore. We had a large barge to the side of our boat in which was our wagons artilery etc. The water became pretty rough towards evening and we ran in behind Ship Island where we were protected from the storm and cast anchor about 5PM.[4]

August 2nd

We lay at anchor off Ship Island until evening, the water being pretty rough. In the evening we raised anchor and proceeded onto Petibois [Petit Bois] Island where we joined that rest of our fource. Here we cast anchor again.

August 3rd

We lay off Petibois Island until 4 PM. During the day a young pelican lit on the boat. Some of the boys caught it and amused themselves for some time by plageing the thing to see it fight. At 4PM our fleet of transports weighed anchor and passed onto Dauplin [Dauphin] Island, off the entrance to Mobile Bay where we landed. The water being shallow our transport could not get near the island and we had to be taken a shore in small boats and when they ran aground then we had to get out and wade the rest of the way. We all got ashore about dark and formed our lines and threw out pickets and lay on our arms until morning. We were now in the present of the ememy as the rebels had possession of a large U S brick fort on the eastern end of the island.[5]

4. Ship Island is located off the coast of Mississippi. Following its December 3, 1861, reoccupation by Federal forces, it served as a base for Union operations in the Gulf. Fort Massachusetts is situated on the island, which, for a time, served as a prison for Confederate soldiers. Edwin C. Bearss, *Decision in Mississippi* (Little Rock: Pioneer Press, 1962), 581.

5. Wiley refers to Fort Gaines. Situated on the eastern tip of Dauphin Island, it was one of the stronger fortifications along the Gulf Coast. Although construction on the pentagon-shaped fort began in 1821, it was not finished by the outbreak of the Civil War, when it was described

August 4th
We moved up to the front about a mile. The left wing of the regiment was deployed as skirmishers to drive in the rebel outposts so as to get out batteries planted in reach of the fort. The right wing supporting the work men who were planting batteries. Fort Morgan another large and very strong US brick fort just across the entrance of the bay about three miles from Fort Gains.[6] The rebels had obstructed the passage of the bay by driving, piling and sinking barges so as to compelled all vessels going in or out to pass close under the guns of Fort Morgan. There was also a small fort called Fort Powell built by the rebels of cottons bales and sand on a little island in the Mediteranian Pass between Dauphin and the main land or Cedar Point through which light boats might pass.[7] These were all in the hands of the rebels and our land fources had been sent there to cooperate with Admiral Farigut in the reduction of these forts. The land fources were under the command of General Gordon Granger* who had his headquarters on a boat on the water. The fources on land were under the amediate command of Gen Maginis. When we landed of Dauphin Island we could see Fariguts fleet of gunboats away out on the Gulf off the mouth of Mobile Bay.

August 5th
After we had got Fort Gains securely invested and our batteries in position the fleet commenced moving up to the attack at an early hour. The intention being to run the blockade, get inside the Bay and distroy the rebel fleet inside the Bay and compelled Fort Gains to surrender. It was a magnificent sight! The fleet moved steady up to the attack with the

---

as a "shell of masonry" without cannon. The brick walls of Fort Gaines stand 22.5 feet high. Arthur W. Bergeron Jr., *Confederate Mobile* (Jackson: University Press of Mississippi, 1991), 12; Park Brochure, Fort Gaines Historic Site, Dauphin Island, Ala.

6. Fort Morgan, located on Mobile Point, opposite the entrance to Mobile Bay from Fort Gaines, also was not finished when the Civil War began. Heavy ordnance, however, was sent to the fort, including two 8-inch columbiads and two 10-inch columbiads. Bergeron, *Confederate Mobile,* 7–9.

7. Situated on Grant's Island, the battery called Fort Powell commanded Grant's Pass (called here Mediteranian Pass by Wiley), which provides entrance to Mobile Bay from the Mississippi Sound to the west. The three-gun battery, consisting of one 10-inch Columbiad, one 8-inch Columbiad, and one 32-pdr rifled piece, was completed on December 17, 1862. On September 25, 1863, following the death of Col. William Llewellyn Powell, who commanded the lower bay defenses, the battery was named Fort Powell. Ibid., 62, 75.

monitors. In front Fariguts flag ship, the Hartford next and the other gunboats following in their order. Admiral Farigut was straped in the riging of the Hartford where he could see all that was going on and give his orders. When the fleet came within range of Fort Morgan the fort opened on them with all their guns and the fleet replying as they moved steadily on and when the boats of the fleet all got within fair range of the fort so that they could all open on the fort and the fort could bring all her guns to bear on the fleet. The sight was awfully grand to those of us who could view it from a safe distance. Our land batteries engaged Fort Gains and droped shell after shell into the fort from all their guns to keep them from operating against the fleet. There was a continuous flash of fire and deafening roar from the guns of both fleet and forts and our land batteries and as the sound reverberated over the water it was terable to hear as well as to behold. Our fleet passed steadily on past the forts inside of the bay where they encountered the rebel fleet which consisted of the Ram Tennisee and gunboats Selma, Morgan, Gains and one cotton clad. The fight between the fleets was short but spirited. The Ram Tennisee was the most formidable of their boats.[8] It attacked Fariguts flag ship Hartford fiercely and tried to sink it by puncturing it with her brow and the fight was fierce between the two ships for a little while until two of the monitors came to the Hartford rescue and they soon disabled the ram and running up on either side of her they throwed out their grapling hooks and fastening on to her they towed her off. The rebel gunboats Morgan and Gains retreated under the guns of Fort Morgan and the Selma and the cotton clad surrendered. The Morgan slipped away at night and ran up the Bay but was run ashore and burned and the Gains was burned by the rebels under the guns of Fort Morgan. Our men repaired the Ram Tennisee and maned it with yankey seamen and ran it down in front of Fort Morgan and let them pelt away on it but they could not fase it. Their balls would bounce off of it like rubber balls off of a house roof. Our loss in the fight included the loss of one monitior sunk by a torpedo carrying down with it over a hundred men and the disabling of one ironclad. The rebels opened on us pretty lively from Fort Gains and

8. Construction of the Confederate ram *Tennessee* was begun in Memphis in 1862 and completed in Mobile, where the boat was commissioned on February 16, 1864. Measuring 209 feet in length and 48 feet in beam, the *Tennessee* carried six inches of armor plating and mounted six heavy Brooke rifles. The powerful ram was flagship for Adm. Franklin Buchanan and was captured in the Battle of Mobile Bay on August 5, 1864. Boatner, *Civil War Dictionary,* 828.

knocked the sand up all around us but we soon got some heavy guns planted and gave them back as good as they sent. The little Fort Powell was evacuated during the night.[9]

August 6th

We continued planting batteries and diging rifle pits. That night we had rather a peculier experience. Our company was detailed with other troops to form a skirkmirsh line across the island with orders to push our way toward the fort as far as we could go driving in the rebel outposts before us and hold our ground until morning. The night was very dark. We could not have seen a rebel or rebel battery ten feet away. The ground was covered by a thick growth of palm leaves which made such a ratteling as we marched through them, that we could be heard a mile away. We proceeded thus for quite aways. The rebel outposts kept quiet until we got close onto them and then they fired on us and fell back towards the fort. We kept on advancing our line until we came on a swamp on part of the line that we could pass and were called to halt but the left of the line not knowing of our trouble proceeded on some distance causing a break in the alinement. When they were halted and an oficer started down the line to see that all was right and when he came to the break in the line he kept straight on some distance in front of us until he came to the swamp then he turned to the right and came towards our line right in front of our company. We could hear him coming tramping through the palm leaves. We did not know who it could be tramping around out there not thinking that it could be any of our men but knowing from the noise that there wasn't more than one or two. So our oficers told us to keep quiet and let them come near our line before we halted them and when he came within a few paces of our line he heard the click of a dozen or twenty muskets as they were cocked right in his face and a dozen voices demand halt who comes there. He was so badly surprised thinking that he had wandered into the rebel lines in the dark he could hardly speak but he made out to say in a hoarce whisper, for God sake

---

9. It was during this fight that Farragut uttered perhaps the most famous phrase in naval history, "Damn the torpedoes, full speed ahead." In this spirited affair, the U.S. Navy suffered the loss of the monitor *Tecumseh*, which was sunk by a torpedo with the loss of 93 men drowned. The Confederate fleet, commanded by Adm. Franklin Buchanan, was scattered. Buchanan lost the *Tennessee* and 312 of his 470 officers and sailors. The admiral himself broke a leg during the battle. Ibid., 558–9.

don't shoot. When he got over his fright a little he explained who he was and how he came to be out there. He was very much relieved when he found whos hands he had run into, so he went back and had the left of the line to fall back in line with us and then spades were brought to us and we dug rifle pits to protect us and we remained there until near daylight when we were relieved, some other troops taking our place.

August 7th

Gen Maginis was taken sick and was relieved from the command of the land forces. Col Grier of our regiment taking command. The rebels sent out a flag of truce to stipualte for the surrender of Fort Gains. It was the sabath day, we had preaching by Chaplin McCullock.

August 8th

Fort Gains surrendered about 8 AM. The rebels marched out of the fort and stacked their arms in front of our lines. The oficers delivering up their swords and were all marched away as prisoners of war. We thought all the time that it was strange that they did not make a stronger defense as the fort was one of the strongest kind and it like as if they might have blown us off the island if had tried but the mistery was solved when they surrendered as they were mostly alot of young boys who had been enlisted in Mobile as city guards, from 15 to 20 years old. The rebels were not expecting an attack on the fort and had sent the boys there to garison the fort while they sent the older troops to oppose Gen [Frederick] Steel* who was threating Mobile from the north. The poor boys looked as if they would like to go home to their mothers but were shiped away to New Orleans as prisoners. Fort Gains was thoroughly cleansed and maned with yankey and the stars and stripes once waved over another of Uncle Sams stolen forts.[10]

August 9th

The land forces were transferred to the other side of the Bay in the rear of Fort Morgan on Mobile Point. We embarked on the Transport James Battle and after going some distance our boat ran aground and stuck fast

10. Col. Charles D. Anderson surrendered Fort Gaines along with 46 officers and 818 enlisted men. In addition to the troops, 26 cannon and a large supply of ordnance stores were turned over to the Federals, along with enough food supplies for twelve months. Bergeron, *Confederate Mobile*, 146.

and another boat coming to take us off stuck fast also and we remained there until about dark when we were transfered to the tin clad No. 42 and remained on board until morning when we were ordered back to Fort Gains by Colonel Grier, commanding the land forces.

August 10th
Returned to Fort Gains and went into camp near the fort. That night there was quite a wind storm and heavy rain. It blew our tents down and we got good and wet.

August 11th
One half of the regiment was detailed to help unload ammuntion from the boats and the other half to clean up the fort and the camp. It rained considerable during the day.

August 12th
We rearranged our camp. The most of the regiment was on duty of one kind or another. It rained the greater part of the day.

August 13th
Things had been very quiet on the other side of the Bay. We were buisy throwing up fortifycations, planting siege guns etc. so as to completely invest the fort and cut off all chances for escape. In the evening the rebel Ram Tennisee having been repaired with a new smoke stack and maned by a yankey crew ran down and paid her compliments to Fort Morgan in the way of a few shells. The rebels replied striking her several times but their balls glanced off of her sloping sides like a rubber ball off of a salt barrel, not damaging her in the least.

August 14th
Nothing of particular interest occurred. The fleet would drop an occasional shell into the fort just to keep the rebel Gen Page* and his men from going to sleep. Things proceeded thus until the 22th. We put in our time with the usual routine of camp and other duties. The smallpox broke out among the negroes on the island and they were sent away to themselves on the west end of the island where they were cared for by our doctors. Oisters were very plentiful in places inside of the Bay. We fished them out of their beds in the mud in considerable quantities and

had oister stew and ositer fried and ositer raw, just as the fancy struck us. But perhaps it is useless to state that perhaps they were not prepared in just as fined stile as they sometimes are in first class restaurants but they were a little change from the army ration. Our stews were prepared by boiling them in the brackish water which we obtained by diging in the sand which obviated the necesity of adding very much salt and after seasoning up well with pepper and breaking some hardtack in it we thought it was good. But on account of our high living and other causes combined, scurry [scurvy] began to break out on us. Scabs and scales began to form under our arms and on our breasts and in spite of all our doctors could do for us it increase. A vegetable diet was what we needed but that we could not get there on that sandbar. Lieutenant Kenyon of company F got so hungry for vegetables that he got permission from the higher oficers to take two or three men and go over onto the mainland on Cedar Point and try to get some vegetables. He took three men and geting in a skiff they passed over to Cedar Point and as they went ashore they were captured by some rebel pickets who were conceled in the bushes watching our movements and were carried of to rebel prisons. One man died in prison and Lieutenant Kenyon and the other man got back to the regiment after a considerable time.[11]

August 22th
Having everything in readiness, the bombard[ment] of Fort Morgan commenced in earnest from both fleet and land batteries and was kept up constantly during the day. We could see the smoke and flames from the burning buildings inside the fort and we did not begrudge them all the glory they were geting out of their stubborn resistance.

August 23th
The bombardment was renewed at daylight and about 7 o'clock a white flag was run up over the Fort and the firing ceased and some oficers from the fort came towards our lines under a flag of truce to stipulate for surrender. But Admiral Farigut thinking he was the one they should stipulate with his flagship began to fire in front of them to warn them to

11. Lt. George C. Kanyon from Knoxville enlisted on August 1, 1862, and was mustered in as sergeant. He was promoted to second lieutenant on March 28, 1863, and on May 17, 1864, was elevated to first lieutenant. He was mustered out on August 15, 1865. *RH*, 63–4; *AG*, 4:668.

return and then they took a skiff and started out toward the Hartford. When Gen Granger ordered one of the land batteries to fire of them and warn them back to land and when they returned Gen Granger and Admiral Farigut had a consultation by signals after which Admiral Farigut came ashore and him and Gen Granger received them jointly. At 3 PM Fort Morgan was formily surrendered and the stars and stripes was run up and once more floated over its ramports.[12] The rebel Gen Page acted rather dishonorably spiking his guns and distroying other property before he surrendered. The rebel garrison consisted of 575 men. We still remained at Fort Gains. On the 23th I was taken sick with malaria feavor and was pretty sick for two or three days.

August 25th

The 77 went aboard the Transport J M Brown [Burr] and crossed over to Mobile Point and took on a lot of picks and spades and proceeded up the bay and crossed over to Cedar Point where we went ashore and marched out some distance on the road towards Mobile. But the rebels having burned a bridge over a bayou so that we could not cross we returned to where we had landed and went into camp until the 27th, putting in our time throwing up breastworks. The land being low and marshly and covered with thickets of brush it was a great place for moskeetoes or regular galinipers as big as an Illinois wasp with pobosis an inch long and from the time the sun went down until it rose again they were worse than rebel bushwhackers. We decided that they were in full simpathy with the rebels, cause the way they wacked it to us poor yanks our faces and hands were all in lumps where they had speared us. We could not have slept at all if we had not had mosqueto bars and at first they would crawl in under our bars in spite of us and about the time we would get asleep and the old fellows would make a charge on us and wake us up suddenly and we would have to get up and drive him out and stop the hole but he would soon be back until we learned to out

12. The surrender of Fort Morgan resulted in the capture of some 600 men and 46 artillery pieces. Although Page suffered the loss of only three men killed and sixteen wounded during the bombardment of Fort Morgan, he justified his actions by writing in his report that he "had no means left of defense." Richard L. Page, "The Defense of Fort Morgan," in Robert U. Johnson and Clarence C. Buel, eds., *Battles and Leaders of the Civil War*, 4 vols. (New York: Century, 1887–88), 4:408–9; Bergeron, *Confederate Mobile*, 150.

general them by piling all around on the edge of our bars and then he could not get at us but made the night hideous with his roaring.

August 27th

Our regiment and two other regiments was ordered across the bay to Mobile Point. I was taken very sick again with malarial feavor. We went aboard the Transport Thomas [Thomas Sparks] and cross over the bay and landed at Pilot Town and marched down the shore about half a mile and went into camp. The day was terable hot and I was just burning up with feavor. When we landed I could not walk but had to be carried to the regimental hospitle on a stretcher and for the next week I was so sick and delerious with feavor I hardly knew what was going on. During the heat of the day the heat of the sun would come through our hospital tent until it was like a bake oven inside and with the heat and feavor and the efect of the quinine cinconia etc., I was in a pretty bad fix. They said I would get so crazy by times that I would crawl out of bed and bore my head in sand like a sand crab. But as my time hadn't come yet to shuffle off the feavor gradually gave away and in the course of some ten days I was able to be on my feet again. On August 31 the regiment moved down near the fort.

10

DUTY IN NEW ORLEANS

The campaigns of spring and summer 1864 had taken a heavy toll on the 77th Illinois. Casualties had been high, sickness widespread, and the soldiers were utterly fatigued by their arduous service. The men were greatly in need of an extended period of rest. Fortunately for William Wiley and his fellow soldiers from Illinois, rest would be theirs. The regiment's next duty was in New Orleans, the South's largest city, where the soldiers would spend the fall and winter guarding prisoners of war. In their spare time, the men of the 77th enjoyed the theater, dances, and other social activities. The paymaster also visited the regiment, which enabled them to indulge in fancy foods and luxury items. As one soldier noted of New Orleans, "of all the places in the world to spend money in, it is the best."[1]

Wiley, however, gives no indication that he took advantage of all that the city had to offer. According to his diary, he stayed close to camp and much to himself during the regiment's service in New Orleans. He also had another short bout with sickness. Yet one cannot help but think that even William Wiley had some fun in the big city.

Despite the social whirl of New Orleans, the harsh reality of military life was never far away. It fell hard on the men in January 1865, when the 77th was consolidated with the 130th Illinois. From then on, the 77th had a new face and a new soul, reflective of the exigencies of a war which all now knew was speeding to its conclusion.

1. *RH,* 327; William T. Rigby to brother, January 4, 1864, Rigby Papers, Vicksburg National Military Park, Vicksburg, Miss.

Sept. 9th

We embarked on the Brig Thomas Sparks a small vessel carrying both steam and canvass but so little steam that the boys said it had to stop a while to gather steam enough to whistle. We passed out of the bay through the Mediteranion [Grant's] Pass onto the Mississippi sounds keeping pretty close to shore with our baby boat.

Sept. 10th

We crossed the bar at the mouth of the Mississippi River at 8PM.

Sept. 11th

We arrived at Morganza Bend at 8 AM where we disembarked and went into camp.[2] I had about recovered from feavor but was still quite weak. The scurvy was geting pretty bad in the regiment but Colonel Grier had sent word to the good women of Peoria about our condition and needs and we soon received a bountiful supply of sanitary goods including a goodly supply of onions and other vegitables which soon knocked the scurvy and left nothing to scratch for but graybacks [lice] which did not surrender to onions and the like. We spent a pretty quite time at Morganza. Our duty was rather light. At one time while there an expedition was sent back to the Atchaffaliah River to try to capture some rebels who had crossed over that river and was encamped on the east side. I was detailed to go but Wm Sims[3] not knowing where they were going and thinking there was going to be a chance to some jahocking came to me and wanted to take my place and not being very strong yet I was not very anxious for the tramp. I told him that he could go providing he could make it all right with the oficers and after considerable trouble he got them to consent. But before they got started he heard some way what they were going for and he got terable worked up and swore he wouldn't go but the oficers told him just to keep still that he was so anxious to go and he would go now and he need not say anything more about it and when they started the boys said he pretended to be terable sick and went along like as if he was trying to vomit but the oficers knowing that he was playing off kept him a going and the other boys kept mocking him till

2. Morganza lies on the west bank of the Mississippi River midway between Port Hudson and the mouth of the Red River.

3. William Sims of Cazenovia was mustered in on August 13, 1862, and was mustered out with the regiment on July 10, 1865. *RH*, 51; *AG*, 4:662.

he give it up. Colonel Grier being absent from the regiment and Captain Stevens of Co E being in command and he and some of the other younger oficers being anxious to get the regiment sent to New Orleans to do garrison duty be thought themselves that this would be a good time to work for that end, so Captain Stevens having lots of cheek and being quite a schemer he went to New Orleans to work the thing up and suceeded in getting the regiment ordered there.

Oct. 7th
We went aboard the Transport Laurrel Hill and started down the river again for New Orleans. Captain Stevens met us at Batonrouge.

Oct. 8th thru the end of November
We arived at New Orleans at 8 AM and marched down to the lower leavee of Pickaune [Picayune] Cotton Press and relieved the 48 Ohio which had been there for some time guarding prisoners. The 48th being sent to Natches [Natchez] Miss. Our duty while there consisted in guarding rebel prisoners who were quartered in an ajoing press and doing guard duty at the Baronest [Baronne Street] Prison and other military prisons, guarding goverment stores etc. The different companys of the regiment were scattered around over thy was to be performed. Some in Picayune Press, some in Alabama Press and some on Levee Street. A good many of the rebel prisoners were those that we had taken at Fort Gains. The presses were surrounded by high brick walls some twelve feet high with broken bottles and the like fastened all over the top of the walls with cement to keep anyone from climbing over which made a very good place to confine prisoners. But we had to keep a strong guard both inside and outside of the wall to keep the prisoners from diging out through the wall and escaping. At first we did not have guards all around the inside and on one or two ocassions they dug through the wall in the night leacing a thin layer of brick on the outside until they got all ready. Then they would kick it out and a lot of them jump through and run in the dark and several got away as their friends in the city would hide them and help them away. Then they had to place guards all around in the inside as well as the outside. There was a lot of desperate fellows among the prisoners and they had heard in someway that their property was being burned and their families were mistreated and they were in a terable way determined to get away and go home to see about it. It was a

rather precarious business to stand guard back under those sheds at night among them fellows with a dozen of so of them watching each guard for an oportunity to snatch our guns away from us and knock us in the head. I well remember one dark night that I stood guard back under there when they seemed to be particular restless. I was satisfied that they had some plot of other that they intended to carry out that night. Fifty or hundred of the worst of them never laid down at all until about midnight and I was satisfied from the way they acted and the way they were dressed and everything that they were preparing for something deperate and along toward midnight they began to get very friendly and try to engage me in conversation. One would come up pretty close and begin to talk and then begin to come up one at a time as if to hear what was being said until several would get together and then they would keep coming closer little by little until I would have to scatter them and make them go back to their bunks but it would not be long until they would be working the same tatics under some other pretense. I could see they were working the same thing with the other guards and I finaly called the oficer of the guard and told him that I was satisfied that there was something up and their intentions was to try to over power the guards for some purpose and told him how they were acting and he said there was no doubt but that I was right and he brought some more guards and made the prisoners go to bed and ordered us to shoot the first man that got out of his bunk before daylight and that ended the trouble for that time. Details were made from the regiment every once in a while to take prisoners off to other prisons. Shortly after we arrived there was a lot of prisoners of our kind and another was sent off to the dry Tortugas and soon after about two hundred rebel prisoners were sent off to some Northern prison. They like all other rebels were terable opposed to being sent north as they thought they would surely freeze to death and it was rather sad to see the parting of them and their families and friends. The wives and children of those that had lived any where near were allowed to come and see them and bid them goodbye which they were obliged to do in the present of the oficers and guards for fear of them bringing them weapons of some kind. Their partings were pretty sad as they seemed to think they would never see them again. Our duty was pretty heavy as we were on duty about every other day and night and with the loss of sleep it began to tell on us pretty visibly in the course of a month or two. Soon after ariving at New Orleans I was taken down with flu and was very bad for a week or so. There was not room for me in the hospitle. But Lieutenant Wright and brother J. P. Wiley took me into their tent and nursed me through. While there they required us to put on considerable stile. We had to carry small swords and on extra occassions we had to put on white gloves and paper collars. We soon concluded that the oficers might be having a soft thing of it but we could hardly see where our soft snap came in. We had good comfortable quarters and good rations but our duty was pretty heavy. The weather was very pleasant there. The coldest night we had that winter it froze but the very least bit of ice in the water troughs. The citizens there thought it was terable cold. They thought we would surely freeze to death standing guard out on the street. But we told them that it just made us feel good.

December 25th
We spent this our third Christmas in the army in moving our camp from the Picaynne Press to Woods Press on Cannall [Canal] Street. Here we had rather better quarters and pleasant surroundings. We were on the princple streets of the city, something like a mile back from the river. After going there we done duty at the Barone Street prison and other places in the central part of the city. But we were kept busiy going on guard regularly every other day but we lived high. They issued us cod fish each day as an extra ration and our mess No. 3 had a yankey cook in the person of Dennis Duff and he prepared us a fine dinner of cod fish and beans each day and we thought it were extra good. The good folks at home sent us a box of good things and among other things there was a four gallon jar of gilt edged butter and as we had hardly tasted butter for something over two years. I think that butter never tasted quite so good to mortal man before or since. It helped out our sad bread and hardtack wonderfully.

1865

January 14th
Quite a furrore and considerable bad feeling was created in the regiment by an order for the consolidating of the 77th and 130th regiments Illinois Vol. Infantry and the mustering out of all supernumerary commissioned oficers and reducing to the ranks all supernumerary noncommissioned

oficers. As each regiment had become reduced in numbers below that was alowed by the regulations. But as we could do nothing but submit we submitted.[4] The 130th lost its identity and we were still known as the 77th. Our companys only commissioned officer Anderson Wright was mustered out. Lieutenant E. S. Dewey who had been Adutant of the 130th was placed in command of our company.[5] He was a good easy soul but was less fit to command the company than any corporal in it. Colonel Grier commanded the regiment and Colonel [John B.] Reed [Reid] of the 130 acted as Lieutenant Colonel.[6] There was a good many pretty rough men in the 130 and we felt as if they were not much credit to us as we had always had a pretty respectable regiment. But had to choke down our dissatisfaction and make the best of it. Along the first of February somethings began to indicate that we might take to the field again before long. There was talk of an expedition to be sent to take the city of Mobile and surrounding works. But our oficers were anxious to stay in the city and were working hard for that not to end. They thought the regiment that would make the finest show would get to stay so we had to put on lots of dog. We had to keep our guns and acoutraments in the best of order. Guns and beyonetts were so bright that they dazzled our eyes and boxes and belts blacked up with a shine and our brass shining like the noon day sun and had to wear white gloves and paper collars.

4. The order of consolidation, Special Order No. 14, issued by Maj. Gen. Stephen Hurlbut (then in command of the Department of the Gulf), reads in part: "The Seventy-Seventh and One Hundred and Thirtieth Illinois Volunteers will be consolidated, and known as the Seventy-Seventh Illinois Volunteers. Brigadier General T. W. Sherman, commanding Defences of New Orleans (who is charged with the execution of this order), will designate such commissioned officers as will be retained in the service, to command the new organization. All other officers will be at once mustered out of service. All supernumerary non-commissioned officers, who were appointed as such at the date of the original organization of their respective companies, will be mustered out of service. All other surplus non-commissioned officers, who have been appointed since the original organization, will be reduced." RH, 331–2.

5. Edward S. Dewey from Greenville enlisted on September 5, 1862, and was mustered in seven days later as adjutant of the 130th Illinois. Following consolidation with the 77th, he served with Company C. When the 130th was reconstituted, he once again was appointed adjutant and served in that capacity until mustered out on August 5, 1865. AG, 6:556, 578.

6. John B. Reid from Greenville enlisted on September 18, 1862, and was mustered in as major of the 130th Illinois on October 25. On July 5, 1864, Reid was promoted to lieutenant colonel, but he was not mustered until January 26, 1865. He served in that capacity until mustered out with the 130th on August 15, 1865. AG, 6:555, 578.

February 10th

All the different regiments about the city were ordered out to perade the principle streets and our oficers getting the idea that which ever regiment made the finest display would get to stay in the city. So they had us to fix up in our best and do our best work. We did not feel afraid of anything there except it was the first US Regulars. We were a little jubus [jealous] of them so we done our big best and got the credit of making the best show of any regiment in line. We felt that we had done it shure but the head oficer seemed to have a different idea from what our officers did and seemed to think that we were the kind they needed in the field. We were one of the first to get orders to prepare to take the field and on Feb 17th a colored regiment was sent to take our place, the 20th CDA.[7] So we packed up our surplus goods and sent somethings home and stored the rest in the city. We remained in our camp until Monday Feb 20th. Our oficers and the most of the men were very much disapointed but as for myself I was about ready to take the field again.

7. The 20th Infantry, United States Colored Troops, had been organized at Riker's Island in New York Harbor on February 9, 1864. Attached to the Department of the East until March, it was then transferred to the Department of the Gulf. Following service at Port Hudson and then in Texas, the regiment returned to Louisiana. In February 1865 it was stationed in New Orleans. Dyer, *Compendium*, 3:1727.

~⍋ 11 ⍋~

THE FINAL CAMPAIGN

Early in 1865, the various companies of the 77th reassembled and embarked on another campaign, which proved to be their last. In this spring of decision, as the armies of the United States moved inexorably toward final victory, Wiley returned to Mobile to assist in the reduction of the powerful earthworks that stood defiant on the east shore of Mobile Bay. Doubtless William, his brother John, and the men from Peoria who formed Company C of the 77th all prayed that a merciful God would spare them in their final combat encounter with southern soldiers.

February 20th
We fell into line about 12 o'clock and marched down to Bulls Head Landing. A good many of the boys had taken a parting swig with their friends before starting and could not step to the music very well. Espically Thomas Holt of Company K.[1] He was so limber that his big knapsack would pull him back until he would double up like a jackknife and down he would go. But he struggle on to his feet again and came on. We went aboard the steamer St. Maries and proceeded down the river and ariving at the mouth of the river. We cast anchor until morning.

February 21th
We weighed anchor at daylight and passed out onto the Gulf. The water was quite rough and a great many of us was soon seasick. Before starting

1. Pvt. Thomas J. Holt from Rosefield enlisted on August 8, 1862, and was mustered out on June 17, 1865. *RH,* 90; *AG,* 4:679.

they issued us a lot of dried herring as a special ration. But they did not lay on our stomachs well when we got onto the rough water. We felt that we had turned the table on the fish instead of the fish throwing up Jonah, Jonah was throwing up the fish. Before we started several men in the regiment was taken sick with small pox but did not know what ailed them and several was taken down on shipboard and some of the other sick boys laid under the same blankets with them before they knew what ailed them. But no more of us took it. The storm increased and the water got rougher during the day. We ran in behind Chandilier [Chandeleur] Island about 4 o'clock and cast anchor. It rained during the night and some of us got pretty wet.

February 22th
It still continued pretty stormy and we lay anchor during the day and the next night. It rained some during the day.

February 23th
Water still pretty rough. We raised anchor at 7-30 and proceeded on to Fort Morgan where we arrived at 5 PM and went ashore in a heavy rain storm. We crawled under a pontoon train near by for shelter and remained there until the next morning but we got pretty wet.

February 24th
It rained considerable during the day. We were assigned our camping place and put up our dog tents, got brush, etc. and fixed up the best we could.

February 25th
Still raining considerably. Henry Largent and some recruits came to the regiment.[2] Our regiment was assigned to the first brigade, third division, thirteenth corps. [Lt.] Colonel Reed was in command of the regiment, Colonel Grier the brigade, Gen Benton* the division and Gen Granger the corps.

---

2. Henry Largent from Limestone had evidently been back home on recruiting duty. He joined Company K on August 9, 1862, and was mustered out on July 10, 1865. *RH,* 90; *AG,* 4:679.

February 26th
It was clear and pleasant. We had inspection at ten PM.

February 27th
Cloudly and cool. We had company drill from 8 till 10 AM and regimental drill from 2 till 4 PM.

February 28th
Cloudly and cool with north wind. We had inspections and muster at 9 AM.

March 1st
We had company drill from 8 til 10 AM and battallion drill from 2 til 4 PM and dress parade at 5 PM.

March 2nd
Cloudly and damp. Company drill from 9 til 11 AM and battallion drill from 2 til 4 PM and dress parade at 5 PM.

March 3rd
Cloudly and misting rain. I was on guard at the pontoon train. Windy at night.

March 4th
Cool and windy. Came off guard duty at 7 AM. Fixed up tent and cleaned up grounds. We heard that Mobile was evacuated. Dress parade at 5 PM.

Sabath March 5th
Cold and windy. Seargent Bender of Company D returned to the regiment from a furlow home.[3] We had preaching at 10-30 by Chaplain. A lot of men from the regiment was detailed to work on a railroad.

March 6th
Weather moderate. Drill and dress parade as usual. I was detailed to work on the railroad but Folks of our company went in my place.

---

3. Sgt. James T. Bender from Lacon joined Company D on August 9, 1862, and was mustered out on July 10, 1865. *RH,* 52; *AG,* 4:663.

March 7th
Cloudly and windy. Drill at 8 AM. Got orders to turn over all extra camp and garison equipage. Rain and high winds at night.

March 8th
Clear and pleasant. Had general inspection at 8 AM by Gen Austerhans.

March 9th
Damp and cloudly. Had company drill at 9 AM. Our oficers turned over their wall tents and drew pup tents. Cold and windy at night.

March 10th
Cold and damp. Laid in our tents the most of the day.

March 11th
Weather more moderate and clear. Gunboats started up the bay towards Mobile in the morning. One brigade of our division started away at 10 AM.

Sabath March 12th
Weather pleasant. We had inspection at 9 AM and preaching at 10 AM and dress parade at 5 PM.

March 13th
Weather moderate with east wind. We had company drill at 9 AM and battallion drill at 2 PM and dress parade at 5 PM. Wm Fen of company D a member of our cornett band died of smallpox.[4] Rain during the night.

March 14th
Wet and stormy. We had no drill.

March 15th
Clear and pleasant. I was detailed to go after rations. High winds and rain during the night.

---

4. Pvt. William P. Fenn from Lacon enlisted on August 22, 1862, and served until his death at Mobile on March 13, 1865. *RH*, 55; *AG*, 4:664.

March 16th
Clear and cold. Company drill at 9 AM. We got orders to be ready to march the next morning at 4 AM with four days rations, 50 rounds of cartridges and two pairs of shoes a piece.

March 17th
Reveilee at 3 AM. March at 4, marched 15 miles and camp for the night. Some eastern troops was just in advance of us. They had started in heavy marching order. The day being rather warm they soon began to lighten up by throwing away their extra blankets, shirts etc. and the road sides was lined with them for miles.

March 18th
We resumed the march at 5 o'clock. Marched some 14 miles and went into camp at 2-30 PM. Rained hard that night.

March 19th
Marched at 5 AM. The ground was very flat and wet. Roads were very swampy in places. Our brigade was marched to a plantation some distance from the road and each man took a rail on his shoulder and we made a noble appearance as we marched through the pine timber each man carrying a rail. We carried our rails for about a mile to a very swampy place in the road where we each one laid our rail down cordaroying the road as we went so that our trains and artilery could pass over. We marched some ten miles and went into camp at 4-30 PM.

March 20th
We remained in camp during the day waiting for our supply train to come up as we had run out of rations. Train caught up in the evening and we drew rations. It rained very hard during the night.

March 21th
Resumed the march at 6-30. It continued to rain until 10 AM. The ground was covered with water and every little while someone would plout into a hole where some artilery wagon had been dug out and would get wet all over. Then the boys would set up the yell. Grab a root, no bottom! We waded along for a mile or two and then we stacked arms and went back and tried to get our trains through. A great many of the

teams had swamped down entirely but failing to get them through we went into camp in the mud. In the evening we went back and pulled a few wagons through by taking the mules off out of the way and attaching long ropes to the wagons, getting 40 or 50 men to each rope. We whooped them out of there in a hurry until we would get them onto solid ground where they could stand up and then we would go back for another one. We worked in this way until we were soaked with the muddy water and went back to camp until morning. We made up our minds that we didn't out ranked a mule very much but it was a little consolation to see Gen Benton get down in the mud and take hold of the rope and help us pull. We concluded he was as good as a mule.

March 22th
We went to building a cordaroy road through the swamp to get our trains and artillery over. Not finding any rails handy we went to cutting down the Pine trees and spiting the sections in havles and laying them side by side. In this way we made two or three miles of road and got our trains over by 2 PM and we marched on two or three miles and went into camp.

March 23th
It was clear and warm. The roads were fair. We marched about 10 miles and went into camp at [on the east branch of] Fish River. That day we were marching through the pine timber where the trees had been barked on the southside to get the pitch to make rosin. A fire got started in the timber and pitch and nearly strangled us but we had to go through it choke or no choke.

March 24th
We remained in camp at Fish River. Billy Jim Houghtaling and some others came to the regiment. There was a rosin manufactory there and quin piled up. Houghtaling raised quite an indignation by telling that it was just the four hundred dollars bounty that took him there. This cause some treats of druming him out of camp.[5]

5. The *Report of the Adjutant General of the State of Illinois* relative to Houghtaling is confusing. In volume 4, which deals with the 77th, he is listed as James W. Houghtaling from Logan, serving in Company E. In volume 6, which deals with the 130th, he is listed as William J. Houghtaling from Peoria, serving in Company B. Both volumes give his date of enlistment as February 23, 1865. Transferred to the 130th Illinois when that unit was revived, he was mustered out on August 15, 1865. *AG*, 4:667, 6:581.

March 25th

Drew a lot of axes and spades and two days of rations and marched at 4 PM. Marched about six miles and went into camp. Our brigade was guarding the train.

Sabath March 26th

Marched at 5-30 AM and caught up with the ballance of our corps at 8 AM. Left the train in charge of the 3rd Brigade and advanced with the main column. We were drawing near to the rebel lines. We closed in on the rebel's works at Spanish Forts in the evening cooperating with Gen Steel's fources who came in from the North.[6] We formed our lines around the rebel's works a mile or two back from the forts and threw up some breastworks by cutting logs and piling them up and throwing dirt over them. We worked until 10 PM and then our band got up on top of our works and surenaded the rebels. A strong skirmished line was placed behind our works and the rest lay on their arms until morning.

March 27th

We fell in line at daylight to receive the rebs if they wished to come after us but they didn't wish to. At 9 AM we advanced on the rebels works. Our brigade in advance of our division. We drove in their outposts without much resistance and formed a line within about half a mile of Spanish Forts. Our part of the line was behind the brow of the hill where they could not rake us with their shot but they dropped their shells down around us rather carelessly cutting the tree tops off over our heads so that we had to cut the trees down to keep the tops from falling on us.

Bounties were used by federal, state, and local authorities to induce enlistments in the Union army and to avoid the need for military conscription. Bounties ranged from as little as $25 at the outbreak of the war to as high as $400 by 1863. It is estimated that the bounties paid by various authorities during the war totaled around $750 million. Boatner, *Civil War Dictionary*, 74.

6. Spanish Fort was situated on the east side of Mobile Bay near where the Blakely River empties into the bay. Consisting of six redoubts connected by rifle pits, the main work (Old Spanish Fort) faced the river, while Redoubts 2 (Fort McDermott), 3 (Red Fort, sometimes referred to as Redoubt Blair), 4, 5, and 6 faced the land side. The bastion mounted six heavy guns, fourteen field pieces, and twelve coehorn mortars. The Confederate garrison comprised a brigade of Louisiana troops, Alabama reserves, and artillerymen, totalling 1,810 men under the command of Brig. Gen. Randall L. Gibson. Bergeron, *Confederate Mobile*, 160, 175.

During the campaign discussed here by Wiley, Maj. Gen. Frederick Steele led a force from Pensacola, Fla., and besieged Fort Blakely. Warner, *Generals in Blue*, 474–5; Boatner, *Civil War Dictionary*, 794–5.

Samuel Akers of our company got so badly overcome with fear when we were closing in on the fort that he just utterly colapsed and we established our line he got down behind a big tree and laid there for two or three days and nights.[7] I never seen anyone so completely overcome with fear. He had got a clip on the head the first fight we got into at Arkansas Port and it knocked all the courage out of him. The oficers took pity on him and let him lay there. The other boys bulleraged and gibed him and tried to talk him out of it but they could not get him away from his tree and had to carry his grub to him. After we had formed our line Gen Benton commanding our division who it was said had been imbibing too freely of fire water to brace up his courage concluded to recanoiter the rebel works. After being helped into the saddle he started and ordered his staff and orderlies to follow him and he rode around in close range of the rebel works the length of our division as fast as his horse could carry him with his staff and orderlies stringing after him getting his color bearer and some of his staff pretty badly wounded. It rained pretty much all day. At night we were ordered forwards onto the top of the hill to throw up breastworks where we worked until midnight falling trees and piling up the logs and digging out a wide ditch behind them and throwing the dirt over in front. Having our works finished pickets were placed in the works and the rest of us lay on our arms until morning.

March 28th

We were called up at 3-30 Am and marched up to our breastworks to guard against an attack from the rebels at daylight. We were relieved at daylight and went back to our position in the hollow. The rebels continued to shell us pretty heavy. We had to dig out places in the hillside and build bomb proofs out of logs by splitting logs and putting the halves over head and thowing dirt over them to sleep in and go into when the rebels shelled us to hard. At night a heavy detail of men was sent to the front to construct a line of rifle pits about half way between out line and the rebel works. After these rifle pits were finished a heavy line of skirmishers would be placed in them to remain there until the next night as we could not go out or back in daylight without encountering the rebel fire.

---

7. Samuel T. Acres from Linn enlisted on August 13, 1862, and was mustered out on July 10, 1865. Perhaps his actions would be referred to today as "battle fatigue." *RH*, 47; *AG*, 4:661.

March 29th

Company I was called out at 4 o'clock AM to remain in the breastworks until daylight. Companies A and H were out on the skirmish line. One of Company H was wounded by a piece of a shell from one of their batteries.

March 30th

Along about the middle of the night the rebels came out of their works and attempted to capture our skirmishers in the rifle pits and a fatigue party that were digging an advance line of rifle pits. They attempted to deceive our men by driving a lot of cattle out ahead of them thinking that we would not see their men until they would get close enough to surprise and capture our pickets but their ruse didn't work as they expected our men seeing their game. The fatigue men fell back to the rifle pits and our skirmishers let loose on them and scattered fresh beef all around there and the rebels seeing that their game had failed soon gave up it up and fell back to their works. When the firing commenced the long roll was beat and we got out to our breastworks in short notice. We grabbed our guns and acoutraments in one hand and our coats in the other and went up over that hill in a hurry. We supposed from the racket, our men was making out in front that the whole rebel fource was making an assault on our party to cut their way out which was doubtless. Their intention if they had succeeded in deceiving and capturing our pickets. So our oficers told us to stand to our works and hold our line until our skirmishers fell back to our line and not to let a rebel reach our lines alive. Every man took his place at the works with his musket cocked and his teeth set with a determination to carry our instructions out to the letter but our skirmishers didn't fall back. They stood to their works so well that the rebs were glad to fall back to their works without any help from us. After the racket was over the regiment all retired to their quarters but Companies C and D. We remained at the works until daylight. One division of the 13 corps and one division from the 16th was sent to assist Gen Steel who was operating against Fort Blackely.[8] We got a lot heavy guns planted during the night.

8. Fort Blakely was situated on the east side of Mobile Bay near where the Tensaw and Apalachee Rivers fork. It is north of and opposite to Bay Minette Creek from Spanish Fort. Fort Blakely consisted of nine lunettes, mounting more than 40 cannon, connected by rifle pits. The whole line covered some three thousand yards and was manned by 2,700 effectives

March 31th
Our batteries opened on the rebelwoeks at daylight and kept it up pretty well. During the day the rebs were replying in good shape and we got a pretty good shelling as we were laying just in rear of our batteries. We had to crawl into our bombproofs. Three of the first Indiana heavy artillery were wounded by having a log knocked onto them from their works.

April 1st
Company B, C, and D went out as skirmkishers at 7 AM. The day was dark and foggy. One of the first Indiana heavy artillery was killed by a musket ball.[9]

Sabath April 2nd
We were on the skirmish line during the day and were relieved at 7-30 PM by the 96th Ohio.[10] The day was clear and pleasant. 319 prisoners came in during the day. They were captured by Gen Steele's fources.

April 3rd
We planted some more heavy guns in our front. Some 600 more prisoners came in from Gen Steele.

April 4th
We went on the skirmish line at 4 PM and remained until 9 PM. All the batteries around the line opened on the rebel works from 5 tii 7 PM.

April 5th
I was on fatigue duty helping to haul gabreals for the fortifycations.[11]

April 6th
One of the 28th Illinois was cut into by a shell. A saloot of 100 guns was fired on account of the fall of Selma Ala.[12]

---

under the command of Brig. Gen. St. John R. Liddell. The fall of Fort Blakely on April 9, 1865, compelled the evacuation of Mobile. Bergeron, *Confederate Mobile*, 182–6.

9. The soldier in question was Pvt. William Hogue of Company C, 1st Indiana Heavy Artillery (formerly 21st Indiana Infantry). Hogue was from Bloomfield and had enlisted on October 7, 1864. *Report of the Adjutant General of the State of Indiana*, 4:456.

10. Organized at Camp Delaware, the 96th Ohio was mustered into service on August 29, 1862. The Ohio regiment served in the same division as the 77th Illinois for much of the war and was mustered out of service on July 7, 1865. Dyer, *Compendium*, 3:1539.

11. Wiley probably refers to gabions, which were large cylindrical objects made of woven cane and vine that were packed with dirt as protection against enemy fire.

12. Selma fell to Union forces under Maj. Gen. James H. Wilson on April 2, 1865. Boatner, *Civil War Dictionary*, 935–6.

April 7th

It was damp and cloudy with some rain. There was heavy firing from the gun boats off to our right. J. W. Avery and J. A. Lindsay of our company were detailed as clerks in the division quartermasters department.[13] Our company went on the skirimish line at 7 PM. Advanced our rifle pits during the night.

April 8th

We were on the skirimish line during the day. There was heavy firing at Fort Blakely at about 1 AM and again at daylight. The rebels tried to cut their way out through Gen Steele lines but failed. Our batteries bombarded Spanish Forts from 6 til 7 PM. Some of our steel guns just above our quarters jared us up good.

Sabath April 9th

The rebels had evacuated Spanish Forts during the night escaping by water.[14] Our fources took posession of the works about 2 o'clock in the morning. Capturing some 30 guns and a lot of amunition. The forts consisted of a system of strong earthworks. The grounds around the forts was planted thickly with torpedoes which they marked with small flags about two inches square so that their men could tell where they were.[15] But an assaulting column would not notice them but would tread on them and explode them. We started for Fort Blakely at 11 AM and after making a fourced march for some two or three hours we discovered that our guide had taken us a rong raod and we had to turn around and marched back several miles to where we had left the right road. We arrived at Fort Blakely about 5 o'clock PM but too late to take part in the assault ont the fort. As it had just been taken a short time before we got

13. J. William Avery from Cazenovia enlisted on August 13, 1862. James A. Lindsay was from Peoria and enlisted on August 14, 1862. Both were mustered out on July 10, 1865, Avery as corporal and Lindsay as private. *RH*, 47, 49; *AG*, 4:661.

14. Brig. Gen. Randall Gibson was able to escape with a portion of his command to the north via a treadway bridge over the Apalachee River to Battery Tracy. However, that fort would be evacuated on the night of April 11, 1865. Bergeron, *Confederate Mobile*, 188.

15. Torpedoes, or mines as they are now called, were first used by American forces during the Civil War. First appearing during the Peninsula Campaign in the spring of 1862, the mines, or "booby traps" as they were also called, consisted of artillery shells with percussion fuses that were buried. The torpedoes were designed to explode with the tread of marching feet or wagons rolling over them. Boatner, *Civil War Dictionary*, 470.

there. We were mean enough to feel glad that it happened as it did as we were not hungering for anymore of that kind of experience. The fight was rather short but hot while it lasted. The fort was a strong earthwork surrounded by a strong abatis of fallen trees, fallen with their tops from the fort and their limbs all turned up and sharpened and also three or four lines of shividefrize.[16] The ground around the fort was just litterly planted full of torpedoes. Gen Steele assaulted the works with three divisions two white and one colored troops.[17] Our loss was quite heavy as the rebels just mowed them down while they were making their way through the obstructions and a great many was blown up by the torpedoes. The colored troops so worked up by the time they got in the fort that their oficers couldn't control them. They set up yell, Remember Fort Pillow and were determined to do as the rebels had done with the colored troops at Fort Pillow. Kill them, surrender or no surrender! They had to bring up a division of white troops to stop them.[18] They took some 4000 prisoners which they marched out into the timber and placed the colored around them to guard them which made the darkeys feel pretty saussy. The rebels were very indignent at being subjected to such disgrace as they considered it and they seemed to be terable afraid of the darkeys. I supposed they knew that the darkeys didn't owe them much simpathy. Some of them discovered some of their old slaves among the colored

16. Chevaux-de-frise were logs about twelve feet long and ten inches thick, drilled through every foot at right angles for sharpened stakes which projected three feet. The purpose of this obstruction was to disrupt approaching lines of infantry. Jack Coggins, *Arms and Equipment of the Civil War* (Garden City: Doubleday, 1962), 102.

17. The assault was made by the First and Second Divisions of the Thirteenth Corps and by Brig. Gen. John P. Hawkins's division of colored troops. Most of these colored soldiers had been slaves on plantations in Louisiana, Mississippi, and Arkansas. Warner, *Generals in Blue*, 218–9; Boatner, *Civil War Dictionary*, 386–7.

18. Wiley refers to the Fort Pillow massacre on April 12, 1864, in which 231 Union soldiers were killed, 100 seriously wounded, and more than 200 captured by Confederates under Nathan Bedford Forrest. Evidence suggests that a large number of these Federal soldiers, many of whom were colored troops, were murdered in cold blood after they had surrendered. Wiley exaggerates the conduct of the black troops on this occasion, for there is no evidence to suggest that the black soldiers acted other than in accordance with the rules of war. Hawkins writes in his report, "The prisoners captured amounted to 21 officers and 200 men—a small number, owing to the fact that when we entered [the works] many of the enemy, fearing the conduct of my troops, ran over to the white troops entering." No violence was committed by the colored troops upon the prisoners of war. Boatner, *Civil War Dictionary*, 295–6; *OR*, vol. 49, pt. 1, p. 287.

soldiers and wanted to be friendly with them. I supposed they thought it was policy under the circumstances and they would come up to them and call them by name and offer to shake hands. But Sam and Tom etc. say stand back dar massa, Ise massa now. Gen Steele took some of the rebels out and made them take up the torpedoes.

April 10th
We remained at Fort Blakely. Wm Patton came to see us. He had just been commissioned Lieutenant and had on a fine new uniform and apulets. His brother Tom concluded that he was putting on too much dog and he concluded to take him down a peg. They had it hot for a while and William jumped on his horse and rode away. Some of us had a notion to kill Tom but he didn't care what we thought.[19]

April 11th
Our brigade started back to Spanish Forts at one Pm to relieve the first Brigade of the seckond division which had been left there. We arrived at Spanish Forts at 4 PM. On arriving there a lot of us was detailed to help plant some heavy guns to bear on a small sand fort the rebels still held out on a small island or sand bar out in the water.[20] We worked until 12 o'clock at night when we were ordered back to camp. When we arrived there we found the regiment in line ready to march to Coxes [Stark's] Landing on the bay some eight miles distant. We arrived at the landing at 3 AM where we went aboard the Boats. Companys C and H on the coaster Kate Dale and the ballance of the regiment on the transport J. M. Brown.

April 12th
The rest of our division came down from Fort Blakely and also the first division of the 13 Corps and went aboard the boats. At daylight we preceeded across the Bay and landed some five or six miles below the city of Mobile. We were on the same boat with the 23 Wisconsin which was

19. William Patton, originally of Company A, 47th Illinois, had been mustered out on December 17, 1864, following his exchange and release as a prisoner of war. On March 22, 1865, he was commissioned a lieutenant and served as quartermaster for the 47th Illinois (Consolidated). He was mustered out a second time on January 21, 1866. *AG*, 3:412, 436.

20. Wiley probably refers to Battery Huger, which was situated on the northern tip of Big Island where the Apalachee and Blakeley Rivers fork.

commanded by a German Major.[21] We were somewhat amused at the
Major as he went from company to company giving them their instructions. He would come to a company and Now poys you youst listen to
me whin we gets on shore you youst brake for de land. They were afraid
the rebels might attact us while we were landing and he wanted his men
to get ashore as quick as they could and form in line. Before we reached
the shore we could see a carriage coming from the city driven at a furious
gate carrying a white flag and we knew what that ment. The rebels had
evacuated the city and the mayor and the city authories came to surrender the city and ask protection.[22] Colonel Grier got the part of the regiment ashore from the Transport J. M. Brown and started for the city on
double quick and left orders for the companys C and H to follow up as
soon as we got ashore. But our boat not being a flat bottom like the
transports we could not get within twenty feet of shore and we could not
youst brake for de land until we constructed piers or foot walks to get
ashore on and we had to move then double quick it to catch up with the
rest of the regiment before they reached the city. But we made the race
and was the first regiment to enter the rebel works. They had a very
strong line of earth works around the city but could not have held out
long against our land and naval forces. The rebel gunboats and transports retreated up the Mobile and Tombigee Rivers. We found the forts
and city entirely deserted by the rebel army and the other troops coming
up we went into camp inside of the rebel works.

April 13th
Was cloudly with frequent showers. We skirmished around and captured
some vegetables and such things. Our division fell in line at 11 AM and
started for Whistler Station on the Mobile and Ohio Railroad some eight
miles distant where we arived at 1 PM and found a regiment of rebel
cavalry who were trying to get some rolling stock and rebel supplies away.
They tried to burn them at our approach but we did not give then time.
They retreated back across a stream a little ways from the station where

21. The 23d Wisconsin was commanded by Maj. Joseph E. Greene. It is likely that Wiley is
mistaken about either the man's rank or the regiment. *OR*, vol. 49, pt. 1, p. 197.
22. Mayor R. H. Slough replied to the Federal demand for surrender by writing: "The city
has been evacuated by the military authorities, and its municipal authority is now under my
control. Your demand has been granted, and I trust, gentlemen, for the sake of humanity, all
the safeguards which you can throw around our people will be secured to them." *RH*, 345.

they made a short stand behind a belt of timber where we had quite a little skirmish with them. They had retreated across the stream and set fire to the bridge but we drove them from the bridge and put out the fire. The 91 Illinois who were in the hotest of it had three men wounded.[23] We killed and wounded ten or twelve of the rebels. We had quite an open field to pass over before we reached the stream and the rebels rattled it to us pretty lively as they were sheltered behind the timber. Our Lietenant Colonel Reed got very much excited and was rushing us on in the face of the enemy without any loads in our guns except a few of us who had loaded as we run. When Colonel Grier who was commanding the Brigade but who always kept one eye on the regiment at such times came dashing up Colonel Colonel sais he don't get excited keep cool keep cool halt your men and have them load their guns. Never rush into a fight with empty guns. Colonel Reed looked like he was pretty badly sold out but he haulted the regiment and had them to load and on we went. But they gave way and retreated when we came close to them and we crossed over the stream and persued them for two or three miles. They broke up into squads and we could see squads off in different directions. They just kept out of our reach but didn't seem to know whether to retreat or come in and surrender. I suppose they felt that the war was realy over as Gen Lee had already surrendered his army of Northern Virginia to Gen Grant at Apomatox Virginia on the 9th of April.[24] And our little fight which we had at Whistler Station was the last fight of the war east of the Mississippi at least and we had begun to think that we could see the end not far off. We fell back to near the station and went into camp. After going into camp they issued us some commisary and some of the men wouldn't drink any and other took a double portion and got gloriously drunk. John Vanarsdall of Co K and some others got the Jim Jams [drunk] and yelled and howeled all night and some of us felt like geting up and shooting them.

23. Organized at Camp Butler, near Springfield, the 91st Illinois was mustered into Federal service on September 8, 1862. Captured en masse in December 1862 by John Hunt Morgan, the regiment was paroled immediately but not declared exchanged until June 1863. The most significant action in which the regiment participated was the operation against Mobile in early 1865. The unit was mustered out on July 12, 1865, and discharged from service at Chicago. Dyer, *Compendium*, 3:1085.

24. News of Lee's surrender did not reach Mobile until April 17.

April 14th

We moved our camp up near the station. I went on picket in the evening. Stood near the edge of the swamp.

April 15th

I was on picket during the day. I started on expedition out into the swamp to see what things looked like out in there. I made my way for some distance jumping from tusic to tusic and from root to root. It was all black colored water between. But I soon found snakes and other kinds of reptiles so plentiful that I concluded to retreat. Thinking that perhaps the solid ground was the healthiest place for a yank. I was relieved from picket duty in the evening. We got mail geting letters from home.

Sabath April 16th

We had the usual inspection at 9 AM and had some preaching by the chaplin at ten AM and 6-30 PM in the Methodist Church.

April 17th

We cleaned up our guns and equipment in the morning. There was a salute of two hundred at twelve o'clock for the down fall of the rebellion as Gen Lee had surrendered to Gen Grant on the 9th and Gen Johnson was stipulating with Gen Sherman for terms of surrender. A truce between them having been declared on the 14th. We got another mail in the evening.[25]

---

25. Sherman and Johnston met near Durham Station, N.C., and signed a "Memorandum or basis of agreement" on April 18 that called for an armistice. This rather curious document was rejected by the authorities in Washington, D.C., on April 24 and the truce was suspended. Johnston then requested a meeting with Sherman that took place at the Bennett House on April 26, and formal terms for capitulation were signed. E. B. Long, *The Civil War Day by Day* (New York: Doubleday, 1971), 678–83.

~ 12 ~

MUSTERED OUT

For all intents and purposes the war was over and a Union victory was secure. After three long years of army life, the men of the 77th perhaps only now entered the most anxious period of their arduous service—the wait to go home. The next several months passed agonizingly slowly for Wiley and his comrades as they waited for their final orders and mustering out.

April 18th
We got orders to be ready to march at 12 o'clock. A flag of truce came in at 10 AM. We got our traps packed and all ready for the march but the order was countermanded.

April 19th
Our division with the exception of the 28 Ill started on the march at 6 AM.[1] Marched some 10 miles up the Mobile River and went into camp for the night. We took considerably forrage by the way such as pigs chickens etc.

April 20th
We resumed the march at 5 AM. Marched some 15 miles. The roads were wet and swampy. We halted at a place called Cedar at 2 PM. Got the

1. The 28th Illinois was organized at Camp Butler, near Springfield, and mustered into Federal service on August 15, 1862. In July 1865, when the 77th was mustered out of service, the 28th Illinois was sent to Texas, where it remained until mustered out in March 1866. Dyer, *Compendium*, 3:1057.

bridge built by 6 PM. Crossed over and went into camp half a mile beond.

April 21th
Marched at 5 AM. It rained hard all day and we got soaken wet. We had to keep our ruber blankets around us to keep our amunition dry which kept us steaming hot. At one time when we were halted for a short time in the pine timber while the rain was coming down in sheets and we were all standing humped up with our backs to the storm like a lot of Texas steers with our hat rims turned down and our ruber blankets around us, every fellow thinking poor me. Wm Wright of company C, a member of the band raised a laugh by crying out in that shrill sharp voice of his, Let er rain theres no one out. After the rain slackened a little we continued the march going some 10 miles and camped for the night at Namnahuba [Nannahubba] Bluff on the Tombigbee River. Our clothes and blankets were soaking wet and we did not put in a very pleasant night. We laid down on the wet hillside and dug ditches around us to keep the water from running under us and laid until morning.

April 22th
We remained in camp. Some of the boys went out to a plantation belonging to a rebel captain and got alot of fresh pork, chicken, etc.

Sabath April 23th
Clear and pleasant. We were ordered to be ready for general inspection at 9 AM but were not inspected. We got the sad news during the day [of] President Lincoln's assassination. It raised a terable feeling of indignation in the regiment as Abraham Lincoln occupied a chief place in every true soldiers heart. A dirg was played at each regiment headquarters and the flags were all drooped or placed at half mast. There was a lot of rebel deserters in camp as they kept deserting and coming in everyday. When they heard the news of Lincoln assassination and seen the excitement among our soliders they looked pretty badly scared perhaps were afraid the soldiers might retalaite on them. They condemned the act in strong language. We supposed they done so for effect but perhaps some were cincere.[2]

2. President Lincoln had been shot by John Wilkes Booth on April 14 while attending a play at Ford's Theatre in Washington. He died the following morning.

April 24th
I went on picket at 9 AM. The day was very pleasant.

April 25th
I came in off picket at 9 AM. We got orders to be ready to march the next morning at 6 AM.

April 26th
Marched at 6 AM. Our brigade guarding the train through to McIntosh Landing on the Tombigbee a distance of 10 miles where we arrived at 2 PM and went into camp about a half a mile from the landing. We gather in considerable forage by the way and fared suntuasly [sumptuously].

April 27th
We remained in camp. The weather was pretty warm and expection to remain there some days. We got brush and made shades over our tents.

April 28th
We remained in camp. Captain [James] Secord and a squad of volunteers from our regiment went up the river some four or five miles in skiffs to try to capture some Jahockers who had been making their headquarters on a small island but didn't find them at home.[3]

April 29th
Our brigade started out on a foraging expedition. We marched out some 15 miles and encamped for the night. Shortly before going into camp in passing a small house quite an old lady came out carrying a small union flag. Some of our oficers rode up to the fence to speak to her and she pointed out a large house up the road aways where she said an old Dr lived who had been a rebel conscripting oficer and that he had come to their house sometime before to try to fource her son to go into the rebel army and that her son being a union man had refused to go and this Dr

3. Capt. James K. Secord of Yates City had been mustered in as second lieutenant of Company F on September 18, 1862. On July 2, 1863, he was promoted to first lieutenant; one year later he was elevated to the rank of captain. He was mustered out at that rank on July 10, 1865. *RH*, 63–4; *AG*, 4:668.

had shot him killing him before her eyes. After going into camp the oficers made inquiries of the darkeys and found that the old ladies tale was
all true.

April 30th
We started back to camp at 5 AM. When we all got back oposite the old
Dr's place, Colonel Grier halted the brigade with our regiment just oposite the Dr's house. The boys knowing what that meant a lot of them soon
scattered off and was soon confiscating whatever they could find in the
way of pigs, chickens, turkeys, geese etc. and some got into his smoke-
house and carried off his bacon. Colonel Grier had rode off some distance from the house and was setting on his horse very unconcerned as
if he did not know anything about what was going on. The old Dr came
out and enquired for the commanding oficer. The under oficers sent him
around here and there where they told him they thought he would find
the commanding oficer. But simply to give the boys time to get in their
work. But after quite a search he found Colonel Grier and laid in his
complaint that his men was trespassing on his property and carrying off
everything they could get a hold of and demanded protection. The Colonel let on to be very much surprised to think his men would interfere
with the Dr property and turning to an oficer near by told him to take a
guard and go and drive those men out of the Dr's premises and not allow
them to interfere with anything. But gave the order in a way that the
oficer knew how to take it. The oficer proceeded in a very leasurly maner
to detail they guard and march them down to the Dr's house and ordered
the boys in a very preemtory maner to get out of there and not to interfere with anything about there and would chase after one squad of boys
while the others were helping themselves and then would chase some of
the rest while them ones loaded up and thus it went until the colonel
thinking they had cleaned him out pretty hard had the bugler to blow in
fall in call and the boys fell in line and we marched off and each of the
guards came back with a ham of a side of bacon on their beyonett. We
marched back to McIntosh landing. The 23 Wisconsin[4] was deployed out
on each side of the road to act as Jahockers to gather up and drive in all

---

4. The 23d Wisconsin was organized in Madison and mustered into service on August 30,
1862. The service of this regiment mirrored that of the 77th Illinois, and the soldiers from
Wisconsin were mustered out on July 4, 1865. Dyer, *Compendium*, 3:1683.

the stock they could find and they brought in a pretty good drove and the teams were loaded with forrage. We arrived at camp at 3 PM and mustered for pay at 4 PM.

May 1st
We remained in camp and rested wrote letters, etc.

May 2nd
We remained in camp. I was taken sick with malarial feavor.

May 3rd
I was still quite sick dosed heavy with quimine sinconia etc.[5]

May 4th
Had but little feavor. The regiment went up the river in a Transport to get corn for the teams. Signed the pay rolls in the evening.

May 5th
I had no feavor. We were paid six months pay during the day.

May 6th
A national salute was fired on account of the surender of the department of the Gulf by the rebels to Gen E. R. S. Canby.*[6] All hostilities was ordered to cease and we felt our work was done.

Sabath May 7th
Was appointed by Gen Canby as a day of thanksgiving and prayers. Thanksgiving for past victories and prayers for a special blessing on the families of fallen comrades. All the Confederate property being surrendered to the government. The rebel fleet which had been run up the Tombigbee River to Demololis [Demopolis] consisting of 17 transports, one gunboat and two rams was brought down to McIntosh landing and turned over to us.[7]

5. Quinine was the standard treatment for malaria.
6. Maj. Gen. Edward R. S. Canby received the surrender of Lt. Gen. Richard Taylor at Citronelle, Ala., on May 4, 1865.
7. Among the vessels turned over to the Federals were *Cherokee, St. Nicholas, Reindeer, Admiral, Dorrance, Jeff Davis, Marengo, Sumter, Waverly, Watson, Magnolia,* and *Duke. RH,* 349–50.

May 8th

Our regiment was detailed to load wood and rosin onto the rebel boats to run them to Mobile.

May 9th

Our division was ordered aboard the rebel boats. We got all aboard and started down the river for Mobile at 12-30 PM. Arrived at Mobile about sundown. The 77 was on the headquarters boat Cherokee. Our capture fleet made quite a display as we sailed down into the bay with our twenty boats. We took a circle around the bay in front of the city. Our flagship in advance and all the others following with bands playing flags flying and men cheering at the top of their voice. After these girations were over with our boats we sailed up to the wharf and was turned over to Uncle Sam. But he didn't reward us with half the prize money as he does with the Navy but we had to take our share in glory so we went ashore and marched out through the city and some two miles to the North and went into camp on Three Miles Creek at 10 PM.

May 10th

Arranged our camp in regular order of regiment brigade and division. Our position being just east of the wagon road running north from the city. I was taken sick with feavor again. Was pretty sick for a few days.

May 11th

We got orders to prepare for an expedition to Texas as the Trans Mississippi department under the command of Gen Kirby Smith had not surrender.[8] We were ordered to draw two pairs of shoes a piece and other clothing sufficient for a two month campaign. All sick not able to stand hard service to be left behind. It is unecessary to say that we were not pleased with this order as we had thought that our campaigning was done. But was rather expecting soon to be ordered to Illinois to be mustered out of the service and this order put quite a damper on our spirits and particularly so with myself as our doctors decided that I would not

8. The Confederate forces under Kirby Smith surrendered to Canby on June 2, 1865. Boatner, *Civil War Dictionary*, 770.

be able to go with the regiment but would have to be left behind or as the report was that those not able to go would be mustered out and sent home and as I had been with the regiment continuously for almost three years and the end seemed so near. I didn't relish the ideah of being seper- ated from the regiment at that time but wanted to remain and go home with the regiment. I tried to persude the doctors to let me go with the regiment and take my chances but I couldn't work them. They said the orders were posative and they tryed to persude me that I had better just submit to be mustered out and go home as I might then regain my health. But if I under took to go with the regiment in the condition I was in I would very likely lose my life. They apreciated my feelings but that would be their advice. I knew that the doctors were right as my health seemed to be compeletly broke down but somehow I felt like I could not make up my mind to submit and as luck or higher power ruled it I did not have to do so.

May 12th
It was clear and cool. Lieutenant Dewey of our company started for New Orleans.[9] We kept hearing all kinds of reports such as that Kirby Smith had surrendered. We had all our unserviceable camp and garrison equi- page condemed to be turned over and sent in requisitions for new camp and garrison equipage clothing, etc.

May 13th
Clear and cool. All the sick not able to go home was sent to the general hospilte at New Orleans. The seckond division of our 13 corps came down from Selma Ala. A transport was burned on the Mobile River near the city.

Sabath May 14th
We had inspection at 9 A.M. The 83 Ohio and 37 Ills. came down from Selma.[10] The rebel soldiers were coming in from all directions. A great

9. The reader will recall that 1st Lt. Edward S. Dewey had been adjutant of the 130th Illinois and came to command Company C of the 77th following consolidation of the two regiments in January 1865.

10. The 83d Ohio, which had served in the same division as the 77th Illinois for much of the war, had been organized at Camp Dennison and mustered into service in August 1862. Consolidated with the 48th Ohio in January 1865, the veterans were mustered out on July 24,

many came a foot and every train that came in on the Mobile and Ohio RR. The tops of the cars would be covered with them. The most of them looked pretty sad. They looked pretty badly used up. Their old butternut clothes were all in rags. They felt very different from what we did. They had staked there all and lost it and were beating there way back as a vanquished army to desolate homes and were expecting soon to return as a conquering host to pleasant homes.

May 15th
We got orders to be ready to march at an hour notice but did not march. We drew some clothing in the evening.

May 16th
We received word of the capture of Jeff Davis in his wifes peticoat. We also heard a rumor that Kirby Smith was assasinated by his own men.[11]

May 17th
Some men of our regiment was courtmartialed for being absent without leave. They had gone into the city and got on a spree and forgot to report for two or three days.

May 18th
A lot of the men of Company F got on a drunk and became mutinous and cursed and threatened their officers at terable rate, Captain Secord was very patient with the poor drunk fools and got the other men to go and talk to them and try to quiet them and tell them what trouble they would get themselves into but they were too drunk to listen to reason. But they got worse and howled and yelled and carried on until Captain Secord had to order out a guard and have some of the worst of them tied

---

1865. The 37th Illinois, also known as the Fremont Rifles, had been organized at Chicago and mustered into Federal service on September 18, 1861. Veterans of Pea Ridge, Vicksburg, and the operations around Mobile, the regiment later moved to Texas (as Wiley feared would happen to the 77th) and was not mustered out until May 15, 1866. Dyer, *Compendium*, 3:1535, 1062.

11. Jefferson Davis, president of the Confederate States of America, had been captured on May 10, 1865, at Irwinville, Ga. Contrary to the rumors which circulated throughout the camp of the 77th Illinois, Davis was not wearing his wife's petticoat.

up. Some of them were tried by courtmartial and sent to the dry tortigas [Tortugas] when they might have been on their way home if they had let whiskey alone and behaved themselves but they could blame no one but themselves. We thought it looked pretty hard for the poor foolish creatures after serving their country faithfully for three long years and just on the eve of being honorably discharged to bring such trouble on themselves and in place of going home with their regiment to be condemned to hard labor on the dry tortugas for six months. It was a pretty strong temperance lesson for some others.

May 19th
The 50th Indiana started for Montgomery Ala.[12] We drew some more clothing in the evening.

May 20th
The rumers about being sent to Texas began to subside and we began to feel in hopes that the regiment would not have to go. We knew that some of our officers were doing all they could to keep us from being sent there. Some of our officers had gone to New Orleans and we knew pretty well that their mission was to use their infuence at headquarters in our behalf and as some of them had been detailed at headquarters while we were quartered in the city. We felt pretty sure that they would suceed in their undertaking.

Sabath May 21th
We had the usual inspection at 9 AM and dress parade at 6 PM. Preaching at 10.

May 22th
Clear and warm. Our camp was a very pleasant one. We were about two miles from the city of Mobile and about one mile from the Mobile River

12. The 50th Indiana Infantry had been organized at Seymour and mustered into Federal service on September 12, 1861. The bulk of the regiment had been captured at Munfordville, Ky., on September 17, 1862. Paroled and sent to Indianapolis, the regiment returned to the field later that year. The regiment's most significant action came during the siege of Spanish Fort and Fort Blakely. On May 25, 1865, the men were consolidated with the 52d Indiana Infantry. Dyer, *Compendium*, 3:1138–9.

and some 40 or 50 rods from Three Mile Creek. Which was simply a bayou at that place being filled with back water from the bay and colored by the water which ran into it from a wide swamp which lay between our camp and the city. The water was as dark as the water that drains from an old strawstack or the ley that our mothers used to filter through ash hopers and the creek and joining swamp was a regular aligator paradise.

May 23th
Clear and pleasant. Our duty was now very light. Simply a little guard and fatigue duty as we did not keep regular picket gards out anymore as hostilities had creased. We just had some cavelry outposts and we did not do much drilling only what was considered necessary for our good in the way of exercise. We had company drill in the cool of the morning and dress parade in the evening.

May 24th
Clear and warm. We had company drill at 7 AM and dress parade at 6 PM. The men not having enough to do the sporty ones got to sliping off as soon as drill was over and going to the city and staying there until time for dress parade in the evening. Some would as the boys expressed it get to much Benzene [alcohol] aboard and forget to come back for dress parade.

May 25th
Clear and warm. We had our usual drill and dress parade. At two PM a terable explosion took place in the city. The government had a large anount of ammunition stored in a large warehouse in the northeast part of the city among other stores was some thirty tons of gunpowder and this became ignited by some unknown means. The concussion was so great that it destroyed nine blocks of the city and of the block in which the building was situated there was not a whole brick left. There was supposed to be several hundred lives lost besides perhaps as many horses and mules. We were something over to miles and the concussion nearly took the tops of our heads off. It was sometime before we got over the effect of the jar. We ran out of our tents as quick as we could gather

ourselves together and looked towards the city and the whole air was filled with bricks timbers boards and everything else which continued to go up for sometime after we ran out before it started down again and shell from the building was thrown in all directions over the city crashing through house roofs and a great many of them exploded in the buildings and streets. One transport on the bay oposite was destroyed and two others badly damaged. The city was full of disbanded rebel soldiers on their way to their homes and there was no means of telling how many of them was killed. As it happened the building was in what was called the warehouse district and was not near the residence part of the town. There was many conjectures as to how the explosion happened but it was only conjecture as there was no one left anywhere near to tell the tale. Some supposed that some of the returning rebels had done it through spite but we thought if he did he would not have the fun of telling the joke. As soon after as I could get a pass i went down to see the ruins. It was a fearful sight to behold. The dead bodies of the men had been gathered up but the dead horses and mules were laying all around and arms and legs and pieces of men and animals was laying everywhere among the ruins and shreds of flesh was sticking to the walls and build-ings all around. We concluded that the Allmighty must have thought that Mobile had gotten off too easy and had concluded to try his hand on her. One of our company Wm Avery was down in the city at the time with one of the comisary teams and him and his team had a very narrow escape.[13]

May 26th
The weather was getting quite warm. We went swimming almost every day either on Three Mile Creek or the Mobile River. The boys at first had their gimnasium at a place on Three Mile Creek near the bridge where they had a spring board fastened in the roots of a tree and extend-ing out over the water and they would run out onto this spring board one after another and give a spring and jump away up in the air and come down into the water head first and dive out of the way of the next man and some of the more daring would get up on the railing of the bridge and jump off a distance of some fifteen or twenty feet and come down into the water head first.

13. Fortunately there were few soldier or civilian casualties in this explosion, which was similar to the one Wiley describes at Vicksburg aboard the *City of Madison.*

May 27th

Clear and warm. We had inspection and drill at 7 AM and dress parade at 6 PM and swimming and gimnastics in the meantime. We kept up our gimnastics at the creek until a big aligator bobed up among a lot of the boys while they were in the water and came near geting his clamp on some of them and then there was a lively scramboing for the shorer and then we transferred our base of operations to the Mobile River where there had been a steamboat near the shore where the water was clearer and we thought we could see the aligators before they got quite so close. The fool boys didn't seem to relish the ideah of diving down into the old fellow big mouth.

Sabath May 28th

We had inspection at 9 AM. Preaching at 10 AM in the shade of the big live oaks near our camp and dress parade at 6 PM.

May 29th

I was detailed for camp gard. The rougher class of men had got to sliping off from camp every day and going into the city and geting drunk and geting into all kinds of trouble. Sometimes alot of them would come back to camp drunk and howl and yell all night so that no one could sleep. Gen Benton concluded to stop it so he ordered each regiment to place a camp guard around their camp and not alow a man to go outside without a pass. But we thought it was too much like punishing the innocent on account of a few mean ones and we concluded it was to late in service for camp guards. Our regimental officers felt about as we did but the genral ordered them to put the gards and they had to obey. So we went on gard and walked our beats in regular order but when we seen any one coming that looked like they wanted out we would turn and walk the other way and forget to look around until they got away. The general got very much out of humor and threaten the officers and gards and everybody if they didn't abey his orders but it didn't do any good. We would stand guard all he wanted us to but that was all we would do. Some of the more reckless of the boys broke up some cartridges and put the powder in an old canteen and sliped over to the general's tent when he was asleep and sliped it under the edge of his tent and fired the fuse and sliped away and let it go off and woke the Gen up sudden. He threatened pretty strong what he would do if he found out who done it but the boys exploded several more around his tent before morning. The General concluded that a camp guard had ceased to be a sucess and didn't order anymore.

May 30th

We had inspection and drill at 7 AM and dress parade at 6 PM. Went a swimming in the afternoon in the Mobile River. We got a long two inch plank at an old sawmill and carried it over to our sunken boat and put one end of it through the hatchway in other end out over the side of the boat and was prepared for our gimnastics again. The ground between our camp and the river was studed with large live oaktrees and was a beautiful place to lounge on our blankets in the shade those hot days and read and write etc.

May 31th

Colonel Reed of our regiment started for New Orleans. That day several regiments embarked for Texas.

June 1st

Capt McCullock and some other oficers of our regiment who had been released from the rebel prison [Camp Ford] at Tiler [Tyler] Texas came to the regiment. We were rejoised to see them once more as they had been taken prisoner something over a year before. The rest of those from our regiment who had been taken prisoner at that time were then in New Orleans.[14]

June 2nd

Had no drill went swimming in Mobile River in the afternoon.

June 3rd

Had grand review in the city of Mobile by General Gordon Granger in honor of Chief Justice [Salmon P.] Chase* who was then visting Mobile. The day was very warm and the roads and streets very dusty and strange as it may appear. We did not seem to enjoy it as much as the spectators.

14. The men who had been captured during the Red River campaign and had survived the hellish conditions at Camp Ford near Tyler, Tex., were mustered out of service on June 17, 1865, shortly after they rejoined the regiment. *RH,* 369.

The streets were lined with citizens returned rebels etc., all whom seemed to enjoy our performance very much even the Johnnies seemed to enjoy that performances better than they had some of our performances on other days. When we got back to camp we were so begrimed with dust and sweat that we made a sorry apperance and were ready for the wash-tub and the bath. The troops on this occasion were under the immediate command of Col Grier of our regiment who was then a brvet brigadier general.[15]

Sabath June 4th
Inspection at 9 AM and preaching at 10 AM and

June 5th
Clear and warm had no drill went swimming.

June 6th
Clear and warm. Orders came from the War Department to muster out all men whos time expired by the 1st of October.

June 7th
Still very warm. Went blackberrying in the forenoon. The ground between our camp and the city was a vast swamp in which the timber had all been cut down at the begining of the war and was a great place for blackberries which we took care of in their season. Some of the more enterprizing men of the regiment got brick mud etc and built ovens and procuring flur and other materials from the city and baked our berries into pies for us on the shares and we had lots of tough pies with our army rations.

June 8th
Drill at 7 AM. The day was clear and very warm.

June 9th
Drill at 7 AM. Went berrying in the afternoon. Had dress parade at 6 PM. The adutant read report of cortmartial. Two of 77 Ill formerly 130

15. Colonel Grier was promoted to brevet brigadier general on March 26, 1865, "for faithful and meritorious services during the campaign against the city of Mobile and its defenses." Roger D. Hunt and Jack R. Brown, *Brevet Brigadier Generals in Blue* (Gaithersburg, Md.: Olde Soldier Books, 1990), 244.

Ill was sentanced to hard labor at Fort Jefferson Florida for 3 months and one for 2 months. With the loss of three months pay each. And one formly 130 to ten days hard labor in camp with the loss of two months pay. We thought poor fools rather dear whiskey to you.

June 10th
Drill at 7 AM. Cleaned guns etc during the day. Went swimming in the afternoon. Dress parade at 6 PM. Further report of cortmatrial read. Two others of Co F 77 Reg Ill were sentanced to 3 months hard labor at Fort Jefferson with the loss of three months pay.

Sabath June 11th
Inspection at 8 AM. Preaching at 9 AM in the shade of live oak trees.

June 12th
Was very warm. I was on guard at divison QM [quartermaster] department.

June 13th
Came off guard at 7 AM. Went berrying in the afternoon.

June 14th
It rained nearly all day. Laid in pup tents to keep dry.

June 15th
Rained all night and for part of the day. Went to the swamp for berries in the afternoon.

June 16th
Cloudly and threatening rain all day. Had company inspection at 8 AM and general inspection at 9 AM.

June 17th
Clear and hot. Done some washing in the forenoon and went to the swamp for berries in the afternoon.

Sabath June 18th
Inspection at 8 AM and preaching at 9 AM.

June 19th
Drill at 8 AM. Built shades over our dog tents in the afternoon.

June 20th
Drill at 7 AM. Washed some clothes in the forenoon. Went berrying in the afternoon. Colonel Grier started for New Orleans at 1 PM.

June 21th
Drill at 7 AM. Went swimming in Mobile River that afternoon.

June 22th
I officiated as cook for mess 3 during the day.

June 23th
I was on the sick list. Drill at 7 AM. Wm McCollister the sulters clerk died at 12 PM of conjestive feavor.

June 24th
I was on guard at divison headquarters. Wm McCollister was burried at 9 AM.

Sabath June 25th
Came off guard at 7 AM. Inspection at 8 AM. Storm in the evening with heavy wind and rain.

June 26th
Drill at 7 AM. Went berrying in the afternoon. Lieutenant [Merritt M.] Clark of Company A returned from New Orleans. Lieutenant [Thomas C.] Mathews of Company I was presented with a fine sword by his company. Jacob Snider [Snyder] made the presentation speech.[16]

16. First Lt. Merritt M. Clark of Galesburg had been mustered into service as a second lieutenant on September 2, 1862. Promoted to first lieutenant on February 2, 1864, he served in that rank until mustered out on July 10, 1865. Thomas G. Mathews of Salem had been mustered in as sergeant in Company I on August 14, 1862. He was promoted to second lieutenant on

June 27th

Drill at 7 AM. Some of company H who had been absent over night came back to camp in a hilarious condition and had a little bedlum of their own and were put under guard for a change. Went swimming in Three Mile Creek in the evening.

June 28th

Done some washing in the morning. That day we got our muster rolls preparitory to being mustered out which made us feel that our soldiering was soon to end.

June 29th

Drill at 7 AM. Done considerable writing during the day.

June 30th

Inspection and muster at 9 AM. Weather very warm.

July 1st

It rained hard during the day. Orders came to mustered out all men whos time expired on or before September 1st. That just missed us by a couple of days as our time would expire on Sept 2nd but Colonel Grier being in New Orleans got a special order from General Sheridan to have the 77 mustered out.[17] We thought our old man was doing pretty well by us as he had suceeded in keeping us from being sent to Texas and had now got a special order for our muster out. Altho we were aware that he had a little personal interest in the matter as he had a new wife waiting for him up in Illinois. An order also came to reinstate the 130 Ill which regiment had been consolidated with the 77 some months before. Their time

---

June 22, 1863, and to first lieutenant on January 22, 1864. Mathews was promoted to captain in Company D, 130th Illinois, when the 77th Illinois was mustered out of service but only briefly served in that rank; he was mustered out on August 15, 1862. Jacob H. Snyder of Elmwood entered service on August 14, 1862, serving as a musician. He was mustered out with the regiment on July 10, 1865. *RH*, 35, 81–3; *AG*, 4:655, 676–7.

17. Maj. Gen. Philip H. Sheridan had been sent from Virginia, where he helped Grant defeat Lee, to Texas, forcing Napoleon III of France to withdraw his support of Maximilian in Mexico. He remained in the South and was named military governor of Texas and Louisiana. Warner, *Generals in Blue*, 437–9; Boatner, *Civil War Dictionary*, 747–8.

not having expired they were to be reinstated as the 130 Ill and all the recruits in the 77 was to be transferred to that regiment.

Sabath July 2nd
Clear and hot. Had preaching at 9 AM and at 7 PM.

July 3rd
Very warm. J. S. Wedley of company C was arrested and put under guard for shooting woodchucks and Homer Higby of Company D for being drunk on guard. [William] Stitler of Company A who was wagon master was arrested and taken to headquarters for assaulting a negro.[18]

July 4th
The regiment was marched to division headquarters to hear a Fourth of July speech by Gen Benton. He made us quite a speech telling us among other good things about one time he knew a slodier to out rank a mule. He said the spring before he was coming from New Orleans to Fort Morgan the ship on which he was on was caught in a terable storm and being very heavily loaded was liken to go down. When they began to throw overboard wagon grain and everything in attempt to ligthen the ship but the storm increasing in fury they began to throw the mules overboard. When he said he noticed a soldier standing off to one side looking very serious and after sometime he said well B G—d this the first time I ever knew a soldier to outrank a mule.

July 5th
The 23th Wisconsin of our brigade being mustered out started for home. We went swimming in the afternoon.

July 6th
Was very warm. We spent the day in camp waiting orders to muster out. There being a great deal of writing to do in making out rolls, discharge papers,etc. A good many men were detailed to assist with the writing.

18. James H. Wedley of Woodford County enlisted on September 27, 1862, and was mustered out on July 10, 1865. Homer H. Higbie from Elmwood served with Company I, not D, as stated by Wiley. He joined the regiment on August 14, 1862, and was mustered out on July 10, 1865. William Stiteler of Knoxville entered service on August 7, 1862, and was quickly elevated to quartermaster sergeant. He evidently performed poorly, as he was returned to the company, where he served until the regiment was mustered out. *RH*, 36, 52, 84; *AG*, 4:656, 662, 676.

July 7th
Clear and warm. I went to the city in the afternoon and went on guard
at Brigade Headquarters at 6 PM. The 96th Ohio was mustered out in
the afternoon.

July 8th
The 96th Ohio started for home at 12-30.

Sabath July 9th
Preaching at 9 AM. The mustering oficer inspected our books and papers
preparatory to mustering us out.

❧ 13 ❧

Going Home

The long-awaited day finally came, and Wiley and his comrades formed ranks to be mustered out of Federal service. Although it was a joyous occasion, a pall hung over the troops as the men reflected on their comrades who lived only in memory. They were haunted by the faces that they recalled, those of men such as George A. Hart, the first man of Company C to die, who succumbed to typhoid before the regiment even left Illinois; of James Vanarsdall, who fell victim to measles and died in an army hospital in Memphis in 1863; of James Drake and James H. Drennan, both of whom were cut down in the bloody assault against Railroad Redoubt at Vicksburg; of the gallant lieutenant colonel Lysander Webb, whose life came to a tragic end at Mansfield; and scores of others like them who sacrificed their lives on the altar of freedom. Theirs were the faces of the young and the not so young, some clean-shaven, others hidden by heavy beards. Wiley could well remember their smiles and laughter, the fears that they confided to one another, and the pride that they felt at being soldiers of the Republic. He was touched by each and every one of them and for the remainder of his long life would remember them fondly.

Thus sadly reduced in numbers, the 77th Illinois headed northward. We join William Wiley on that journey home.

July 10th 1865
The 77 Regiment Ill Vol Inft was mustered out of the United States service at one PM. The members of the band were presented with their instru-

ments by adutant H. P. Ayres in the name of the regiment.[1] This was a
day that we had long looked forward to when we could feel that our work
which we had enlisted to do was done and we could lay down our arms
and return to our homes and we felt hapy in the thought that our work
was well done. We had nothing to be ashamed of. We had done well our
part in atchieving a glorious victory in preserving and strengthing our
institutions and restoring peace to our land and felt hapy in the thought
of soon returning to our homes and friends from whom we had been
seperated for 3 long weary years. But yet we could not keep a feeling of
sadness at the thought of breaking up our organization and seperating
perhaps many of us never to meet again. As there is a strong bond of
friendship ataches between soldiers after a three years campaigning together cemented by mutual experiences hardships and deprivations
which no one could fully apreciate but those that had experienced them.
There was a good many of our comrades who had come to us as recruits
during our terms of service as well as those from the 130 Ill who had
associated with us for some months who would have to remain behind.[2]

July 11th
The 91 Ill was mustered out. We remained in camp awaiting transport-
ion. Went swimming in the evening as a kind of farewell to the old Mobile River.

July 12th
Reveilee at 4 AM. Got breakfast. Swung knapsacks and what was left of
the original 77 fell into line for the homeward march. There was hardly
enough of us to form one company. A small number compared with the
nine hundred and over which we marched away from Camp Lions at
Peoria Ill about three years before whos graves marked our pathway from
Memphis to Mobile. Biding good bie to those we were to leave behind
and with cheers for those remaining and counter cheers for those starting
for home. We marched down to the landing in the city and embarked

1. Henry P. Ayres from Galesburg had enlisted as a private on August 5, 1862, but one month
later was mustered in as corporal in Company A. Promoted to sergeant major on January 14,
1863, he was elevated to first lieutenant on May 15 of that same year and was named adjutant.
He served as A.A.A.G. on both the brigade and division levels but was mustered out with the
regiment on July 10, 1865. *RH*, 32; *AG*, 4:654–5.
2. The men of the 130th Illinois were mustered out on August 15, 1865.

on the Transport White Cloud for New Orleans. The 91 Ill and 19 Iowa embarked on the same boat. The 77 had the upper deck the 91 Ill the middle deck and the 19 Iowa the lower. The lower deck where the Iowans were stowed not being quite full the officers in charge of the transportation ordered 40 or 50 mules to be put aboard.[3] But the foolish Iowans thinking perhaps since they were mustered out of Uncle Sams service that like Gen Benton's man they did out rank a mule they refused to ride with the mules. But the officers had the mules put aboard then the Iowans got their western blood up and swore that if they didn't take the mules off they would put them overboard. But the officers refused to take them off and the Iowans put on their bayonetts and drove the mules off in a hurry the officers and their men having to run to keep out of the way of the mules. Then our fool boys and the 91st cheered the Iowa boys which made the officers still mader and they sent some other troops aboard to keep the Iowa boys back while they put the mules aboard again. The boys knowing that the guards had to obey orders and not wanting to fued with them they fell back until the mules were put aboard again and a lot of the Iowa boys surrounded the guards and told them to keep still and the rest of them put the mules off again. Then the officers sent a whole regiment aboard and had them to load their guns and ordered them to shoot down the first man that interferred. Things began to look pretty blustery down on the lower deck about this time. Both parties seemed determined not to give in. The colonel of the Iowa regiment [John Bruce] ordered his men into line and marched them off of the boat and told the transportation officers to put the d———m mules on if they wanted to that they would wait for another boat.[4] So that settled the mule question and the mules had the lower deck all to themselves. But in the meelee runing the mules on and off they broke what is called the hogchain of the boat which is a strong iron rod which runs from the brow to the stern of the boat and up over the main deck to support the

3. Bentley gives the number of horses and mules as five hundred. *RH*, 378.

4. Col. John Bruce, a native of Stirlingshire, Scotland, who resided in Keokuk at the outbreak of civil war, enlisted on August 17, 1862, and was mustered in as captain of Company A. Promoted to major five months later, Bruce was elevated to lieutenant colonel on March 10, 1864, and in July of 1865 became colonel of the regiment. For "gallant and meritorious services during the war," he was brevetted brigadier general and mustered out of service on July 10, 1865. *Roster and Record of Iowa Soldiers in the War of the Rebellion*, 6 vols. (Des Moines, 1908–11), 3:237, 241; Hunt and Brown, *Brevet Brigadier Generals in Blue*, 87.

ends of the boat. This breaking let the ends of the boat sink down leaving great cracks through caben in the center of the boat. We didn't think the old craft looked very safe in that condition to start out to sea in. But soldiers were cheap then the war was over and they had no farther use for us so they sent us a drift in our crippled boat at 2 PM. We passed down the Bay and out through Grants Pass into the Mississippi Sounds about sundown keeping as close to shore as it was safe on account of the condition of our boat. About 7 PM there was a strong appearance of a storm arising and ran in as close to shore as we could and cast anchor. The squall didn't amount to much but soon passed by but the sailors seemed to be badly scared. I supposed they knew the danger better then we. When the squall was coming up the soldiers who gotten pretty near past being scared at anything were laughing and joking as usual. When an old Irish sailor stoped and looked at some of them and said you damed fools don't you see that storm coming if it strikes us we will all go to hell in a minit. Some fool soldier answered back O let er come were here first. The old sailor remarked poor damn fools and went on about his business. The storm having passed we weighed anchor at about midnight and passed on our way.

July 13th
Passed Ship Island and pass Cagoula [Pascagoula] at daylight and Fort Pike[5] at 10-30 and arived at Haycock Landing on Lake Ponchartrain at 2 PM where we disinbarked and took the train for New Orleans where we arived about 3 PM and went aboard the Lady Franklin at the lower leavy where we left our traps and spent the evening stroling around through the city where we spent the winter before. Some of the boys got on a bum and got run in. Some of them tried to resist the police and got pretty well pummeled with the billy.

July 14th
We remained at New Orleans until 11-30. That forenoon the old union flag which had been pulled down from the Custom House at the breaking

5. Situated at the entrance to Lake Pontchartrain, Fort Pike was named in honor of Zebulon Pike, for whom Pike's Peak is also named. Construction of the fort began in 1818 and was completed in 1827. The fort had a maximum capacity to mount 48 cannon but during the Civil War held fewer than that number. Oral interview with Ed Smith, park historian, November 13, 1998.

out of the war having been found again was raised over the building with appropriate ceremonies and our regimental band had the honor of making the music for the occassion.[6] At 11-30 AM we started on up the Mississippi River. Our boat was a very slow craft.

July 15th

At 7 AM we arived at Batonrouge La. where we had spent some two months in 1864 where we stoped for a short time. Our boat had orders to take on 100 men of the 11 Ill Inft at Batonrouge but other arangements having been made for their accomdations we went on without them. Passing Port Hudson the scene of Gen Banks great siege in 1863 at 12 PM and Morganza Bend where we had camped for a short time in the fall of 1864 at 2 PM and the mouth of Red River up whos winding course we had some varied experiences the spring of 1864 at about dark.[7]

Sabath July 16th

We passed Nachez at 6 AM and Grand Gulf at 3-30 PM where Gen Grants army crossed the Mississippi River on the march around Vickburg in the spring of 1863. That night we had to lay low on account of fog.[8]

July 17th

We arived at Vicksburg at 9 AM. This was an interesting place to us. It was the scene of our first and greatest campaign where we had endured so many hardships during the winter spring and summer of 1863 and where lay burried so many of our comrades. The sight of the place brought back to us the memory of all these scenes. The weary march the

6. The Custom House had been seized by state forces in January 1861. On April 29, 1862, Flag Officer David Glasgow Farragut, whose ships of the West Gulf Blockading Squadron compelled the surrender of New Orleans, took possession of the building for the United States and raised the Stars and Stripes. The flag that had flown over the building in 1861 was later located and was raised in the formal ceremony described here by Wiley. Charles L. Dufour, *The Night the War Was Lost* (Garden City: Doubleday, 1960), 27, 327.

7. The siege of Port Hudson extended from May 23 to July 9, 1863, when the Confederate garrison under Maj. Gen. Franklin Gardner surrendered to Banks. Union victory at Port Hudson, coupled with Grant's victory at Vicksburg, gave the North undisputed control of the Mississippi River.

8. Wiley is in error. Although Grand Gulf was Grant's desired landing site for the inland campaign against Vicksburg, Union forces were unable to silence the forts there. The Union commander moved farther south and crossed the Mississippi River at Bruinsburg.

hard fought battles and the tiresome siege. This was one of the rebels most important strongholds and they defended it stubbornly and to the bitter end until their last mule was eaten up and fought us from both front and rear. Our boat stoped at the city about an hour and then crossed over to the other side of the river to take on coal. Brother John and I stoped off in the city to see cousin Wirt Wpderaph[9] and took dinner with him and started back to our boat and having to wait for the ferry boat to take us across the river. It kept us a little late and when we got about half across our boat pulled out and left us but when we got across we found several others of the regiment who were left behind like ourselves. So we held council of war and decided to foot it across Youngs Point and try to hail the boat on the oposite side. Youngs Point was formed by the river striking the bluffs below the city and making a short bend running back past the city almost paralell with itself for some distance leaving a narrow point of land about half a mile wide oposite the city. So we had about half a mile to go while the boat had some five or six miles. We bid cousin Wirt goodbye and struck out up Butlers Canall[10] telling him if we did not catch our boat we would see him later but we got across in good time and signaled our boat which ran in close to shore slowing up and ran out a gangplank and we scrambled on and proceeded our way up the river taking a last look at the ole leavie along the river at Youngs Point and Milikens Bend where we had burried so many of our commrades during the winter and spring of 1863. We had to lay too a part of the night on account of the darkness.

July 18th
We passed on up the river passing Lake Providence at 6-45 AM and Greenville Miss at 6-30 PM.

July 19th
We passed Napolian [Napoleon, Arkansas] at 8 AM and the mouth of White River at 10 AM.

---

9. This name does not appear in the Vicksburg City Directory for the years marked by civil war. As with the Wiley brothers, it is possible that Wirt was a Federal soldier whose unit was then in Vicksburg, en route home.

10. Also known as the Williams-Grant Canal.

July 20th

We arived at Hellena Miss [*sic*] at 2 AM where we stoped for about one hour and passing on we arived at Memphis Tenn at 7 PM. We stoped at the city about an hour and droped down to Fort Pickering where we took on some coal and started on up the river at 10 PM.

July 21th

Was very warm. We proceeded on up the river all day and night.

July 22th

We passed Columbus Ky at 12-15 PM and arived at Cairo Ill at 4 PM. We soon fell in line and marched off the boat onto Illinois soil. Our band playing Home again, Home again from a far and distant clime. We had just been 8 days and five hours runing form New Orleans to Cario a distance of 1000 miles and when we looked on the black mud of Ill we felt that we were almost home again. At Cario we were loaded into some dirty boxcars without anykind of seats and didn't even give us any straw as they do with the hogs when they ship them. It made us think of the way we left Peoria three years before althro we had seats on that first occassion if they were pretty rough and hard but thinking that perhaps we were enough tougher to make up for that little difference. We left Cario at 7 PM over one of the roughest roads that mortal man ever rode over. We had some of the boys to hang their heads out of the side door of the car while some of us held them by the heels to see if our car wasn't off the track and bumping over the ties but they reported that she were runing allright. So when we got tired out seting and standing around we wraped our blankets around us and laid down in the dirt and bumped and bounced around until morning. I lay down in one end of the car and in the morning I found myself in the opsite end. How I got there we will leave for cojecture.

Sabath July 23th

We arived at Centrulia at daylight. Stoped there for breakfast and proceeded onto Decater where we arived at 11-30 took dinner and changed cars for Springfield geting pasenger cars for a change. We arived at

Springfield at 4 PM. Were ordered into camp at Camp Bulter.[11] We ran back to camp and left the cars and set up our dog tents on the banks of the Sangamon River in the rain and it continued to rain during the night.

July 24th

It rained considerably during the day. Col Grier who had been onto Peoria came to the regiment and took a vote of the regiment as to whether we would go to Peoria as a regiment or disband at Springfield. The vote was almost unanimus for going to Peoria as a regiment. A good many of companies H and B[12] objected to going to Peoria as it would be out of their way but as the good people of Peoria were making arangments to give us a nice reception on our return. We thought it would not be right to dispoint them. Company C took a vote during the day as to who should received honorary promotions to fill the offical vacancies in the company and it was decided to promote according to rank and fill out the minor offices with those that had been reduced to the ranks at the time the 77 and 130 Ill Vol Inft were consolidated as one regiment on Jan 14th 1865. Accordingly honorary commissions was bestowed by the Governor on J. P. Wiley as Captain, Joseph Hutchison as First Lieutenant, Alfred [Albert] Shepherd as seckond Lieutenant and the remaining noncommission officers were promoted and the vacancies filled from the ranks by the order of Colonel D. P. Grier commanding the regiment.

July 25th

We signed the payrolls and returned over our guns and accoutraments. I was quite sick not able to be up. We felt sad to part with our guns which we had carried so long. If I had been able to go to the ordnance

11. Camp Butler was the second-largest military training camp in Illinois. Situated six miles northeast of Springfield, near the Sangamon River, the camp was named for Illinois state treasurer William Butler, who had helped select the site for it. The first of thousands of troops arrived for training on August 5, 1861, and the following year the facilities were also used to house Confederate prisoners of war. During the war, 848 Confederates died as prisoners at Camp Butler and were interred in the post cemetery. At the end of hostilities, many of the regiments that had been raised in Illinois were mustered out at Camp Butler before returning home. *The Camp Butler National Cemetery* (Philadelphia: U.S. Army Memorial Affairs Agency, 1973).

12. Companies B and H were recruited largely in Woodford and Putnam Counties, northnortheast of Peoria. It appears that the men of these two companies were just eager to get home.

department and go through the red tape performance which was required I should have kept by gun and accoutraments as I have wished many times since that I had done so. But I was so badly played out and feeling so miserable that I didn't care very much for anything.

July 26th

We still remained in camp waiting our turn for pay and final muster out by the state. It had rained all night and continued to rain and everything was wet and disagreeable for both the well and sick.

July 27th

It was still raining. I was still quite sick and miserable. I thought that if some of them head officers felt as bad as i did and had to lay in the mud they would want to hurry things up a little faster and get home where they could be taken care of. But they were well housed and well fed and well paid and they were not in near as much of a hurry as we were.

July 28th

The rain had ceased and I was feeling some better. Was able to be on my feet again. We turned over our pup tents the last of Uncle Sams goods that remained in our possession and went down to the city at 10 AM and got our pay and sheep skins by 12 PM and was mustered out of the State service and spent the afternoon in the city listening to speeches etc. Took a special train for Peoria at 8 PM. We were now civil citizens of Illinois once more and paid our own passage and travled like men. We traveled all night sleeping but little in our seats.

July 29th

At 3 AM we arived at Chenook where we changed cars taking the TP&W [Toledo, Peoria, and Western] RR for Peoria. We arived in Peoria at 8 AM where we found our friends in goodly numbers to welcome us home again. Ariving at the depot we left the cars and fell into line and marched up to Rouses hall[13] where the ladies national Liegue had prepared a sumtuous breakfast for us to which we done ample justice as it was a little late and we had not sat down to such a meal for three years

13. Located on the corner of Main and Jefferson Streets, Rouses Hall was an opera house built in 1857. Oral interview with Laurie Trimble, reference librarian, Peoria Public Library, November 16, 1998.

at least. The Democrats calling themselves the good samaritans in order to try to gain the good will of the returning soldiers for politcal ends had prepared breakfast in another hall and made strenuous efforts to get the boys to go and eat with them but we had not forgotten who had been our friends and whos blessings and help had followed us all through our service and we took breakfast with the ladies national liegue. After breakfast we marched to the Corthouse Square where we listened to a considerable amount of speach making. The flag which had been presented to our regiment by the ladies of Peoria was returned to them in an appropriate speech by Captain Stevens of Company E. It was not the same beautiful flag that it was when presented to us three long years before. But badly soiled and torned riddled by shot and shell and stained with patriotic blood. But its wounds were honorable and only added to its glory. It had been through many a hard conflict and hand never been lowered to the enemy and we could return it to them with no feeling but that of pride. Captain Stevens was followed by Alexander McCoy,[14] Chaplain McCulloch, Mr. Thomas McCulloch and others in patriotic speeches after which we were given dinner at the Central Hotel. After dinner the old 77 Regiment disbanded each going their several ways to meet and greet their loved ones from whom they had been seperated so long and to take up civil life and it duties where they had laid it down three long years before.

14. Alexander McCoy was the local representative in the state legislature. A native of Ohio, born in 1818, he was educated at Washington College (today Washington and Jefferson) in Pennsylvania. McCoy taught language in Ohio for several years before turning to law as a profession and was admitted to the bar in 1850. He moved to Illinois and established a lucrative practice in Peoria. He was elected state's attorney for the 16th Judicial District and later served as the local prosecutor. He died in Pasadena, Calif., on February 10, 1893. Ibid.

EPILOGUE

Having faithfully performed his duty as a soldier, William Wiley became once again a common citizen of Illinois. Although his health was severely weakened, he quickly returned to his prewar pursuits and resumed farming in Logan Township near Peoria. On January 23, 1868, he married Leannah Patton in nearby Elmwood. Reverend William G. Pierce, former chaplain of the 77th Illinois, performed the ceremony. The couple had only one child, a son, Samuel Wirt, who was born on May 6, 1875.[1]

The rigors of farming exacted a heavy physical toll on Wiley, and his health continued to deteriorate. William M. Pinkerton, who had served with Wiley in Company C, became his neighbor in Logan Township after the Civil War. Pinkerton later wrote of his comrade, "After we were mustered out and came home, William Wiley lived for about six years within about one 1/2 mile of me and I know that he was in very poor health."[2]

Eventually, Wiley was unable to continue farming without assistance. He moved into nearby Summersville (present-day Hanna City), west of Peoria, where relatives and neighbors could help take care of his family and the ailing veteran could visit the doctor as needed, which was frequently. Looking to provide for his wife and son, Wiley, urged by his brother John, filed an application for an invalid pension on May 18, 1881, citing "liver complaint and dispepsia," a result of the malaria contracted

1. Supplemental Questionnaire for Pension Application completed by William Wiley on June 16, 1898, in Wiley Pension Records.
2. Affadavit by William M. Pinkerton, May 28, 1883, in Wiley Pension Records.

during the winter of 1862–63 while on duty in the Lower Mississippi River Valley.[3]

As required, Wiley was examined by a surgeon on September 6, 1881. Dr. John Neglay reported, "In my opinion the said Wm. Wiley is partially incapacitated for obtaining his subsistence by manual labor from the cause [liver complaint and dyspepsia] above stated." The partial disability was rated by Dr. Neglay as "3/8" which translated to compensation of $3.00 per month.[4]

The U.S. Department of the Interior, which was responsible for soldiers' pensions, checked the records of the War Department to verify Wiley's service and claims to disability. Adhering to a strict standard of evaluation, officials examined the bimonthly returns and even the morning reports of the 77th Illinois to determine the frequency and duration of his absence from the regiment due to sickness. They also reviewed the files of the Surgeon General's Office, which showed him absent due to illness only for the period of April 17 to May 8, 1863. (As we have seen, Wiley often stayed on duty with the regiment while sick, his brother John and others assuming his duties.) Further weakening his claim was the fact that Wiley was unable to secure letters of support from the regimental surgeon Charles Winnie and assistant surgeon John Stoner, who could not recall his case.[5]

Realizing that his application was in jeopardy, Wiley sought the assistance of those who could support his claims. Former captain of Company C Joseph M. McCulloch swore out an affidavit on Wiley's behalf on August 15, 1881. Recalling the widespread sickness that had plagued the regiment during its service along the Mississippi River, McCulloch noted that his regiment "was at that time in a very malarial atmosphere." Although the captain well remembered that the "command suffered very much at the time on account of meager sanitary and medical arrangements," he could not "remember distinctly" any particulars concerning Wiley's health.[6]

Numerous other affidavits were filed on his behalf between 1881 and

3. Declaration for an Original Invalid Pension filed by William Wiley on May 13, 1881, recorded on May 18, 1881, in Wiley Pension Records.

4. Examining Surgeon's Certificate by Dr. John H. Neglay, September 6, 1881, in Wiley Pension Records.

5. General Affidavit by William Wiley, April 19, 1884, in Wiley Pension Records.

6. Affadavit by Joseph M. McCulloch, August 15, 1881, in Wiley Pension Records.

1883, including one by his brother John, which stated: "Said claimant was an ablebodied man before & at the time of enlistment. About January 1st, 1863, in the Chickasaw Swamp in Miss. he contracted malarial fever for which he was treated on a river boat named the Duke of Argyle. He was unfit for duty about five months." Wiley's older brother was quick to mention that William "remained with the regiment on the sick list" from January 1 until April 16, 1863, when the critical condition of his health required that he be hospitalized. At the time of his return to the regiment in the rear of Vicksburg, John noted that his brother remained in "feeble health." His former bunkmate, James R. McCracken, confirmed that following Wiley's return to the regiment "he was never strong thereafter, and had spells of same fever."[7]

Dr. T. R. Plummer, who had served as the Wiley family physician since 1859, provided strong evidence on William's behalf in an affidavit on September 28, 1883. The doctor stated that he knew Wiley "to be an able bodied man previous to his enlistment into the Service." Immediately following his return from the Army, noted Plummer, William had applied to him for medical treatment. The doctor wrote that William was found to be "suffering from indigestion & torpid liver also inflammation of his eyes the diseased condition of the stomach & liver." This condition, he affirmed, "continues up to the present time with but little if any improvement which renders him in my opinion unable to perform manual labor more than about two thirds of the time." Dr. Plummer concluded by noting that Wiley "was at the time of his enlistment and previous then to [be] free from any disease of the stomach & liver."[8]

Despite the evidence of Wiley's disability, his application for an invalid pension was rejected on May 23, 1884, on the grounds that there was "no ratable disability from alleged cause." The ruling was based largely on a medical examination of Wiley ordered by the Pension Office and conducted on March 3, 1883. The panel of three surgeons, which included Dr. Edgar L. Phillips, simply noted that their examinations revealed that Wiley's "[t]ongue, abdomen, liver, and spleen [were] normal. Muscles firm. Hands hard and indicate that he is a person who does considerable manual labor. General appearance good." In their opinion, Wiley's physical abilities "entitle him to no rating."[9]

7. Affidavits by John P. Wiley, September 28, 1883, and James R. McCracken, March 21, 1883, in Wiley Pension Records.

8. Affidavit by T. R. Plummer, September 28, 1883, in Wiley Pension Records.

9. Examining Surgeon's Certificate, March 8, 1883, in Wiley Pension Records.

Malaria causes periodic chills, with fevers that can reach 106° F. Attacks, which last two or more hours, are followed by headache, muscular pain, and nausea. Between attacks the victim feels better but is weak and anemic. In some cases, those afflicted with malaria become weaker with each attack. It is possible that on March 3, when he was examined by the panel of surgeons, Wiley was between flareups of the disease and thus his physical condition was fairly normal. If so, this could explain their findings.

On June 27, 1890, Congress enacted more lenient legislation governing soldiers' claims which made it easier to qualify for a disability pension. On August 2, Wiley again filed for an invalid pension, citing the same reasons as on his previous application—"disease of the liver and stomach rheumatism." Five months later, despite what his family and friends believed was an obviously poor physical condition, his application was again rejected. It was the opinion of the examining physicians that William was not "disabled in a ratable degree under Act of June 27, 1890." Their examination, conducted on December 3, 1890, reported that Wiley's "[t]ongue [was] natural; liver not enlarged and not tender. All abdominal organs apparently in good condition. No icterus; skin natural. No piles. Heart and lungs healthy. All joints, ligaments, muscles and tendons normal. No evidence of rheumatism. General appearance healthy. Hands toil hardened."[10]

By 1895, Wiley's health had become so poor that he and his wife depended almost entirely on others for support. The couple had moved to Monmouth in Warren County, just west of Galesburg, where they resided at 330 North 5th Street. The old veteran came under the medical care of Dr. E. J. Blair, who throughout March of that year treated Wiley for gastritis. The doctor recorded in his journal, "stomach extremely irritable, patient became anemic & prostrated, skin yellow, liver enlarged & torpid. Glandular organs generaly locked up resulting in general debility." Blair later affirmed that similar attacks occurred in December 1896 and in April 1897.[11]

On July 7, 1897, Wiley once more filed for an invalid pension through

10. Declaration for Original Invalid Pension filed by William Wiley on July 28, 1890, recorded August 2, 1890; Examining Surgeon's Certificate, December 3, 1890, in Wiley Pension Records.

11. Physician's Affidavit by Dr. E. J. Blair, not dated but stamped received in the Pension Office October 29, 1898, in Wiley Pension Records.

the Washington law firm of Taber & Whitman, claiming "[p]artial in-
ability to earn support by manual labor," a result of "disease of digestive
organs and general debility." The slow process of verifying information,
evaluating affidavits, and conducting medical examinations began anew.
The review of Wiley's application and supporting documentation took
a full year to reach the stage where he was instructed to submit to a
physical examination by a medical board of three doctors.[12]

Wiley reported for the examination on July 20, 1898. He recounted
for the doctors the situation in which he contracted malaria and the
effects of the disease over the years following his service in the Civil War.
In describing the nature of his ills, William informed them that "I have
nervous dyspepsia, my liver is torpid. I have nervousness and am compelled to live on a restricted diet and I am troubled greatly with nausea
and flatulency." This condition was confirmed by the board, which consisted of Drs. E. L. Emerson, A. P. Nelson, and E. M. Hanson. In their
report, the doctors detailed the condition of their patient:

> The lower margin of stomach is very tender, tongue is coated and
> breath foeted. The skin is dry and jaundiced and stomach and bowels are
> distended and tympanitic. The liver is greatly enlarged, is increased in size
> fully 1/4 of a total and is very tender. There is obstinate constipation and
> dyspepsia, rate of disease of liver and stomach 16/18. Claimant is emaci-
> ated, old, feeble, poorly nourished and weak, is nervous and trembling,
> rate general debility 17/18. Claimant is almost totally incapacitated for the
> performance of any manual labor. Urinalysis, sp. gr. 1020, light straw
> color, acid, no sugar, albumen, pus, blood or tubecasts. Pulse rate standing
> is 80, after exercise, 90; Apex beat of heart is, 1-1/2 in. below and 1-1/2 in.
> to right of nipple line. Area of cardiac dullness is normal, heart is normal.
> Chest measure at rest is 34-1/2 in., forced inspiration, 36 in., forced expira-
> tion, 33. Lungs are normal. Claimant is free from any evidence of vicious
> habits. We find no other disabilities.[13]

While William awaited a decision from the Pension Office, tragedy
struck his family. On November 10, 1897, his wife died. Leannah had
been a faithful companion who toiled alongside her husband in the fields
and nursed him throughout their marriage. Her health had no doubt

12. Declaration for Original Invalid Pension filed by Taber & Whitman, July 7, 1897, in Wiley
Pension Records.

13. Examining Surgeon's Certificate, July 20, 1898, in Wiley Pension Records.

been broken by the rigors of farming and an adult life spent in poverty. Hers was truly as hard a life as William's, yet her love for him had been constant and strong. The loss of his wife left Wiley not only heartbroken, but now totally dependent on his son S. Wirt, his brother John, close friends, and neighbors for even the basic necessities of life.[14]

In hope of helping to secure the approval of William's pension, his personal physician, Dr. Blair, submitted a statement in support of Wiley's application. He stressed that the ailing veteran "is a frail man & always will be—stomach continues to be weak & irritable & it is only with the greatest of care that said soldier is able to get enough nourishment to give him strength to walk the streets." The speed of the approval process, however, failed to be affected by the efforts of those who worked on his behalf.[15]

The long-sought pension was finally approved in July 1899, and made effective as of July 10, 1897—the date that Wiley's application had been filed by Taber & Whitman. William was awarded a pension of $10.00 per month, on which he would live for the remainder of his life. Ironically, his brother John, who was not disabled by service, filed application for a pension around the same time as William and secured approval on September 1, 1898, at the rate of $8.00 per month.[16]

Death mercifully came to William Wiley on November 12, 1902. In life he had been a remarkably common man, and as those who loved him also passed away, Wiley faded from memory, joining that vast host of men and women of whom the only reminder is a simple stone in an obscure cemetery. Wiley's service in the Civil War had been the defining moment of his life; and service to his nation was the legacy that he would leave his son S. Wirt. At least for the moment, William Wiley has been resurrected through the publication of these pages. May they establish for him a place in history which is his due for his sacrifice and suffering as a soldier of the Republic.

14. Supplemental Questionnaire for Pension Application, completed by William Wiley on June 16, 1898, in Wiley Pension Records.

15. Physician's Affidavit by Dr. E. J. Blair, not dated but stamped received in the Pension Office October 29, 1898, in Wiley Pension Records.

16. Pension Certificate No. 984626; E. W. Morgan, Acting Commissioner, Widow Division (possibly State of Illinois as it is not on U.S. Pension Office letterhead), to Mrs. Sarah E. Patton, April 12, 1929, in Wiley Pension Records.

Biographical Appendix

CHARLES BALLANCE, a prominent resident of Peoria, was authorized by Gov. Richard Yates in the summer of 1862 to raise a regiment of infantry. "He had devoted his time and energies to this object," wrote William Bentley, but "inasmuch as Mr. Ballance was an old man, and as a lawyer of note, an influential citizen, it was thought that he could do more good for the country by remaining at home than by going into the field." In recognition of his recruiting work, he was commissioned colonel of the 77th Illinois on August 18, 1862, but not mustered. On September 3, 1862, he took formal leave of the regiment and, by prior arrangement with the governor, transferred command to David P. Grier. *RH,* 16–8; *AG,* 4:654.

NATHANIEL P. BANKS was commander of the Department of the Gulf. Born in Waltham, Mass., on January 30, 1816, he went to work at an early age in the cotton mill at which his father was superintendent. Although he had little formal education, he studied law and was admitted to the bar. Entering the political arena, Banks was first elected to the state legislature, where he became speaker of the house, and then to Congress, where he also rose to become Speaker. He served as governor of Massachusetts from 1858 until the outbreak of war, when Lincoln appointed him as a major general of volunteers. He proved of great value in raising troops and money for the war effort, but he was a colossal failure as a field officer. His 1864 Red River campaign was a fiasco that resulted in his removal from command. Following the war, Banks returned to Congress, where he served for six terms and later was appointed U.S. Marshal. He retired from public life in 1890, "owing to an increasing mental disorder," and died three years later at his home in Waltham. Warner, *Generals in Blue*, 17–8; Boatner, *Civil War Dictionary*, 42.

BRIG. GEN. WILLIAM P. BENTON, who commanded the Third Division, Thirteenth Corps, was born near the hamlet of New Market, Frederick County, Md., on December 25, 1828. Raised in Indiana, Benton fought as a private during the Mexican War, seeing considerable combat in the drive toward Mexico City. Returning to Indiana, he devoted himself to the study of law, was admitted to the bar, and even served as a judge. At the outbreak of the Civil War, he was commissioned colonel of the 8th Indiana Infantry. After initial service in the East, he was sent west and fought at Pea Ridge. Promoted to brigadier general on April 28, 1862, Benton commanded a brigade during the Vicksburg campaign. Elevated to division command, he was later brevetted major general of volunteers on March 26, 1865. He died of yellow fever on March 14, 1867, while in New Orleans serving as a government agent. Warner, *Generals in Blue*, 30–1; Boatner, *Civil War Dictionary*, 60.

BRIG. GEN. FRANCIS P. BLAIR JR. was the son of Francis Blair, who had been an advisor to Andrew Jackson, and the brother of Montgomery Blair, who served as Lincoln's postmaster general. Born in Lexington, Ky., on February 19, 1821, Blair was a graduate of Princeton. After studying law at Transylvania, he entered into practice with his brother in St. Louis. Entering the political arena, he was elected to Congress in 1856 and again in 1860. His family was credited by President Lincoln with saving Missouri for the Union. Blair's efforts in raising troops in Missouri resulted in his commission as a brigadier general on August 7, 1862. Three months later he was elevated to a major general, at which grade he led a division in Sherman's corps during the Vicksburg campaign. An aggressive fighter, he earned the frequent praise of both Sherman and Grant and went on to direct a corps during the March to the Sea. Following the war, he served briefly as a United States senator from Missouri. Warner, *Generals in Blue*, 35–6; Boatner, *Civil War Dictionary*, 67.

MAJ. GEN. JOHN S. BOWEN commanded one of Pemberton's four divisions that manned the defense line around Vicksburg. During the Vicksburg campaign, he had commanded the troops who had stood tall at

Grand Gulf when the Federals attempted to come ashore there on April 29, 1863. He offered stiff resistance during the Battle of Port Gibson on May 1 and fought brilliantly at Champion Hill on May 16. Although his troops were roughly handled in these engagements and at Big Black River Bridge on May 17, they were the most reliable men in Pemberton's army and the Confederate commander came to view Bowen as his most capable subordinate. The Georgia native was an 1853 graduate of the U.S. Military Academy at West Point who resigned from service three years later to pursue a career as an architect in St. Louis. At the outbreak of hostilities, he became colonel of the 1st Missouri Infantry and commanded a brigade at Shiloh. Bowen contracted dysentery during the siege of Vicksburg and died on July 13, 1863, nine days after Vicksburg surrendered. Warner, *Generals in Gray,* 29–30; Boatner, *Civil War Dictionary,* 75.

COL. JOHN BRYNER of the 47th Illinois was originally captain of a company from Peoria known as "The National Blues." He was appointed colonel of the 47th Illinois on July 27, 1861, by Gov. Richard Yates and was mustered in at that rank on October 2. From June until October Bryner commanded the post at Peoria and assisted in raising and organizing a number of regiments. Although a rigid disciplinarian, he gained the respect and admiration of his men. Campaigning soon took its toll on the colonel, however, who contracted malaria while on duty in Mississippi. Compelled to leave the service due to poor health, he tendered his resignation on August 17, 1862, and on September 2 took leave of the regiment at Rienzi, Miss. One member of the unit recalled that on Bryner's departure "there was not a dry eye in the regiment."

Bryner reentered service as a first lieutenant in the 139th Illinois on May 18, 1864, and served as the regimental quartermaster until mustered out on October 28, 1864. When the men of the 47th Illinois reenlisted as veterans in the spring of 1865, "a petition signed by every officer and man was sent to Col. Bryner, asking him to again assume command." The petition was also sent to Gov. Richard J. Oglesby, who gave his consent. On March 17, 1865, Bryner was reappointed colonel, but he took sick that very day and died on March 19. *AG,* 3:409, 7:124; Bryner, *Bugle Echoes,* 1, 13, 27, 50.

STEPHEN GANO BURBRIDGE was born in Scott County, Ky., on August 19, 1831. A lawyer by training, he was commissioned colonel of the 26th

Kentucky Infantry at the outbreak of hostilities, which command he led
into battle at Shiloh. Promoted to brigadier general, he led a brigade at
Chickasaw Bayou, Arkansas Post, and during the Vicksburg campaign.
In 1864, he was named commander of the District of Kentucky, a post
he held until the end of the war. During his tenure of command in Kentucky he initiated a number of harsh policies and was "actively loathed
by a majority of the population over whom he had extensive civil and
military powers." Warner, *Generals in Blue*, 54–5; Boatner, *Civil War Dictionary*, 106.

Maj. Gen. Edward R. S. Canby, a native of Boone County, Ky., graduated 30th out of 31 cadets in the West Point class of 1839. He participated
in the Indian-removal process and fought Seminoles in Florida. During
the Mexican War, Canby served as a staff officer and was awarded the
brevets of both major and lieutenant colonel. He was appointed colonel
of the 19th U.S. Infantry at the outbreak of the Civil War and commanded the Department of New Mexico. On May 31, 1862, he was promoted to brigadier general and ordered to the East. Performing only staff
duty until May 1864, Canby was promoted to major general and given
command of the Military Division of West Mississippi. After reorganiz-
ing Banks's army in the wake of the Red River campaign, he ordered the
move against Mobile and, in the operations discussed here by Wiley, his
troops compelled the surrender of the city. He was murdered by the
Modoc Indians in California on April 11, 1873. Warner, *Generals in Blue*,
67–8; Boatner, *Civil War Dictionary*, 118.

Salmon P. Chase, former U.S. senator and governor of Ohio, was appointed by President Abraham Lincoln as secretary of the treasury. Although he ably served the president, Chase and Lincoln always seemed
at odds. On June 30, 1864, Lincoln accepted the fourth resignation submitted by Chase, much to the secretary's surprise. Six months later, Lincoln named Chase chief justice of the Supreme Court, a position in
which he served until his death in 1873. Stewart Sifakis, *Who Was Who
in the Civil War* (New York: Facts on File, 1988), 117–8.

Born on October 27, 1825, John Coburn was a native of Indianapolis.
He graduated from Wabash College in 1846, following which he pursued
a career in law, serving first as a lawyer and then as a judge. Elected

colonel of the 33d Indiana at the outbreak of the war, Coburn distinguished himself as both a regimental and a brigade commander. On March 13, 1865, he was brevetted brigadier general for "gallant and meritorious services during the war." In 1867, he was elected to the U.S. House of Representatives, where he served four consecutive terms. He died on January 28, 1908, and is interred in Crown Hill Cemetery in Indianapolis. Hunt and Brown, *Brevet Brigadier Generals in Blue,* 119.

WASHINGTON COCKLE was one of the more illustrious citizens of Peoria in 1862. Born in New York on May 2, 1811, Cockle enjoyed the benefits of a quality education, after which he taught for several years. He then studied law and was admitted to the bar in 1832. Five years later, at the age of twenty-six, he migrated to Illinois and eventually settled in Peoria. Engaged in a variety of enterprises, from real estate to railroads, banking to pork packing, he also owned a distillery and a newspaper, through which he amassed wealth. Popular with the citizens of Peoria County, Cockle was elected to two terms in the state legislature and one term in the Illinois senate. A Democrat in the tradition of Stephen A. Douglas, he broke with the party on the question of slavery and joined the Republican ranks. He was later appointed postmaster of Peoria. He spoke in support of the Lincoln administration, and his patriotic fervor was instrumental in raising troops for the war effort. He died at the age of seventy-five on July 15, 1886. *History of Peoria County,* 446–7.

A native New Yorker, GORDON GRANGER was born in Joy, Wayne County, on November 6, 1822. A graduate of West Point, he stood thirty-fifth out of forty-one cadets in the celebrated class of 1845. He served in the Mexican War and was awarded two brevets for meritorious service. From then until the outbreak of the Civil War, Granger served on the western frontier and fought against the Indians. In September 1861, he was appointed colonel of the 2d Michigan Cavalry. Later he commanded the cavalry of the Army of the Mississippi during the operations against New Madrid, Island No. 10, and the subsequent advance on Corinth. Promoted to brigadier general of volunteers on March 26, 1862, he was awarded the coveted second star of a major general six months later. Granger earned acclaim at Chickamauga where, without orders, he advanced to the relief of George Thomas on Horseshoe Ridge. He played a major role in the capture of Mobile. Warner, *Generals in Blue*, 181; Boatner, *Civil War Dictionary*, 351–2.

MAJ. GEN. ULYSSES S. GRANT was the most successful general under whom Wiley served during the war. Born in Point Pleasant, Ohio, on April 27, 1822, he stood twenty-first of thirty-nine cadets at his graduation from West Point in 1843. He earned two citations for gallantry and one for meritorious conduct during the Mexican War. His career took a turn for the worse in the postwar period; stationed on the West Coast, he began to drink heavily. Rather than be court-martialed, he resigned his commission in 1854. From then until the outbreak of the Civil War, Grant failed in a number of business ventures and wound up as a clerk in his father's leather store in Galena, Ill.

On June 17, 1861, Grant was appointed colonel of the 21st Illinois Infantry, from which he rose rapidly to brigadier general and to major general. Grant won the first major Union victory of the war when he compelled the surrender of Fort Donelson in February 1862. Two months later he gained another victory in the bloody Battle of Shiloh. The following year he seized Vicksburg through a brilliant campaign. In 1864 he was elevated to lieutenant general and given command of all Union forces. Battling his way to the gates of Richmond and Petersburg, Grant forced his opponent, Gen. Robert E. Lee, to evacuate the Confederate capital and on April 9, 1865, received the surrender of the Army of Northern Virginia at Appomattox Courthouse to end the war.

After the war, Grant served two terms as U.S. president. His final years, however, were marked by misfortune, during which he fell into bankruptcy. Dying of cancer, he raced to finish his memoirs, the sale of which he hoped would provide for his family. Although he finished the manuscript, he died before it was published. Following his death at Mount McGregor on July 23, 1885, he was buried in an imposing tomb in New York City. Warner, *Generals in Blue*, 183–6; Boatner, *Civil War Dictionary*, 352–3.

DAVID P. GRIER served as colonel of the 77th Illinois throughout its course of service. Born in Danville, Pa., on December 26, 1836, Grier was engaged in business in Elmwood, Ill., northwest of Peoria, when Fort Sumter was fired upon on April 12, 1861. Quick to recruit a company, he was elected its captain. But when the company was proffered to Gov.

Yates of Illinois, it was not accepted as the state's quota had been filled. Grier and his company then traveled to St. Louis, where they were mustered into service in June as Company G, 8th Missouri Infantry. He led his company into battle at Forts Henry and Donelson, at Shiloh, and at the siege of Corinth. The youthful captain, who wore short dark hair and a mustache, proved himself a man of courage and ability. Thus when the 77th Illinois was authorized, his name was advanced for the position of colonel. In Peoria and the surrounding area, there was, according to William Bentley, "a strong feeling in the Regiment, both among the officers and men, in favor of David P. Grier." Their feeling prevailed. By arrangement with the governor, shortly after Ballance was commissioned colonel of the regiment, command of the 77th was transferred to Grier. He was commissioned colonel on September 2 and mustered in on September 12. *RH,* 16, 17, 28, 29; *AG,* 4:654; Hunt and Brown, *Brevet Brigadier Generals in Blue,* 244.

JOHN HOUGH of Peoria was mustered in as a first lieutenant in Company B, 17th Illinois Infantry, on August 26, 1861. Poor health, however, compelled his resignation on April 16, 1862. Five months later he reentered service as a first lieutenant and adjutant of the 77th. His military bearing and efficiency led to his appointment by presidential order as assistant adjutant general on the staff of Maj. Gen. Andrew Jackson Smith on May 15, 1863. *RH,* 32; *AG,* 4:654.

EBON CLARK INGERSOLL, born in Dresden, N.Y., in 1831, was the son of a Congregational minister. His mother died when he was only four and he moved frequently with his father from one pastorage to another in New York, Ohio, Wisconsin, and Illinois. Interested in law, Ingersoll was admitted to the bar and later effected a partnership with his younger brother Robert in Shawneetown, Ill. In 1858, the brothers moved their practice to Peoria where both men quickly rose to prominence. Elected to Congress in 1864, Ingersoll served three consecutive terms. He died in 1879. Aaron Wilson Oakford, "The Peoria Story," Special Collections, Peoria Public Library, Peoria, Ill., 551–7.

JOSEPH E. JOHNSTON, a native of Virginia, was a classmate of Robert E. Lee at West Point and graduated thirteenth out of forty-six cadets in the class of 1829. Wounded five times during the Mexican War, he was brevetted repeatedly and by the outbreak of civil war he held the staff rank of brigadier general in the Army of the United States. Resigning on April 22, 1861, he was commissioned a brigadier in the Provisional Army of the Confederacy and in August was appointed a full general. Johnston commanded the army responsible for the defense of Richmond until he was badly wounded in May 1862 at Seven Pines.

Returning to duty in November, Johnston was named commander of the Department of the West and placed over both Braxton Bragg's army in Tennessee and John Pemberton's army in Mississippi. Sent from Tennessee by the authorities in Richmond to salvage the rapidly deteriorating situation in Mississippi, Johnston arrived in Jackson on the night of May 13, 1863. Rather than fight to save the capital city, Johnston wired the secretary of war, "I am too late," and ordered Jackson evacuated. While Vicksburg was besieged, he raised a relief force in the Jackson-Canton area. Although this force was a potential threat to Grant's army around Vicksburg, Johnston did not act aggressively and virtually abandoned Pemberton to his fate. Warner, *Generals in Gray,* 161–2; Boatner, *Civil War Dictionary,* 441.

COL. WILLIAM J. LANDRAM was no stranger to the soldiers of the 77th Illinois, as he commanded their sister regiment, the 19th Kentucky. A native of Lancaster, Ky., born on February 11, 1828, he was a veteran of the Mexican War. A lawyer by training, Landram later served as a U.S. Internal Revenue collector. In photographs, he appears to be a plain, unassuming man who wore wavy dark hair and a beard with no mustache. He proved an officer of note and commanded a brigade for much of the Civil War. On March 13, 1865, he was brevetted brigadier general of volunteers for "gallant and meritorious service during the war." He died in his hometown on October 11, 1895. Hunt and Brown, *Brevet Brigadier Generals in Blue,* 344.

MICHAEL LAWLER was born on November 16, 1814, in County Kildare, Ireland. When he was an infant, his parents moved to the United States and settled in Illinois. In addition to farming, Lawler ran a general store in Shawneetown. He was active in the militia and distinguished himself as a captain in the 3d Illinois Volunteer Infantry during the Mexican War. Mustered in as colonel of the 18th Illinois at the outbreak of the Civil War, he led his regiment into battle at Fort Donelson. Promoted to brigadier general, Lawler led a brigade during the Vicksburg campaign that gained fame at Big Black River Bridge. Elevated to division command, he was stationed in Louisiana and Texas for the remainder of the war, where he was a strict disciplinarian. Brevetted major general in 1865, Lawler retired to his farm, where he died on July 26, 1882. Warner, *Generals in Blue*, 276–7; Boatner, *Civil War Dictionary*, 472–3.

MAJ. GEN. JOHN A. LOGAN, known affectionately by his men as "Black Jack," commanded the Third Division, 17 Corps, during the Vicksburg campaign. Considered the North's "premier civilian combat general," he was born on February 9, 1826, in southern Illinois. A veteran of the Mexican War, Logan's passion was for politics. He served in the Illinois legislature and in the U.S. Congress, supporting Stephen Douglas for president in 1860. Although a Democrat, he supported the war effort and fought at Bull Run as a volunteer. He later recruited the 31st Illinois and was commissioned colonel. Logan rose rapidly through the ranks and demonstrated both leadership and bravery on many hard-fought fields, including Belmont, Fort Donelson, and the siege of Corinth. Following the Vicksburg campaign, he led with great distinction the 15 Corps during the operations against Atlanta and even temporarily commanded the Army of the Tennessee. Returning to Congress following the war, he served in both houses. In 1884 he was nominated as James Blaine's vice president in the unsuccessful Republican bid for the White House. Warner, *Generals in Blue*, 281–2; Boatner, *Civil War Dictionary*, 486–7.

MAJ. GEN. JOHN A. MCCLERNAND was one of the war's more colorful and controversial officers. A lawyer by training, he also edited the *Gallatin Democrat and Illinois Advertiser* prior to the Civil War. It was politics, however, that attracted the young man and his many talents. A fiery orator, he proved to be a gifted politician. He served as an Illinois assemblyman for seven years beginning in 1836 and was elected to the U.S. House of Representatives as a Jacksonian Democrat in 1843, serving four consecutive terms.

In 1859, he was reelected to Congress and quickly rose to power in the House of Representatives, only to be defeated for the speakership in 1860. Upon the outbreak of war, he resigned his seat and took up the sword. The politician-turned-soldier looked to the field of battle to win victories and headlines in his quest for the White House, and threw his considerable influence behind the Lincoln administration's war policy. Although McClernand was a Democrat, Lincoln considered him an ally in the maintenance of midwestern support for the Union and appointed him a brigadier general of volunteers to rank from May 17, 1861. He soon demonstrated both personal bravery and a willingness to fight at Belmont, Fort Donelson, and Shiloh, developing into an able combat officer.

In the fall of 1862, McClernand was authorized by Lincoln to raise and command a force for operations on the Mississippi River aimed at Vicksburg. The troops he raised were shipped to Memphis. Prior to McClernand's arrival, however, this force was commandeered by Sherman and led to defeat on the banks of Chickasaw Bayou. During the Vicksburg campaign, McClernand commanded the Thirteenth Corps. Although he performed admirably and with great credit to himself, Grant relieved him in June 1863, following publication of a congratulatory letter that had not been cleared through army channels. McClernand returned to command of the Thirteenth Corps in 1864 and led it during the latter part of the Red River campaign. He resigned his commission on November 30, 1864. Following the war he remained active on both the state and national levels in Democratic Party politics but did not seek elected office himself. In 1876 he served as chairman of the national convention that nominated Samuel J. Tilden for president. John McClernand died in 1900, having lived long enough to see the field of his most stirring triumph and stinging defeat, Vicksburg, established as a national military park. Warner, *Generals in Blue*, 293–4; Boatner, *Civil War Dictionary*, 525.

CHARLES F. McCULLOCH of Cazenovia, brother of J. M. McCulloch, was mustered in as first sergeant on August 13, 1862. He seemingly experienced a checkered career, for according to Bentley's regimental history McCulloch was promoted to second lieutenant on March 17, 1863, and commissioned captain on April 8, 1864, but not mustered in at that rank. Yet on May 11, 1865, several months after the regiment was consolidated with the 130th Illinois, he was commissioned a first lieutenant, then was mustered out on June 17, 1865, as a second lieutenant. The records of the Adjutant General's office are no less confusing, as they state that he was promoted to second lieutenant on March 17, 1863, and to captain on April 8, 1864, at which rank he was mustered in on January 4, 1865. He is stated to have served as captain until mustered out on June 17, 1865. *RH*, 47; *AG*, 4:660.

JOSEPH M. McCULLOCH was from Cazenovia and was mustered into Federal service as captain of Company C on September 1, 1862. He is mentioned more than any other man in the pages of Wiley's diary. Captured on April 8, 1864, at Mansfield, McCulloch commanded the Union prisoners of war at Camp Ford in Texas from October 1864 until his release in May 1865. Returning to the regiment near Mobile, he was promoted major to date from January 1865 and was discharged on either June 17 or July 7, 1865. *RH*, 31, 46; *AG*, 4:654, 660.

GEORGE F. McGINNIS was born on March 19, 1826, in Boston. He later moved to Chillicothe, Ohio, with his father and went on to serve as a lieutenant and then captain in the 2d Ohio Infantry during the Mexican War. After the war, he moved to Indianapolis where he manufactured hats. At the outbreak of the Civil War, McGinnis became colonel of the 11th Indiana Infantry and led the regiment into battle at Fort Donelson and at Shiloh. In the spring of 1863, he was elevated to brigadier general and led a brigade during the Vicksburg campaign. Although he rose to division command, he was not elevated in rank and was mustered out as a brigadier general on August 24, 1865. He spent the remainder of his life holding public office, including service as postmaster of Indianapolis. McGinnis died on May 29, 1910. Warner, *Generals in Blue*, 299–300; Boatner, *Civil War Dictionary*, 532.

DAVID McKINNEY of Peoria was mustered in as quartermaster of the 77th Illinois on September 12, 1862. He spent much of his career on detached service as acting assistant quartermaster for the Second Brigade, Fourth Division, Thirteenth Army Corps. Promoted to captain on May 15, 1865, McKinney was also elevated to assistant quartermaster and served as post quartermaster at the mouth of the White River and at Duvall's Bluff, Ark. Although Bentley's regimental history states that he was mustered out on January 15, 1866, the records of the Adjutant General's office cite July 10, 1865. *RH*, 32; *AG*, 4:654.

JAMES B. McPHERSON was born on November 14, 1828, in Clyde, Ohio. He graduated first in his class at West Point in 1853, and following the outbreak of civil war he rose rapidly through the ranks. On October 8, 1862, he was promoted to major general. After commanding a corps during the Vicksburg campaign, he led the Army of the Tennessee during the Atlanta operations. He was killed in action on July 22, 1864. Warner, *Generals in Blue*, 306–8; Boatner, *Civil War Dictionary*, 538.

Born in either 1840 or 1841, **FREDERICK W. MOORE** was a clean-shaven young man from Green Township, Hamilton County, Ohio, when he was appointed a second lieutenant in Company G, 5th Ohio Infantry, a three-month regiment, in April 1861. Promoted to first lieutenant in September 1861 and captain in April 1862, he resigned his commission to accept the appointment of colonel in the 83d Ohio on August 22, 1862. Moore was brevetted brigadier general on March 26, 1865, and mustered out of service four months later.

Following the war, he received an appointment as second lieutenant in the 19th U.S. Infantry and served with that unit from July 1866 until April 1867, when he resigned. Thomas B. Marshall, regimental historian of the 83d Ohio, wrote of Moore's post–Civil War service: "He was stationed in some place in the West but after going through such stirring scenes as he did for four years, and ranking as Colonel for so long and many times with a whole brigade under his command, this monotonous life of a subaltern and with such surroundings did not at all appeal either to his sense of patriotism or to his own aspirations."

Returning to civil life, Moore practiced law in Cincinnati and later became a judge. He died in Cincinnati on May 6, 1905, and is interred in Spring Grove Cemetery. Marshall, *History of the Eighty-third Ohio Volunteer Infantry*, 27–8, 190; Hunt and Brown, *Brevet Brigadier Generals in Blue*, 425; *Official Roster of the Soldiers of the State of Ohio in the War of the Rebellion*, 12 vols. (Cincinnati, 1886–95), 6:571.

Originally a businessman from Lexington, **COL. JOHN HUNT MORGAN** immediately took up arms for the Confederacy upon the outbreak of war, leading a cavalry brigade on numerous raids into Tennessee and Kentucky. Morgan's most famous escapade was his 1863 raid through Indiana and Ohio, during which he was captured near New Lisbon, Ohio, on July 23. Imprisoned in the Ohio State Penitentiary in Columbus, he escaped on November 26. On September 4, 1864, he was killed by Federal troops in Greenville, Tenn. He is interred in his home town of Lexington. He was brother-in-law to Confederate generals A. P. Hill and Basil Duke. Warner, *Generals in Gray*, 220–1.

BRIG. GEN. PETER J. OSTERHAUS commanded the Ninth Division, Thirteenth Corps. Regarded as the "most distinguished of the foreign-born officers who served the Union," Osterhaus was a native of Prussia who fled his homeland following the unsuccessful revolts of 1848. Mustered into service as a major in 1861, he quickly rose through the ranks, first to colonel of the 12th Missouri Infantry, and then to brigadier general in June 1862. Having seen action at Wilson's Creek and Pea Ridge, Osterhaus was wounded at Big Black River Bridge on May 17, 1863, and command of his division fell temporarily to Brig. Gen. Albert Lee. Warner, *Generals in Blue*, 352–3; Boatner, *Civil War Dictionary*, 613.

BRIG. GEN. RICHARD L. PAGE was born in Clarke County, Va., on December 20, 1807. He became a midshipman in the U.S. Navy in 1824, and served until the outbreak of the Civil War. Upon the secession of Virginia in April 1861, he resigned his commission and entered the Confederate navy as an ordnance officer with the rank of commander. Nicknamed "Ramrod" and "Bombast Page," he became a brigadier general in the Provisional Army on March 1, 1864, and was given command of the outer defenses of Mobile. Following surrender of the fort, Page was imprisoned at Fort Delaware, from which he was released on July 24, 1865. After the war he served as superintendent of schools in Norfolk. General Page died on August 9, 1901, at the age of 94. Warner, *Generals in Gray*, 226–7.

REAR ADM. DAVID DIXON PORTER commanded the Mississippi Squadron, which operated independently of but in cooperation with Grant's Army of the Tennessee during the Vicksburg campaign. A native of Pennsylvania, he was the son of Commodore David Porter and the foster brother of David Glasgow Farragut. Having served in the U.S. Navy since 1829, Porter commanded the mortar fleet which assisted in the capture of New Orleans early in 1862. Promoted to rear admiral, he served during the Vicksburg campaign and was a key factor in the Union's success, for which he received the thanks of Congress. After participating in the Red River campaign in 1864, he was given command of the North Atlantic Blockading Squadron and fought at Fort Fisher. Porter was elevated to vice admiral in 1866 and later served as superintendent of the Naval Academy at Annapolis. Appointed Admiral of the Navy in 1870, he died in 1891 and is interred at Arlington National Cemetery near the Custis-Lee mansion. Boatner, *Civil War Dictionary*, 661.

WILLIAM REYNOLDS was born in Roxbury, Pa., in 1830. His father and grandfather had been elders in the Presbyterian Church and William seemed destined to follow in their footsteps. His family moved to Peoria when William was six, and he soon entered the Peoria Academy. Upon completion of his education, he went to Pennsylvania and worked in Philadelphia. In 1852, he returned to Peoria and entered the grain-and-meatpacking house established by his father. Church work, however, was his true calling and he became a leader in the Young Men's Christian Association. Upon the outbreak of hostilities between the states, William served in the U.S. Christian Commission, administering to the spiritual needs of the soldiers. He frequently visited the troops at the front, supplying them with religious tracts, vegetables, and medicine. He remained active in church work for the remainder of his life and died on September 28, 1897. Oakford, "The Peoria Story," 171–4.

MAJ. GEN. WILLIAM T. SHERMAN was born in Lancaster, Ohio, on February 8, 1820. At the age of nine, he lost his father and was taken in by the neighboring family of U.S. senator Thomas Ewing. Sherman graduated from the U.S. Military Academy, ranking sixth out of forty-two cadets in the class of 1840. Resigning his commission in 1853, he worked as a banker in California, then as a lawyer in Kansas, and finally as superintendent of what is now Louisiana State University prior to the outbreak of civil war.

On May 14, 1861, he was reappointed to the army as colonel of the 13th U.S. Infantry. He led a brigade into battle at Bull Run and commanded a division at Shiloh, where his actions won him the friendship of Ulysses S. Grant, with whom his fortunes would be linked. Sherman directed the expeditionary force which advanced on Vicksburg in the winter of 1862 and led the Fifteenth Corps during the Vicksburg campaign of 1863. He later became commander of the Army of the Tennessee and directed an army group during the Atlanta campaign and on the March to the Sea.

Following the Civil War, he was elevated to lieutenant general and on March 4, 1869, he became a full general. He went on to serve as general in chief of the army for fourteen years, retiring on February 8, 1884. Sherman died in New York City on February 14, 1891, at the age of seventy-one. He is buried in St. Louis. Warner, *Generals in Blue*, 442–4; Boatner, *Civil War Dictionary*, 750–1.

ANDREW JACKSON SMITH, who became one of the North's premier generals in the western theater, was a native of Pennsylvania. Born in Bucks

County on April 28, 1815, he graduated thirty-sixth out of forty-five cadets in the West Point class of 1838. He served with the 1st Dragoons
fighting Indians on the frontier and during the Mexican War, rising to
the rank of major by 1861. Appointed a brigadier general of volunteers
on March 17, 1862, he was destined to command on both the division and
corps levels. Described as "small and brusque," his physical appearance
belied his tenacity and he demonstrated exceptional abilities as a combat
officer. Elevated to major general of volunteers on May 14, 1864, he was
brevetted major general in the regular army that same year. As one historian wrote, "His career attracted little notoriety compared to that of
many of his colleagues; nevertheless, he was one of the most competent
division and corps commanders in the service." Warner, *Generals in
Blue*, 454–5 (quotation); Boatner, *Civil War Dictionary*, 768.

GEN. EDMUND KIRBY SMITH was born on May 16, 1824, in St. Augustine,
Fla. A graduate of West Point, Smith stood twenty-fifth out of forty-one
cadets in the class of 1845. Awarded two brevets for gallantry during the
Mexican War, he returned to West Point and served as an assistant pro-
fessor of mathematics until 1852. From then until the outbreak of hostilities between the states, Smith served on the frontier against Indians.

On April 6, 1861, he resigned his commission as major in the 2d U.S.
Cavalry and accepted a commission as lieutenant colonel in Confederate
service. Promoted to brigadier general, he was badly wounded at Manassas, where he demonstrated personal bravery. Elevated to major general
in October 1861 and given command of the Department of East Tennessee, Smith led an invasion of Kentucky in the late summer of 1862 and
gained a victory at Richmond on August 30. However, after initial success which carried him to the banks of the Ohio River opposite Cincinnati, Smith, along with Braxton Bragg, was defeated at Perryville.

Promoted to lieutenant general, he was placed in command of the
vast Trans-Mississippi Department, in which capacity he served for the
duration of the war. Elevated to full general on February 19, 1864, Smith
was practically the last Confederate general in the field to surrender his
command, on May 26, 1865. Warner, *Generals in Gray*, 279–80; Boatner,
Civil War Dictionary, 769–70.

FREDERICK STEELE was a New York native born in Delhi on January 14,
1819. He graduated thirtieth out of thirty-nine cadets in the West Point

class of 1843, nine positions behind his classmate Ulysses S. Grant. A veteran of the Mexican War who won two brevets for gallantry, Steele commanded a battalion of regulars in the Battle of Wilson's Creek in August 1861. The following month, he became colonel of the 8th Iowa Infantry, and in January 1862 he was elevated to brigadier general. Steele commanded a division at Chickasaw Bayou and Arkansas Post during the Vicksburg campaign of 1863. Placed in command of all U.S. forces in Arkansas, he captured Little Rock and fought several engagements in the southwest portion of the state in support of Banks's Red River campaign. Toward the end of the war Steele led a division in the campaign against Mobile. He remained on duty following the Civil War and served as colonel of the 20th Infantry. He died on January 12, 1868, after a fall from his buggy caused by an attack of apoplexy. Warner, *Generals in Blue,* 474–5; Boatner, *Civil War Dictionary,* 794–5.

Son of former president Zachary Taylor, MAJ. GEN. RICHARD TAYLOR was also the brother-in-law of Confederate president Jefferson Davis. Upon the outbreak of hostilities, Taylor was appointed colonel of the 9th Louisiana Infantry and led his regiment to Virginia. Arriving too late to participate in the Battle of Manassas, he would not see action until the spring of 1862 in Stonewall Jackson's celebrated Valley campaign, in which he led a brigade. Promoted to brigadier general and later major general, Taylor was assigned to command the District of West Louisiana where, in the assessment of Ezra Warner, "he made a notable record with a paucity of troops and supplies." Perhaps his most noteworthy accomplishment during the war was his brilliant series of operations against Nathaniel Banks during the Red River campaign. Promoted to lieutenant general, Taylor was placed in command of the Department of Alabama, Mississippi, and East Louisiana. He faced great odds in defending this key area and on May 4, 1865, surrendered his forces to Union general E. R. S. Canby. Warner, *Generals in Gray,* 299–300; Boatner, *Civil War Dictionary,* 827–8.

LYSANDER WEBB was a native of Berkshire County, Mass. Orphaned at an early age, he was adopted by a Colonel Sheperd, a businessman "supposed of immense wealth." Reared in affluence, Webb attended Yale, where he studied for three years before being called home due to the death of his adoptive father. His adoptive mother soon died as well, and the estate was left in "a lamentable state of affairs." Webb found himself penniless but quickly secured employment in the editorial room of the *Republican,* one of New England's leading newspapers, in Springfield. The following year, he began a Republican newspaper in Waukegan, Illinois. Described as "a singularly handsome man, with brown hair and eyes, and an engaging manner that few could resist," Webb gained respect as a journalist. His reputation enabled him to establish another Republican paper, the *Transcript,* in Peoria—which at that time was considered "the stronghold of Democracy." "The magnetism of the new editor was felt at once," wrote one resident of the town, "and for the first time, Peorians had a paper of which they were proud."

The young editor married Virginia Ballance, whose father was a noted lawyer and first colonel of the 77th Illinois. Webb began to study law at the instigation of his father-in-law and was admitted to the bar just prior to the war. Elected lieutenant colonel on September 3, 1862, Webb was mustered in on September 12. Throughout the course of his service, he sent lengthy letters home for publication in the *Transcript,* through which the people of Peoria and the surrounding area were kept informed of the regiment's activities. Well-liked and respected by the men of the 77th, Webb was killed on April 8, 1864, in the Battle of Mansfield. *RH,* 29–31; *AG,* 4:654.

INDEX